. . . a comprehensive and thoughtful anthology . . . the selections offer a varied but consistent picture of the current radical world view.

—*The Kirkus Reviews*

A walloping collection of 16 short, explosive extracts of hardcore writing by writers crucial to the New Left . . . the concepts behind the headlines. Definite, and stimulating as a bed of hot coals.

—*Publishers' Weekly*

THE NEW LEFT READER

Edited by Carl Oglesby

Grove Press, Inc. New York

Library of Congress Catalog Card Number: 78–84890
First Evergreen Black Cat Edition, 1969
Second Printing

Manufactured in the United States of America

Acknowledgements

"The Politics of Responsibility" from *Letter to the New Left* by C. Wright Mills, Copyright © 1960 by *New Left Review*, reprinted by permission of *New Left Review*.

"The Politics of Responsibility" from *The Causes of World War III* by C. Wright Mills, Copyright © 1958 by C. Wright Mills, reprinted by permission of Simon & Schuster, Inc.

"Conclusion" from *One-Dimensional Man* by Herbert Marcuse, Copyright © 1964 by Herbert Marcuse, reprinted by permission of Beacon Press.

From *Strategy for Labor* by André Gorz, French text Copyright © 1964 by Editions du Seuil, English translation Copyright © 1967 by Beacon Press, reprinted by permission of Beacon Press.

"Contradiction and Overdetermination" from the forthcoming *For Marx* by Louis Althusser, translated by Ben Brewster, reprinted by permission of Pantheon Books, a division of Random House, Inc.

"The Unknown Marx" by Martin Nicolaus, Copyright © 1968 by *New Left Review*, reprinted by permission of *New Left Review*.

From *The May Day Manifesto* by Stuart Hall, Raymond Williams, and Edward Thompson, Copyright © 1968 by May Day Manifesto Committee, reprinted by permission of Penguin Books, Ltd.

"The Concept of the Left" from *Toward a Marxist Humanism*, Copyright © 1968 by Leszek Kolakowski, reprinted by permission of Grove Press, Inc.

"Algeria Unveiled" from *A Dying Colonialism*, by Frantz Fanon, French text Copyright © 1959 by François Maspero, English translation Copyright © 1965 by Monthly Review Press, reprinted by permission of Monthly Review Press.

A Note on the styling of this book: For the convenience of the reader, each article, although reprinted from a different source, has been styled consistently, for uniformity of American spelling and usage. Citations on the publishers and publication dates of books mentioned are given wherever possible, but with editions of "classics," like the works of Marx and Engels, etc., no specific editions have been cited, as many are available in both hardcover and paperback.

Contents

The Idea of the New Left

WHY NOT SIMPLY the *current* Left? What makes it new?

The themes of last century's radicals remain vivid in this half of the twentieth century. The Left has always wanted something called progress, aspired to something called human mastery over something called social destiny, seen itself as the winner in the long distance, viewed its general program as being the same thing as humanity's proper historical agenda.

A new pattern of stresses has emerged in the post-World War II world. They may imply the larger point that this same world had changed structurally since the fixing of the basic radical definitions, that it needed to be understood again, conceptualized and acted upon from a standpoint uncommon to classical Marxism and through political modes suggested no more by the experience of the Bolsheviks than by that of the parliamentary socialists or the Stalinists.

No one was thinking of anything like this when the name New Left began to acquire small currency in the America of the early Sixties, where politics had grown so used to having no Left at all that any Left at all would already be a novelty. Leftwards of Congress's famous Class of '48 lay the ruins of Henry Wallace; beyond, a few small magazines and some fugitives.

This has all been explained, of course: the purge of communists from the trade-union movement, the explicit national resumption of domestic and foreign anti-Bolshevism, McCarthyism, etc.

But why did the workers permit the purge, the people authorize the anti-Bolshevism, their leaders allow the top-down liquidation of McCarthy to provide, above all, for the continuation of McCarthyism by more subtle means, etc.? The explanations do not explain themselves.

Everywhere in Europe at the end of World War II the heroes of the anti-Fascist resistance movements were the Reds. Allied war propaganda had stressed the progressive nature of the Alliance, the reactionary nature of the Axis Powers. The Soviet army had won the West's respect, the Soviet people its admiration, the Soviet government its acceptance as the voice of a Great Power. The economic ruination of the Continent, the urgency and magnitude of the forthcoming reconstruction effort seemed a self-evident case for precisely that sort of state planning for which an important strain of socialism had made itself famous.

How could the Left have been destroyed?

The centerpiece of radical politics was in that period what it had been for a century, namely, the conception of capitalism as an inherently contradictory system which was fated to destroy itself. With businesses required steadily to lower their rate of profit in order to compete, but, on the other hand, required to maximize profits in order to grow, capitalism could not protect itself from chronic social disaster—warehouses bulging with inventories everyone needed but no one could buy, machines standing idle, and unemployed workers everywhere. The maturing of the fateful economic crisis would destroy the false consciousness that had depoliticized the proletariat and deflected it from its historical mission, the making of the socialist revolution.

It is almost a carrion-bird politics. Distant and above it all for the moment, the revolutionary cadre circles, awaiting the hour of his predestinated dinner. Capitalism weakens, lay-offs and inflation converge, a rash of strikes—the bird moves in. But not so fast: the government also moves. A different money policy, stepped-up federal spending, a public-works project, selective repression of the militants—the bird resumes his higher orbit.

How could there be a practical politics for a radicalism whose most honest slogan must have been "This is a bubble which must burst"?

The Left was liquidated in the fifties because it was defenseless. It was defenseless because its most essential claims amounted to so many dire conjectures or predictions or prophecies, whether sound or not is beside the point. A politically practical Left must be able convincingly to say, "This is not even a good bubble." But how could the American Left have said that, since it had traditionally endorsed a program whose simplest driving objective was for the same economic security "for the masses" which the "masses" in question believed themselves already to possess? If the argument for socialism is reduced in practice to the argument that capitalism cannot deliver the goods, then there is no practical argument for socialism when the goods are being delivered. Radicals tirelessly explained, first, that the general level of national prosperity was not so incredible as all that (the South, the inner cities, the blacks), and second, that this prosperity was, in any case, much less the flower of an organically healthy system than of the Cold War politics which allowed an irrational system to subsidize its incapacities through the Pentagon. Take away this annually swelling defense budget, and what will happen then to this vaunted "neocapitalism"? The first point, however, could not meet the rejoinder that things were better here than anyplace else and getting better, and the second point could hardly have been defended for long unless the American radicals had been willing to attack the main assumptions of the Cold War, something which was scarcely a task for men whose highest hopes had so recently been abused by the Stalinist consummation in Russia, and something which would scarcely have mobilized the revolution anyway.

Even during the Eisenhower Fifties, when a flagging growth rate and occasional recessions gave some substance to a conventional left-wing critique, the intellectual initiative lay with those whose chief point was that, within the West, there were no more fundamental economic problems to be solved. Granting sometimes, in parenthetical asides, that the situation elsewhere might be different, political critics like Daniel Bell argued that we had come upon "the end of ideology," meaning simply that an achieved welfare-state capitalism, equipped with Keynesian control devices, had met all the objections of the nineteenth century and the Thirties, and there being apparently no new objections, the matter was closed. Herbert Hoover's concept of a corporate society, a working national coalition of business, labor, and government meritocracies, had so nearly materialized that ideological thought in the grand manner, not even to mention revolutionary politics, was henceforth required to yield to another kind of task, the extension of administrative and technical expertise. The only practical question still left on the agenda was no longer "How must we restructure our relations of production?" but rather "How can we most efficiently maintain the present course, steadily extending to now-excluded groups the self-evidently adequate system we have already contrived, tested, proved, and installed?" On this base of domestic tranquillity, American foreign policy could return with confidence to a modernized Wilsonian line: anti-Bolshevism with the loophole of détente, commercial and political integration of the world's Great Powers, and continued extension of the Atlantic world's mastery (*noblesse oblige*, of course, the mastery must be technologically generous and financially paternal) over the whole of the earth.

But no one can now say there was anything placid about the consciousness, the spirit, of the American Fifties, a decade which belonged also, though we tried hard to ignore the fact, to such other peoples as the Chinese, the Vietnamese, the Cubans, the Algerians, the decolonizing African states.

On the contrary. It was in that period, for example, that the phenomenon of middle-class juvenile crime emerged, posing a great mystery to liberalism's conviction that crime came from material want. Young white gangs in the best of the suburbs? What sense did that make? Crime was for the poor, for it was only the gall of poverty that could motivate the risks of crime. And the same generation which authored this mystery seemed almost purposively quiet as to its motives. The Silent Generation —queried, analyzed, and rebuked in a thousand commencement-day addresses—stood mute, unexplained, and innocent before its accusers; and choosing neither to know itself nor to be condemned, it made its uniform not only the gray flannel suit but also the beard and the fatigue jacket. The Silent Generation: Perhaps there was not so much silence after all. At least, this was also the Beat Generation—owners of that supremely ambiguous title which said: We are beaten and shall endure.

Of course it could not have been clearer to their interpreters that these Beaten and Beatified renegades—Kerouac, Ginsberg, Ferlinghetti—had precisely no political ambitions. The question hardly occurred. Who imagined that Norman Mailer would become—a Candidate? What the Beat Generation wanted was a bit of free social space for a few spiritual and literary experiments. Like any subcult, it was a nuisance, an insult, a circus, and a kind of pantomimed moral criticism: Culture Gypsies, not Candidates. So it seemed.

Elsewhere in the same period, still another demurrer from happy consciousness was being entered: "If We're So Rich, What's Eating Us?"—very typical title of a very typical mid-Fifties middlebrow essay (this one, for *Harper's*, by economist

Robert Lekachman). Vance Packard assembles three politically absent-minded indictments against an unspecified suspect: *The Waste Makers, The Status Seekers, The Hidden Persuaders* ache with unliberated conclusions about a certain form of civilization. Much more insightfully but still without a sharp conception of the political imperatives he had encountered, David Riesman reconsidered individualism and probed the loneliness of the American crowd. By the end of the decade, these themes were so commonplace as to have become the property of all points of view—Left, Right, and Center.

Everybody knew it: something was wrong.

But how could that be, since everybody also knew that there was no more need for ideology? A soft, deft pessimism became the main philosophical stance of the best of the non-Beat novelists and poets. Salinger, Roth, Updike, Bellow, Lowell, and Roethke—variously schooled on Freud but not Riech, Eliot but not Neruda, and Dewey but not Marx—developed remarkably cognate points of view, a set of implicit judgments amounting to an informal canon of the modern sensibility. The inner experience is paramount. Neurosis is man's ordinary condition and can even be husbanded to a certain eerie grace. History has been preempted by science and magic, which have fused into psychoanalysis.

Through such moves, the gap between what the world looked like and what it felt like was not so much bridged as converted into a national park for the exploratory cultivation of ambiguity, the characteristically modern adventure. There was a fey sort of loveliness, it seemed, which survived even economic perfection. One could even grow enamoured of all this melancholy. Had it remained for modern man to discover the allures of *angst*, of defeat? The famous antihero whom the Fifties had created in its image: was he the central figure in a circus? Or in a trial?

We were not to be very long in doubt.

The political imagination, necessarily banished from even so chilly an Eden, had therefore disguised itself as nostalgia, to reinfiltrate first consciousness and then discourse with a happy orgasm in its pocket like a concealed weapon—a threat and a promise, this orgasm, and in both aspects revolutionary.

There had been no end of ideology at all. Rather, ideological thought—*critical thought with historical structure*—had merely gone out of its conventional métier to prepare its negation of contemporary Western life. The advent of what we have lately been asked to call the "post-scarcity" or "post-industrial" state had confronted critical analysis with a subject matter before which the conventional methods of political economics and sociology were insufficiently descriptive. A subject matter, moreover, whose features ran so far beyond the conceptual power of ordinary politics that it required a wild leap of the imagination to see that it was precisely politics that was being put into question. Salinger's Holden Caulfield, Mailer's White Negro, Kerouac's Dean Moriarty, Bellow's Augie March or Herzog: Do they *enjoy* capitalism?

No misunderstanding: The informal pattern of negations which such figures constituted was almost never explicitly political, nor was there much of even an underlying reprieve for the period's conception of a "radical" politics. No doubt there is some reserve of special compassion for the man who does not yet have enough, but no one supposed that his suffering was beyond the available remedies or that curing it might need structural changes in our mode of economic organization. The fear, rather, was that curing it might not even help very much. Indeed, the white writer in his white ambience would more than once see something enviable in the situation of the affluent society's outsiders. Apparently these outsiders had more soul than those who had made it—passion instead of bitchiness, a vivifying community of social pain instead of the naggingly selfish itch of a $100-a-week neurosis. To be materially secure was evidently to be spiritually bland. How unsatisfying. The point is that the assumptions of the then-current radical viewpoint could catch the political drift of this ennui scarcely any better than the assumptions of the more familiar liberal viewpoint could dissipate it. Revolution? Something the workers were supposed to make in order that they never again be wiped out by economic (but not spiritual) depression. The radical? Either a Dostoyevskian fanatic or someone who believed that capitalism would fail to rationalize the industrial society—either a freak or a bore. Socialism? What happens to imperial states shorn of their empires. Communism? An extravagant horror produced by killer utopians.

The deepening American malady seemed beyond all known therapies. It did not even seem to have a political name.

But when a lonely and doubtless very brave American radical, C. Wright Mills, began to put political pieces together in a political way, he could hardly have guessed how quickly—a matter of half a decade?—a rising generation would move to refute one of his cardinal political observations. Refute: for even through the remarkable moral and physical energy which sustained him, one could not fail to understand that Mills saw himself as a political desperado whose most difficult struggle was against a very persuasive despair. The first and continuing need of those whom his polemic would bring to activism would be to prove the possibility of what he considered next to impossible, a radical movement with some serious power behind it.

How could there be a radical politics without mass support? Then where were America's potentially radical masses? The poor? They have been chronically hard to organize, and even granting their possible mobility, Mills could see no barrier to their being geared into the same mass-consumer society which had emasculated everyone else. The blacks? The odds again seemed to be with the system: over and over it had shown its skills at legalistic maneuver and cooptation; and what could the blacks demand except inclusion, access to the general beehive? Labor? Bureaucratized and politically docile, the trade-unionist seemed happy to forget his prewar militancy; socialism could find no more indifferent and the Cold War no more ardent a partisan.

There remained, thought Mills, only the academic intellectuals. But what good were they? They did not even begin to constitute a class in the political sense, and as one career group among others, their postwar record had been dreary. They had professionally supported the official American equation of revolution with Stalinism; they had learned, moreover, how to fatten off the Cold War, and at their radical best, they drew the line at an unexhilirating social democracy whose most lively pursuit seemed to be the sycophantic care and feeding of welfare-state capitalism. Still, their training—and their vanities—made them on some terms prepared to answer for their views of the world. Considering themselves to be responsible to the humane criteria of classical liberalism, maybe they could be made to think some second and third thoughts. And then perhaps to make a few small waves.

Mills described from his sociological orientation essentially the same world which Herbert Marcuse faced from his philosophical one, namely, the internal rationalization of an externally irrational culture. How to make bigger bombs, crazier cars, greedier consumers: the impressive capacities of science and technology were routinely brought to bear on such projects, but the culture lacked entirely the methodological and institutional means for posing practical questions about these pursuits in themselves. One could grumble about the Bomb and Madison Avenue manipulation; people grumbled about such things all the time. But what could be done? A letter? A petition? A committee?

Reason itself seemed arrogantly to have forgotten mere man in its sublime quest for pure knowledge. To every frail challenge which an addled humanism could muster, pure knowledge answered: sentimentality. The imperious "value-free" positivism, which still gives Western science its apologies, explained that the *idea* of "man's destiny" is an unworkable abstraction about which proper science has nothing to say. Wholly permeated with the bourgeois ideology which it therefore refused to recognize as such, science's chief assumptions, already laid out by Galileo in the seventeenth century, remained that the physical world was given and that the scientist merely interrogated it by means of hypothesis and test to discover its nature, the end objective being an integrated, global system of verified propositions. Not, for example, a better world. No doubt a provisionally successful treasure hunt, however disinterested, would make the world better. But however interesting an incidental that might be, it remained an incidental; and it could not occur to science in any practical, operational way that it remained continuously a human instrument—merely human—created and developed precisely by that same social man whom it refused to recognize as having any principled claims upon it, and that, as such, its definitive purpose might be (of all things) a *moral* one: less to discover than to *create* the "truth" of nature, the meaning of the cosmos—of human history.

That far had the spirit of the Enlightenment declined. The method of thought which the eighteenth century had imagined would liberate mankind turned out in the twentieth—we allow for ivy-day ceremonializing about miracles—not even to understand the idea of such a project. Challenge the Manhattan Project and CBW research? But not as a scientist, for between scientific thought and moral thought there is and can be no structural link. Was it not the final divorce of the two domains which defined the platform of science at the onset of the modern era? To put science again at the mercy of a moral system, whether profane or sacred, is to restore the politics of Inquisition and the need for martyrs.

Precisely. It is science's old and current servitudes which continue to demand its special war of liberation: liberation from an imperial system of social classes, from the subordination of its work to the conflict-based imperatives which class societies produce.

A humdrum example from technology: The effect of America's overland transportation system—fast cars, fast roads—is to create a worsening array of problems at the urban ganglia upon which the impeccable ribbons all converge. Neighborhoods are first lacerated, then buried under the thickening whirls of concrete and steel; the air is casually poisoned; fatalities are perpetually of epidemic scale; nevertheless, transportation is bad and gets worse. This is the objective result of our having spent the transportation share of the national budget in a certain way. There were other ways we might have spent our money—on a fast-train system, for example—if the purpose had really been to get the best transportation system, and if such decisions were really made by the disinterested science and rational technology to which we pretend we have ceded our collective social fate. That we never even had a chance to pose the alternatives is above all a *political* fact whose simple meaning is that the combined political power of the auto makers, the road builders, and the oil refiners is peerless. This combine tells us that we really *want* to ride around in mustangs, cougars, and other untamed animals (our totemistic animal cultism surpasses, even in its rituals, the known primitive atavisms)—and being civilized, we gracefully swoon. Take the auto industry as a paradigm: "What's good for General Motors is good for America," said Charles Wilson, making up in clarity what he may have lacked in finesse. The Inquisitor did not disappear at all. He was merely victorious. This "value freedom" claimed by science is nothing but a churchy dogma whose function is to disguise the difference between the special interests of a dominant class and the general interests of mankind.

Nothing new, of course, not even the magnificence of the disguise, which as usual is least understood by those who are most victimized by it. Thus, the pessimism of Mills and Marcuse. Contemporary Western culture appears to be distinguished by its failure to produce a class whose essential objectives transcend the capacities of the given order and whose presence would therefore force a structural transformation of the relations of production. Dismal surprise: a political situation which was supposed to materialize only under the auspices of the revolution has arrived prematurely, making the prospects of the revolution dimmest exactly within the culture which stands in greatest apparent need of the revolution. If Mills saw some chance that the academic intellectuals might successfully challenge, if not the System, then at least its policy, Marcuse could scarcely venture so far from despair: "[The] absolute need for breaking out of this whole does not prevail where it could become the driving force of a historical practice, the effective cause of qualitative change. Without this material force, even the most acute consciousness remains powerless."[1]

So. Does this amount to the concrete actualization of that famous whimper? Or are the disciples of an exhausted critical tradition chewing sour grapes?

But there is a third possibility. What if a changing world configuration of forces has been creating new social needs—and the political possibility of pursuing them—which remain invisible only to the old system of anticipations?

Isaac Deutscher closed a 1965 commentary on the Vietnam War with the following observation:

> We may not be able to get away from the severe conflicts of our age and we need not get away from them. But we may perhaps lift those conflicts above the morass into which they have been forced. The divisions may once again run within nations, rather than between nations. We may give back to class struggle its old dignity. We may and we must restore meaning to the great ideas by which mankind is still living, the ideas of liberalism, democracy, and communism.[2]

Peculiar: Before class struggle can recapture an old dignity which it has apparently lost, and before the vivifying ideas can recover their meaning, also lost, we will (somehow) have to return class conflict to that national framework which it has apparently burst through. We find Deutscher here in the grips of nostalgia for a world which was at once industrialized *and* politically convulsed—Europe before and between the great wars. Elsewhere in the same collection of essays, he is no less disturbed by the current form of class struggle but more lucid as to its reversibility:

> The impossibility of disentangling progress from backwardness is the price that not only Russia and China but mankind as a whole is paying for the confinement of the revolution to the underdeveloped countries. But this is the way history has turned; and now nothing can force its pace.[3]

[1] Herbert Marcuse, *One-Dimensional Man* (Boston: Beacon Press, 1964), p. 253.

[2] Isaac Deutscher, *The Ironies of History* (New York: Oxford University Press, 1966), p. 163.

[3] *Ibid.*, p. 120.

No doubt. The problem is to try to deal somehow with this development; and it may be that the conceptual apparatus of Marxism as practiced up to the advent of the Cold War, when not only the whole of Europe but the entire world found itself fixed helplessly by the politics of class, cannot meet such a need.

The practical core of classical Marxism is the presumption of an irreconcilable conflict between capital and labor. The two must fight. If they are not fighting at some moment, that must only be owing to capital's skills at momentarily obscuring the fateful class opposition. That opposition nevertheless remains basic until the revolution liquidates it by liquidating the forms and instruments of class domination, and it is therefore present even when it seems to be absent. To explain the absence of this fight, Marxism resorted to a conceptual distinction between objective and subjective conditions, corresponding to true (or class) consciousness versus false consciousness at the level of politics and infrastructural (economic) reality versus superstructural (social) reality at the level of culture. That distinction carried with it the belief that subjective awareness must at some point encompass objective fact, that class consciousness must finally overcome false consciousness, that the pivotal realities of class relations in the system of production must at some juncture be fully and openly expressed in the politics of class conflict. The revolution will thereupon have been prepared.

Regardless of the validity of this conceptualization, the fact is that it had lost, at both the theoretical and practical levels, the power to criticize itself. It amounted to an hypothesis which could not be negated, therefore a false hypothesis. There was simply no way to put a time scale underneath the test of history. The workers will move to take control of the means of production? When, ultimately? But what can "ultimately" mean? Predictions and excuses multiplied, each more "rigorous," more "scientific" than the last. Since the situation was always in turmoil, since the air was always filled with rumors of crisis and speculations of disaster, the anticipatory stance into which the Western revolutionary had frozen himself never became embarrassing. Like Vladimir and Estragon waiting for Godot, he could never be sure that the very next moment might not divulge the practical means to that victory which his "final analysis" always guaranteed. Meanwhile, tactical battles of all sorts needed to be waged; one could keep busy. And beyond the furies of the moment, giving them scale and a meaning to which he and his comrades alone were privy, a horizon about which everything but its distance was known held the revolutionary cosmos firmly in place.

But the waiting game to which the Western communist parties had committed themselves in the aftermath of the Truman Doctrine and the Marshall Plan was, of course, by no means theoretically derived, nor was it merely a response to the success of American reconstruction of West European capitalism. The motive was simpler.

The communist parties of the Continent had matured in a period when all socialist hopes were pinned to the survival of the Soviet Union. Even for a long time after the advent of Stalin, a living strain of European Bolshevism still held that protecting the world's solitary socialist state required prompt revolutions in Europe's industrial heartland. But by the end of World War II and the emergence of the U.S.S.R. as a troubled but evidently stable Great Power, an unchanged aim was being served by a wholly reversed strategy. The security of the U.S.S.R., as central an aim as ever, was now held to require the *passivity* of European (and Asian) revolutionaries. "Socialism in one country," as Deutscher points out, was the slogan by means of which Stalin announced socialism's intention to cooperate with capitalism's intention to contain the revolution. The U.S.S.R.'s self-containment, expressed finally as the doctrine of coexistence, could hardly have been a more explicit directive to revolutionaries elsewhere *also* to coexist. A hard-fisted irony had closed: revolution needs the security of the U.S.S.R., but the security of the U.S.S.R. outlaws revolution.

Thus, the European communist parties, confronting a massive array of problems—theoretical, organizational, practical, ethical—found themselves both tempted and driven to a politics without a future. With no clear goals beyond those of more rational industrialization which Cold War capitalism seemed to have subverted, with few methods of political struggle beyond the parliamentary ones which were capitalism's proudest legal achievement, with no concrete response to the internationalizing of the class struggle which would not immediately contradict the U.S.S.R.–first dogma (standard until the Twentieth Party Congress and "polycentrism"), the communist parties of Europe (and Latin America) came upon an impasse which they could not surmount or even very honestly survey.

But it seemed they could make camp before this impasse—even build a rather comfortable suburb in the outskirts of this Cold War capitalism. Coexistence, initially a concession to a passing strategic necessity, had finally become an unconditional demand. Struggle had been supplanted by dialogue. According to Alain Geismar, an activist in the French uprising of spring, 1968, "Under its present organization, the French Communist Party has emerged as the anti-communist structure *par excellence*."

In essence, the institutionalized European Left of the postwar period could not relate to the internationalizing of the class war because it had itself become objectively counterrevolutionary.

The fury of events, of course, did not therefore subside. Outside the West, other peoples would understand themselves to be the only liberators of their destiny; and within the West, another generation would be unable to see why the U.S.S.R. deserved so much protection—or why their own sharpening needs for a changed world should remain locked in the hands of those who no longer seemed so interested in changing it.

The New Left is properly so called because in order to exist it had to overcome the memories, the certitudes, and the promises of the Old Left. Russia-firstism had been made insupportable by Hungary and then unintelligible by the Sino-Soviet split, well before Czechoslovakia was to make it grotesque. The doctrine of coexistence had therefore lost such binding practical authority as it had formerly possessed. The internationalizing of the class war, momentous event, along with the directly connected triumph of international monopoly as the prime mode of Western economic organization, called implicitly for a new conception of the participants in the ongoing conflict of classes. "You are nothing without the workers," advises a grand old revolutionary warhorse who won in colors in the anti-Fascist resistance, and who cannot fathom why his sons should now say, "Who precisely are they?"

The confidence needed to pose such a question could not come overnight, not even in Europe, where the methods of critical philosophy were much more available than in the United States. An American generation with obscure new projects roiling in the back of its mind, not finding itself suitably identified within the class typologies of a barely audible domestic radicalism, would initially misunderstand its political motivation as bad conscience about the blacks.

The high tide of the civil-rights movement began in February 1960 with the Greensboro sit-ins which led to the formation of the Student Nonviolent Coordinating Committee (SNCC). It ended with the Democratic Party's Atlantic City convention in August 1964, when the Mississippi Freedom Democratic Party's solid case for the unseating of the regular delegation was overridden in a well-televised exhibition of backroom politics. The main political event of the following summer was the Watts rebellion.

SNCC and SDS (Students for a Democratic Society) were answering to the name New Left early in the Sixties, but this needs two cautions. Both groups shared a pathological distrust for what they sneeringly called ideology. This was often noted by the early commentators, who understood it no better than did the New Left itself. It was accounted to be anti-intellectualism and the activists cheerfully accepted that account. In fact, it was a necessary defense against the power of an exhausted but nonetheless practiced ideology, the net effect of whose truths might easily have been to send the activists packing to the socialist clubs, where they would have been made either skillful at writing themselves off as change agents, or bored. They wanted neither. They wanted instead to go south and get their hands and their heads—their lives—into the dangerous, the moral, and therefore the authentic. The instinct from the beginning was to discover the streets, and there was nothing at all anti-intellectual about this. It embodied rather a refusal to tolerate the further separation of thought from its consequences: books argued with each other and lied and in any case did not make much of a difference; only direct experience was incontrovertible.

The second caution: there was simply nothing very radical or in need of ideology about the Movement's civil rights, Heroic Period, 1960–1964. What was so leftist about SNCC's "one man, one vote" demand? Or the abiding SDS principle of participatory democracy, the view that people should make the decisions that affect their lives? No one bothered to notice in those days that such a principle, fully understood, would lead through draft-card burning toward a demand for workers' control of the means of production.

From the beginning, the Movement gave the System the benefit of every doubt. An SDS slogan in 1964: "Part of the way with LBJ." There were always Movement people who understood that the seemingly innocuous demands were saturated with deeply radical implications, but it was not before 1965 or 1966 that this consciousness began to be widely shared. "Take the bourgeoisie at its word," Marx says somewhere, and this is precisely what the movement did, in its nearly spotless ignorance of Marx. Did it matter—as the schooled and knowing leftists insisted it did—that the early integrationist or student-power demands were only reformist or corporative? English New Leftist Tom Fawthrop, commenting on the June 1968 student rising at the University of Hull, wrote, "We chose the real politics of revolutionary democracy as opposed to the sham politics of revolutionary semantics. Every real struggle, every engagement with the power structure is worth a hundred revolutionary slogans."

German New Leftist Rudi Dutschke makes a point about this process which applies at least as forcibly to the American experience, and probably just as well to the French, English, Spanish, Mexican—and Czechoslovak. The new activists acquired their radical anti-authoritarianism at the end of police sticks that are swinging from one end of the earth to the other in behalf of everything dead and dry, in defense of social orders that prosper by denying life its possibilities and that greet every new aspiration with increasing indifference, derision, and violence. The policeman's riot club functions like a magic wand under whose hard caress the banal soul grows vivid and the nameless recover their authenticity—a bestower, this wand, of the lost charisma of the modern self: I bleed, therefore I am.

This is a ferocious but effective way to be a student—to be *educated.* By the end of the Chicago Democratic Party convention in August 1968, such young white activists as may still have supposed they were making this curiously unexamined revolution in the name of the blacks or the Vietnamese—or even the workers who (out of "false consciousness" no doubt) were cheering on the police—had had second thoughts pounded into their heads. The bad conscience which had seemed motive enough in the earlier period had been supplanted by a weightier sense of their own cultural need and hence of their own political mission. It was for themselves, these sons and daughters of the well-appointed classes, that the revolution would have to be made; for short of surrender—spiritual suicide—they seemed to have no other way to survive.

Whereupon the *need* for ideological thought, growing bit by bit as the Movement cantilevered itself steadily further from the liberal value system which had given it its first platform, had finally restored the *possibility* of ideological thought. The essentially personalistic apology for action which had satisfied all earlier engagements had become—one could *feel* this—insufficient. Its power to motivate and defend had dwindled with respect to the changing character of Movement actions and mood. An undistinguished idealism, really a fetish of innocence, could support Selma but not Watts, the campus teach-ins but not the Columbia insurrection. An existential morality had precipitated a chain of collisions which could finally be explained only in terms of historical politics. It had become necessary for a "youth movement" to discover—or create—a class identity.

Thus, having begun with a misreading of Camus, the American New Left at last begins to take up Marx, more than a little fearful that yet another misreading will be required, but hoping to sustain an additive revision. Can such a project succeed? Will a habituation to old certitudes even disallow the attempt? In any case, the clubs and committees have convinced the Movement that dialogue has certain limits and that a politics rooted in class imperatives is more likely to prosper than a politics rooted in that sort of moral fineness which is one product of the idleness of the few.

What is at stake is the political self-confidence of the Movement. Does the white "middle-class" New Left constitute the embryonic beginnings of a class-for-itself? Does it embody the beginnings of an identifiable historical practice which can neither be transferred to another class nor abandoned nor permanently defeated? Or, on the contrary, is this Movement merely the suds, the effervescing, of a globalized class war in which the entire West plays the role of capital and the entire neocolonial South that of labor, and whose basic features therefore differ only in scale from the class conflict of the nineteenth century?

The sharpest form of the question: in view of modern radicalism's unchallenged doctrine that the revolution is to be made by the army of industrial labor, how does the new radical dare to proceed (putting it mildly) in the conspicuous absence of that army?

First things first. *He does proceed.* Perhaps he has no choice and he is pure fatality; perhaps there is no fatality and he is pure will. His self-estimate may be sophisticated and in error or primitive and correct. His position may be invincible, absurd, both, or neither. It does not matter. He is on the scene, caught in events and definitively beyond silence, no longer awaiting some advance demonstration of the prudence or the consequences of engagement. It is not as if he is about to decide something as a precondition of doing something. The hands are out, the chips are down, the New Left is at the table with all the other gamblers.

So much for history.

For the New Left's future, its destiny, it must serve here to say that the debate intensifies at the same tempo as the confrontation, and that the confrontation is by this time clearly general in the West. Barring, by this time, not even England, which made its impressive debut in the spring of 1968, there is no advanced capitalist country which has not given rise to an increasingly self-aware and militant postwar movement centered physically in the universities and politically in anti-authoritarianism. At the same time, none of these countries (*not* excluding France!) has produced a living socialist movement centered in the factories. Further, each of the youth movements coalesced initially around some variation of an anti-imperialist issue (the May demonstrations at Essex, for example, began in protest against a talk given by a government germ-warfare expert). That is, the igniting spark has always jumped to the interior, to the imperial metropolis, from friction points at the frontier, and it has been only in the aftermath of anti-imperialist beginnings that these movements began to develop a more clearly self-interested political stance. This is doubly true of the American New Left. Reacting first against the oppression of the blacks, whose ghettoes are like so many colonial native quarters, and then against the attempted suppression of the Vietnamese independence struggle, white activists have only recently discovered in practice the ubiquity of oppressive authoritarianism—discovered that for all the obvious modal differences, they share the victimization of the most humiliated slave.

There are four basic positions on the identity of the New Left.

The first is held by a variety of left-wing liberals and Millsian radicals who believe either that the System can produce a worthwhile self-reform, or (the case with the Millsians) that the absence of radical alternatives forces one to hope that it can. The New Left is understood then as a generator of challenges, of critical energy and ideas which may bear some fruit within the evolving structures of enlightened capitalism.

Second, the most familiarly radical position, is that the industrial workers remain the essential driving force of an inevitable socialist revolution. The student movement's main current purposes must be the building of a radical base among intellectuals and the making of such ties with the factories and the black groups as may be possible.

Third, an exclusively New Left position, is that the composition of the work force has been significantly altered by the massive assimilation of industry and technology. Students and workers are from now on one and the same. "There are no student problems," begins *The Appeal from the Sorbonne.* The factory of the post-industrial state is the multiversity. Students are the new working class.

Fourth is a position which has not yet been argued in a sustained way, although it is perhaps suggested in some of the writings by André Gorz, Louis Althusser, and Martin Nicolaus. Diverging from the conclusions but not the methods of Marx, this view would share with the new-working-class theory the notion that students can no longer be understood as if the modern university retained all the key features of the medieval university. Students constitute the beginnings of a new historical class, produced by a workers' revolution which (within the West) is not still to come but which has already taken place. Such a view implies several departures from classical Marxism. First, it denies that bourgeois society in anything like the original model still exists: bourgeois society was above all a scarcity society, a fact which determined its chief legal, political, and economic features. What we have now, inadequately termed post-scarcity and post-industrial, is, in fact, merely the fulfilled industrial society. Second, it denies that bourgeois society (or any other) is the last of the contradictory social system. On the contrary, there is more reason to believe that each historically successful revolution will produce a new class with a new conception of need and possibility, new objectives which will motivate new historical practices. Third, it denies that the mission of the proletariat was to make the socialist revolution. The objective evidence indicates, rather, that its mission was to industrialize society—a mission which brought it into sharp conflict with the bourgeoisie. Fourth, it denies that current world politics can be understood as a clash of rival socio-ethical systems. Capitalism and socialism, as defined by their practice, are different means, corresponding to different material and political situations, for pursuing the common and general aim of industrialization. Fifth, far from hero-worshipping the proletariat, the new class (unnamed and no doubt at this point unnameable) repudiates in part and in part carries forward the proletarian culture in much the same way that the proletariat both absorbed and transcended bourgeois culture. That an embryonic new class will seek alliance with the proletariat in its struggle with the bourgeoisie—this has the same kind of meaning as the fact that the embryonic proletariat made alliance with the bourgeoisie in the latter's struggle against Versailles.

So much—at the moment—for speculation.

Whether as de-classed provocateur, as an attendant upon another class's temporarily stalled revolution, as a new version of that other class, or as something new, the New Left will create itself through its actions in an arena defined as well as occupied by other forces. Even as this is written—mid-fall of 1968—George Wallace's Presidential campaign has conclusively established the presence of a serious fascist movement: militarism, chauvinism, racism—all bound together by a deformed populist nostalgia which gives this movement both its menace and its irony. At the same moment, Establishment liberalism has altogether lost its former poise, as well as its control of the nation's primary political media. Overnight, the nation's majority coalition, the Democratic Party, has become all but an also-ran. The next four years no doubt will be filled with a continuing crisis within the Atlantic economy and either the agonies of disengagement from Vietnam or the extension of the war to China, thence quickly to the world as a whole. Against this backdrop, domestic politics will be dominated by the continuing rise of the Right and a bewildered Establishment's attempts both to appease populist reaction and New Left militancy and to reassemble a functioning Center coalition, one shade to the left of Nixon. In terms of the day-to-day necessities implied by this over-all conjuncture, the New Left will have to discover or create its historical identity. What we already know is simply that it has one—that through the appropriately discoherent New Left movement, the postwar generations have implicated themselves in history's permanent showdown between fatality and will.

A note on the selections. In the first part, each of the seven pieces is an effort to lay out part of the portrait of life in the industrial countries. All, but notably those by Althusser, Nicolaus, and Leszek Kolakowski, are therefore in some part meditations on history, process, and methods of seeing form.

In this of all periods in the modern era, the West may not think of itself as being alone in the world. Our acute awareness of the Others has been thrust upon us by the Others' fury.

They do not permit us to forget that their situation is a leading aspect of our own. Castro and Fanon speak from that situation with perfect authority. Two major statements by black American radicals—Malcolm X and Huey Newton—are included in this second part, "The Revolutionary Frontier," because black Americans remain essentially a colonized people: Harlem is New York City's *Kasbah* in almost all respects but the geographical.

Except for Newton and Fanon (who died at thirty-seven in 1961), all the authors represented in the first two parts are over forty. Most of those in the final part, "A New Revolution?," are all under twenty-five. The university-based New Left, whatever else it may do, has already produced a fertile body of often strikingly original analysis. The included selections deal with all the major themes which preoccupy it.

Everyone will notice that only six of the seventeen selections are American. This is partly because the collection is made for Americans, who presumably have easy access to the basic American texts. There is, of course, still a larger reason. The English routinely use American coinages like sit-in, teach-in, drop-out, and—fuzz. (Pig will no doubt follow.) The Battle of Telegraph Avenue in Berkeley in 1968 began as a mass demonstration of solidarity with the French students. Demonstrators at the Democratic Party's convention carried signs that linked Chicago and Prague. The New Left is an international movement.

Carl Oglesby

PART ONE:

Understanding Leviathan

The Politics of Responsibility

C. WRIGHT MILLS

As technically strong a sociologist as America has produced, Mills was stronger yet as a polemicist. No writer had nearly his influence on the generation that produced the sit-in movement, the Peace Corps, and the first crop of New Leftists.

The following selection is a compound of two extracts, the first taken from the 1960 edition of his book, The Causes of World War III,[1] *and the second (in which he reproduces an extensive passage from that book) from a later pamphlet, "Letter to the New Left." Taken together, the two extracts perfectly strike the mood which, when he was writing, had hardly been heard of in America but which has since become general on the campuses; and with faultless accuracy, they lay out an agenda for thought and action which today has only acquired a still more piercing relevance.*

WHAT I HAVE BEEN trying to say to intellectuals, preachers, scientists—as well as more generally to publics—can be put into one sentence: drop the liberal rhetoric and the conservative default; they are now parts of one and the same official line; transcend that line.

There is still a good deal of talk, so fashionable several years ago, about the collapse of "Right" and "Left"; about "conservative" and "radical" being no longer viable as intellectual and political orientations. Much of this talk, I believe, is part of the default of intellectual workmen, a revelation of their lack of imagination. As a political type, the conservative, in common with the indifferent, is generally content "to be like other men

[1] New York: Simon and Schuster, 1960.

and to take things as they are," for he believes that the status quo has been built slowly and that as such it is as beneficent an arrangement as can fairly be expected. In brief, and in the consistent extreme, the conservative is a man who abdicates the willful making of history.

The radical (and even the liberal) is a man who does not abdicate. He agrees that many human events, important events at that, may indeed be the results of so many little acts that they are indeed part of fate. But he also sees that more and more events in our epoch are not matters of fate; that they are the results of decisions made and not made by identifiable men who command the new means of decision and of power.

Given these means of administration, production, violence, it seems clear that more and more events are due less to any uncontrollable fate than to the decisions, the defaults, the ignorance—as the case may be—of the higher circles of the superstates. To reflect upon the present as history is to understand that history may now be made by default. Understanding that, we no longer need accept as "necessary" the lesser evil. We no longer need to accept historical fate, for fate is a feature of specific kinds of social structure, of irresponsible systems of power.

These systems can be changed. Fate can be transcended. We must come to understand that while the domain of fate is diminishing, the exercise of responsibility is also diminishing and in fact becoming organized as irresponsibility. We must hold men of power variously responsible for pivotal events, we must unmask their pretensions—and often their own mistaken convictions—that they are not responsible.

Our politics, in short, must be the politics of responsibility. Our basic charge against the systems of both the United States and the U.S.S.R. must be that in differing ways they both live by the politics of irresponsibility.

In East and in West, nowadays, the idea of responsibility is in a sad condition. It is either washed away in liberal rhetoric, or it becomes a trumped-up bloody purge. But we must hold to it; we must be serious about it; we must understand that to use it requires knowledge and inquiry, continual reflection and imagination.

Those who decide should be held responsible to those men and women everywhere who are in any grievous way affected by decisions and defaults. But by whom should they be held responsible? That is the immediate problem of political power.

In both East and West today, the immediate answer is: by the intellectual community. Who else but intellectuals are capable of discerning the role in history of explicit history-making decisions? Who else is in a position to understand that now fate itself must be made a political issue?

No longer can fate be used either as excuse or as hope; neither our hopes nor our fears are part of anything inevitable: we are on our own. Would it not be elementary honesty for the intellectual to realize this new and radical fact of human history and so at least consider the decisions that he is in fact making, rather than to deny by his work that any responsible decisions are open to him?

Democracy requires that those who bear the consequences of decisions have enough knowledge to hold decision-makers accountable. If men hope that contemporary America is to be a democratic society, they must look to the intellectual community for knowledge about those decisions that are now shaping human destiny. Men must depend upon knowledge provided by this community, for by their own private experience they can know only a small portion of the social world, only a few of the decisions that now affect them.

Yet leading intellectual circles in America as elsewhere have not provided true images of the elite as men in irresponsible command of unprecedented means of power. Instead, they have invented images of a scatter of reasonable men, overwhelmed by events and doing their best in a difficult situation. By its softening of the political will, the conservative mood of the intellectuals, out of which these images have arisen, enables men to accept public depravity without any private sense of outrage and to give up the central goal of Western humanism, so strongly felt in nineteenth-century American experience: the audacious control by reason of man's fate.

Nowadays, there is much generalized anguish because there were Causes in the Thirties but not any more. What all this means, I think, is that in the Thirties the Causes were all set up as programs and little intellectual or moral effort was required to focus them, to pursue them. At present, the social energy to develop such Causes does not seem to be available. As a result there is the often-bemoaned dreariness of the recent cultural scene and the obvious international fact of the political default of cultural workmen of the West. This complaint and this default rest upon the unmet need to specify private troubles out of the vague uneasiness of individuals; to make public issues out of indifference and malaise; and to turn uneasiness and indifference themselves into troubles, issues, and problems open to inquiry.

Both private uneasiness and public indifference rest upon an unawareness of imperiled values and of that which is imperiling them. What is needed is political thinking that is also culturally sensible. That this does not now exist is a result of the failure to assert the values as well as the perils. I cannot help but think that this failure represents another instance in the West of the ascendancy of the international hayseed.

There is a showdown on socialism, on its very meaning as well as its chances, going on in Eastern Europe, in Russia, in China, in Cuba.

There is a showdown on capitalism in Western Europe, in North America, in parts of the pre-industrial world.

But for those concerned with the politics of culture and the culture of politics, the most important showdown has to do with the problems that lie in the international encounter of the two superstates. This encounter involves not only two coexisting kinds of political economy; it poses not only the problems of how the world is to be industrialized. This world encounter is also an encounter of models of human character. For the kinds of human beings that are going to prevail are now being selected and formed in the United States and in Russia. And within both these societies there is coming a showdown on all the modern expectations about what man can *want* to become.

In America and in Russia—in differing ways but often with frightening convergence—we now witness the rise of the cheerful robot, the technological idiot, the crackpot realist. All these types embody a common ethos: rationality without reason. The fate of this ethos and of these types, what is done about them and what they do—that is the real, even the ultimate, showdown on "socialism" and on "capitalism" in our time. It is a showdown on what kinds of human being and what kinds of culture are going to become the ascendant models of human aspiration. It is an epochal showdown, separating the contemporary period from "the modern age." To make that showdown clear, as it affects every region of the world and every intimate recess of the self, requires a union of political reflection and cultural sensibility of a sort not really known before. That union is now scarcely available in the Western or in the Soviet intellectual community. Within both world blocs, there *are* attempts to achieve it and to use it. Perhaps these attempts are the showdown on human culture itself.

. . . The most important issue of political reflection and of political action in our time [is] the problem of the historical agency of change, of the social and institutional means of structural change. There are several points about this problem I would like to put to you.

First, the historic agencies of change for liberals of the capitalist societies have been an array of voluntary associations, coming to a political climax in a parliamentary or congressional system. For socialists of almost all varieties, the historic agency has been the working class—and later the peasantry, or parties and unions composed of members of the working class, or (to blur, for now, a great problem) of political parties acting in its name, "representing its interests."

I cannot avoid the view that both these forms of historic agency have either collapsed or become most ambiguous. So far as structural change is concerned, neither seems to be at once available and effective as *our* agency anymore. I know this is a debatable point among us, and among many others as well; I am by no means certain about it. But surely, if it is true, it ought not to be taken as an excuse for moaning and withdrawal (as it is by some of those who have become involved with the end-of-ideology); and it ought not to be by-passed (as it is by many Soviet scholars and publicists, who in their reflections upon the course of advanced capitalist societies simply refuse to admit the political condition and attitudes of the working class).

Is anything more certain than that in 1970—indeed, at this time next year—our situation will be quite different, and—the chances are high—decisively so? But of course, that isn't saying much. The seeming collapse of our historic agencies of change ought to be taken as a problem, an issue, a trouble—in fact, as *the* political problem which *we* must turn into issue and trouble.

Second, it is obvious that when we talk about the collapse of agencies of change, we cannot seriously mean that such agencies do not exist. On the contrary, the means of history-making—of decision and of the enforcement of decision—have never in world history been so enlarged and so available to such small circles of men on both sides of The Curtains as they now are. My own conception of the shape of power, the theory of the power elite, I feel no need to argue here. This theory has been fortunate in its critics, from the most diverse political viewpoints, and I have learned from several of these critics. But I have not seen, as of this date, an analysis of the idea that causes me to modify any of its essential features.

The point that is immediately relevant does seem obvious: what is utopian for us is not at all utopian for the presidium of the Central Committee in Moscow, or the higher circles of the Presidency in Washington, or, recent events make evident, for the men of SAC and CIA. The historic agencies of change that have collapsed are those which were at least thought to be open to the *Left* inside the advanced Western nations, to those who have wished for structural changes of these societies. Many things follow from this obvious fact; of many of them, I am sure, we are not yet adequately aware.

Third, what I do not quite understand about some New Left writers is why they cling so mightily to "the working class" of the advanced capitalist societies as *the* historic agency, or even as the most important agency, in the face of the really impressive historical evidence that now stands against this expectation.

Such a labor metaphysic, I think, is a legacy from Victorian Marxism that is now quite unrealistic.

It is a historically specific idea that has been turned into an a-historical and unspecific hope.

The social and historical conditions under which industrial workers tend to become a-class-for-themselves, and a decisive political force, must be fully and precisely elaborated. There have been, there are, there will be such conditions. These conditions vary according to national social structure and the exact phase of their economic and political development. Of course we cannot "write off the working class." But we must *study* all that, and freshly. Where labor exists as an agency, of course we must work with it, but we must not treat it as The Necessary Lever, as nice old Labour Gentlemen in Britain and elsewhere tend to do.

Although I have not yet completed my own comparative studies of working classes, generally it would seem that only at certain (earlier) stages of industrialization, and in a political context of autocracy, *etc.*, do wage-workers tend to become a-class-for-themselves, *etc.* The *etceteras* mean that I can here merely raise the question.

It is with this problem of agency in mind that I have been studying, for several years now, the cultural appartus, the intellectuals, as a possible, immediate, radical agency of change.

For a long time, I was not much happier with this idea than were many of you; but it turns out now, at the beginning of the 1960's, that it may be a very relevant idea indeed.

In the first place, is it not clear that if we try to be realistic in our utopianism—and that is no fruitless contradiction—a writer in our countries on the Left today *must* begin with the intellectuals? For that is what we are, that is where we stand.

In the second place, the problem of the intelligentsia is an extremely complicated set of problems on which rather little factual work has been done. In doing this work, we must, above all, not confuse the problems of the intellectuals of West Europe and North America with those of the Soviet bloc or with those of the underdeveloped worlds. In each of the three major components of the world's social structure today, the character and the role of the intelligentsia is distinct and historically specific. Only by detailed comparative studies of them in all their human variety can we hope to understand any one of them.

In the third place, who is it that is getting fed up? Who is it that is getting disgusted with what Marx called "all the old crap"? Who is it that is thinking and acting in radical ways? All over the world—in the bloc, outside the bloc, and in between—the answer is the same: It is the young intelligentsia.

I cannot resist copying out for you, with a few changes, some materials I recently prepared for a 1960 paperback edition of a book of mine on war:

> In the spring and early summer of 1960, more of the returns from the American decision and default are coming in. In Turkey, after student riots, a military junta takes over the state, of late run by Communist Container Menderes. In South Korea, too, students and others knock over the corrupt American-puppet regime of Syngman Rhee. In Cuba, a genuinely left-wing revolution begins full-scale economic reorganization, without the domination of U.S. corporations. Average age of its leaders: about thirty—and certainly a revolution without Labor As Agency. On Taiwan, the eight million Taiwanese under the American-imposed dictatorship of Chiang Kai-shek, with his two million Chinese, grow increasingly restive. On Okinawa, a U.S. military base, the people get their first chance since World War II ended to demonstrate against U.S. seizure of their island; and some students take that chance, snake-dancing and chanting angrily to the visiting President: "Go home, go home—take away your missiles." (Don't worry, 12,000 U.S. troops easily handle the generally grateful crowds; also the President is "spirited out the rear end of the United

> States compound"—and so by helicopter to the airport.) In Japan, weeks of student rioting succeed in rejecting the President's visit, jeopardizing a new treaty with the United States, and displacing the big-business, pro-American Prime Minister, Kishi. And even in our own pleasant Southland, Negro and white students are—but let us keep quiet: it really *is* disgraceful.
>
> That is by no means the complete list; that was yesterday; see today's newspaper. Tomorrow, in varying degree, the returns will be more evident. Will they be evident enough? They will have to be very obvious to attract real American attention: sweet complaints and the voice of reason—these are not enough. In the slum countries of the world today, what are they saying? The rich Americans, they pay attention only to violence—and to money. You don't care what they say, American? Good for you. Still, they may insist; things are no longer under the old control; you're not getting it straight, American: your country—it would seem—may well become the target of a world hatred the like of which the easy-going Americans have never dreamed. Neutralists and Pacifists and Unilateralists and that confusing variety of Leftists around the world—all those tens of millions of people, of course they are misguided, absolutely controlled by small conspiratorial groups of trouble-makers, under direct orders from Moscow and Peking. Diabolically omnipotent, it is *they* who create all this messy unrest. It is *they* who have given the tens of millions the absurd idea that they shouldn't want to remain, or to become, the seat of American nuclear bases—those gay little outposts of American civilization. So now they don't want U-2's on their territory; so now they want to contract out of the American military machine; they want to be neutral among the crazy big antagonists. And they don't want their own societies to be militarized.
>
> But take heart, American: you won't have time to get really bored with your friends abroad: they won't be your friends much longer. You don't need *them;* it will all go away; don't let them confuse you.

Add to that: In the Soviet bloc, who is it that has been breaking out of apathy? It has been students and young professors and writers; it has been the young intelligentsia of Poland and Hungary, and of Russia, too. Never mind that they have not won; never mind that there are other social and moral types among them. First of all, it has been these types. But the point is clear, isn't it?

That is why we have got to study these new generations of intellectuals around the world as real live agencies of historic change. Forget Victorian Marxism, except when you need it; and read Lenin again (be careful)—Rosa Luxemburg, too.

"But it is just some kind of moral upsurge, isn't it?" Correct. But under it: no apathy. Much of it is direct nonviolent action, and it seems to be working, here and there. Now we must learn from the practice of these young intellectuals and with them work out new forms of action.

"But it's all so ambiguous—Cuba, for instance." Of course it is; history-making is always ambiguous. Wait a bit; in the meantime, help them to focus their moral upsurge in less ambiguous political ways. Work out with them the ideologies, the strategies, the theories that will help them consolidate their efforts: new theories of structural changes of and by human societies in our epoch.

"But it is utopian, after all, isn't it?" No, not in the sense you mean. Whatever else it may be, it's not that. Tell it to the students of Japan. Tell it to the Negro sit-ins. Tell it to the Cuban Revolutionaries. Tell it to the people of the hungry-nation bloc.

from One-Dimensional Man

HERBERT MARCUSE

Marcuse's importance to the New Left has probably by this time been badly overstated. He is not the kind of writer whose books explode one out of the study, and his richly elaborated pessimism can even make the study seem, in this society, the only sane place to be.

But if he has produced few activists, he has informed many. He is someone to be read after the membrane of silence or noncommitment has been ruptured and he is a major source of the New Left's conceptualization of its world and its tasks.

THE ADVANCING ONE-DIMENSIONAL society alters the relation between the rational and the irrational. Contrasted with the fantastic and insane aspects of its rationality, the realm of the irrational becomes the home of the really rational—of the ideas which may "promote the art of life." If the established society manages all normal communication, validating or invalidating it in accordance with social requirements, then the values alien to these requirements may perhaps have no other medium of communication than the abnormal one of fiction. The aesthetic dimension still retains a freedom of expression which enables the writer and artist to call men and things by their name—to name the otherwise unnameable.

The real face of our time shows in Samuel Beckett's novels; its real history is written to Rolf Hochhuth's play *Der Stellvertreter* [*The Deputy*]. It is no longer Imagination which speaks here, but Reason, in a reality which justifies everything and absolves everything—except the sin against its spirit. Imagination is abdicating to this reality, which is catching up with and overtaking Imagination. Auschwitz continues to haunt, not the memory but the accomplishments of man—the space flights; the rockets and missiles; the "labyrinthine basement under the Snack Bar"; the pretty electronic plants, clean, hygienic, and with flower beds; the poison gas which is not really harmful to people; the secrecy in which we all participate. This is the setting in which the great human achievements of science, medicine, technology take place; the efforts to save and ameliorate life are the sole promise in the disaster. The willful play with fantastic possibilities, the ability to act with good conscience, *contra naturam,* to experiment with men and things, to convert illusion into reality and fiction into truth, testify to the extent to which Imagination has become an instrument of progress. And it is one which, like others in the established societies, is methodically abused. Setting the pace and style of politics, the power of Imagination far exceeds Alice in Wonderland in the manipulation of words, turning sense into nonsense and nonsense into sense.

The formerly antagonistic realms merge on technical and political grounds—magic and science, life and death, joy and misery. Beauty reveals its terror as highly classified nuclear plants and laboratories become "Industrial Parks" in pleasing surroundings; Civil Defense Headquarters display a "deluxe fallout shelter" with wall-to-wall carpeting, ("soft") lounge chairs, television, and Scrabble, "designed as a combination family room during peacetime (sic!) and family fallout shelter should war break out."[1] If the horror of such realizations does not penetrate into consciousness, if it is readily taken for granted, it is because these achievements are (a) perfectly rational in terms of the existing order, (b) tokens of human ingenuity and power beyond the traditional limits of Imagination.

The obscene merger of aesthetics and reality refutes the philosophies which oppose "poetic" Imagination to scientific and empirical Reason. Technological progress is accompanied by a progressive rationalization and even realization of the imaginary. The archetypes of horror as well as of joy, of war as well as of peace, lose their catastrophic character. Their appearance in the daily life of individuals is no longer that of irrational forces—their modern avatars are elements of technological domination, and subject to it.

In reducing and even canceling the romantic space of Imagi-

[1] According to *The New York Times,* November 11, 1960, displayed at the New York Civil Defense Headquarters, Lexington Avenue and 55th Street.

nation, society has forced the Imagination to prove itself on new grounds, on which the images are translated into historical capabilities and projects. The translation will be as bad and distorted as the society which undertakes it. Separated from the realm of material production and material needs, Imagination was mere play, invalid in the realm of necessity, and committed only to a fantastic logic and a fantastic truth. When technical progress cancels this separation, it invests the images with its own logic and its own truth; it reduces the free faculty of the mind. But it also reduces the gap between Imagination and Reason. The two antagonistic faculties become interdependent on common ground. In the light of the capabilities of advanced industrial civilization, is not all play of the Imagination playing technical possibilities, which can be tested as to their chances of realization? The romantic idea of a "science of the Imagination" seems to assume an ever more empirical aspect.

The scientific, rational character of Imagination has long since been recognized in mathematics, in the hypotheses and experiments of the physical sciences. It is likewise recognized in psychoanalysis, which is in theory based on the acceptance of the specific rationality of the irrational; the comprehended Imagination becomes, redirected, a therapeutic force. But this therapeutic force may go much further than in the cure of neuroses. It was not a poet but a scientist who has outlined this prospect:

> Toute une psychanalyse matérielle peut . . . nous aider à guérir de nos images, ou du moins nous aider à limiter l'emprise de nos images. On peut alors espérer . . . *pouvoir rendre l'imagination heureuse,* autrement dit, pouvoir donner bonne conscience à l'imagination, en lui accordant pleinement tous ses moyens d'expression, toutes les images matérielles qui se produisent dans les *rêves naturels,* dans l'activité onorique normale. Rendre heureuse l'imagination, lui accorder toute son exuberance, c'est précisément donner à l'imagination sa véritable fonction d'entraînement psychique.[2]

[2] "An entire psychoanalysis of matter can help us to cure ourselves of our images or at least help us to limit the hold of our images on us. One may then hope *to be able to render imagination happy,* to give it good conscience in allowing it fully all its means of expression, all material images which emerge in *natural dreams,* in normal dream activity. To render imagination happy, to allow it all its exuberance, means precisely to grant imagination its true function as psychological impulse and force." Gaston Bachelard, *Le Matérialisme rationnel* (Paris: Presses Universitaires, 1953), p. 18.

Imagination has not remained immune to the process of reification. We are possessed by our images, suffer our own images. Psychoanalysis knew it well, and knew the consequences. However, "to give to the Imagination all the means of expression" would be regression. The mutilated individuals (mutilated also in their faculty of Imagination) would organize and destroy even more than they are now permitted to do. Such release would be the unmitigated horror—not the catastrophe of culture, but the free sweep of its most repressive tendencies. Rational is the Imagination which can become *a priori* of the reconstruction and redirection of the productive apparatus toward a pacified existence, a life without fear. And this can never be the Imagination of those who are possessed by the images of domination and death.

To liberate the Imagination so that it can be given all its means of expression presupposes the repression of much that is now free and that perpetuates a repressive society. And such reversal is not a matter of psychology or ethics but of politics, in the sense in which this term has here been used throughout: the practice in which the basic societal institutions are developed, defined, sustained, and changed. It is the practice of individuals, no matter how organized they may be. Thus the question once again must be faced: how can the administered individuals—who have made their mutilation into their own liberties and satisfactions, and thus reproduce it on an enlarged scale—liberate themselves from themselves as well as from their masters? How is it even thinkable that the vicious circle be broken?

Paradoxically, it seems that it is not the notion of the new societal *institutions* which presents the greatest difficulty in the attempt to answer this question. The established societies themselves are changing, or have already changed the basic institutions in the direction of increased planning. Since the development and utilization of all available resources for the universal satisfaction of vital needs is the prerequisite of pacification, it is incompatible with the prevalence of particular interests which stand in the way of attaining this goal. Qualitative change is conditional upon planning for the whole against these interests, and a free and rational society can emerge only on this basis.

The institutions within which pacification can be envisaged thus defy the traditional classification into authoritarian and democratic, centralized and liberal administration. Today, the opposition to central planning in the name of a liberal democracy which is denied in reality serves as an ideological prop for repressive interests. The goal of authentic self-determination by individuals depends on effective social control over the production and distribution of the necessities (in terms of the achieved level of culture, material and intellectual).

Here, technological rationality, stripped of its exploitative features, is the sole standard and guide in planning and developing the available resources for all. Self-determination in the production and distribution of vital goods and services would be wasteful. The job is a technical one, and as a truly technical job, it makes for the reduction of physical and mental toil. In this realm, centralized control is rational if it establishes the preconditions for meaningful self-determination. The latter can then become effective in its own realm—in the decisions which involve the production and distribution of the economic surplus, and in the individual existence.

In any case, the combination of centralized authority and direct democracy is subject to infinite variations, according to the degree of development. Self-determination will be real to the extent to which the masses have been dissolved into individuals liberated from all propaganda, indoctrination, and manipulation, capable of knowing and comprehending the facts and of evaluating the alternatives. In other words, society would be rational and free to the extent to which it is organized, sustained, and reproduced by an essentially new historical Subject.

At the present stage of development of the advanced industrial societies, the material as well as the cultural system denies this exigency. The power and efficiency of this System, the thorough assimilation of mind with fact, of thought with required behavior, of aspirations with reality, militate against the emergence of a new Subject. They also militate against the notion that the replacement of the prevailing control over the productive process by "control from below" would mean the advent of qualitative change. This notion was valid, and still is valid, where the laborers were, and still are, the living denial and indictment of the established society. However, where these classes have become a prop of the established way of life, their ascent to control would prolong this way in a different setting.

And yet, the facts are all there which validate the critical theory of this society and of its fatal development: the increasing irrationality of the whole; waste and restriction of productivity; the need for aggressive expansion; the constant threat of war; intensified exploitation; dehumanization. And they all point to the historical alternative: the planned utilization of resources for the satisfaction of vital needs with a minimum of toil; the transformation of leisure into free time; the pacification of the struggle for existence.

But the facts and the alternatives are there like fragments which do not connect, or like a world of mute objects without a subject, without the practice which would move these objects in the new direction. Dialectical theory is not refuted, but it cannot offer the remedy. It cannot be positive. To be sure, the dialectical concept, in comprehending the given facts, transcends the given facts. This is the very token of its truth. It defines the historical possibilities, even necessities; but their realization can only be in the practice which responds to the theory, and, at present, the practice gives no such response.

On theoretical as well as empirical grounds, the dialectical concept pronounces its own hopelessness. The human reality is its history and, in it, contradictions do not explode by themselves. The conflict between streamlined, rewarding domination on the one hand, and its achievements that make for self-determination and pacification on the other, may become blatant beyond any possible denial, but it may well continue to be a manageable and even productive conflict, for with the growth in the technological conquest of nature grows the conquest of man by man. And this conquest reduces the freedom which is a necessary *a priori* of liberation. This is freedom of thought in the only sense in which thought can be free in the administered world—as the consciousness of its repressive productivity, and as the absolute need for breaking out of this whole. But precisely this absolute need does not prevail where it could become the driving force of a historical practice, the effective cause of qualitative change. Without this material force, even the most acute consciousness remains powerless.

No matter how obvious the irrational character of the whole may manifest itself and, with it, the necessity of change, insight into necessity has never sufficed for seizing the possible alternatives. Confronted with the omnipresent efficiency of the given system of life, its alternatives have always appeared utopian. And insight into necessity, the consciousness of the evil state, will not suffice even at the stage where the accomplishments of science and the level of productivity have eliminated the utopian features of the alternatives—where the established reality rather than its opposite is utopian.

Does this mean that the critical theory of society abdicates and leaves the field to an empirical sociology which, freed from all theoretical guidance except a methodological one, succumbs to the fallacies of misplaced concreteness, thus performing an ideological service while proclaiming the elimination of value judgments? Or do the dialectical concepts once again testify to their truth—by comprehending their own situation as that of the society which they analyze? A response might suggest itself if one considers the critical theory precisely at the point of its greatest weakness—its inability to demonstrate the liberating tendencies *within* the established society.

The critical theory of society was, at the time of its origin, confronted with the presence of real forces (objective and subjective) *in* the established society which moved (or could be guided to move) toward more rational and freer institutions by abolishing the existing ones which had become obstacles to progress. These were the empirical grounds on which the theory was erected, and from these empirical grounds derived the idea of the liberation of *inherent* possibilities—the development, otherwise blocked and distorted, of material and intellectual productivity, faculties, and needs. Without the demonstration of such forces, the critique of society would still be valid and rational, but it would be incapable of translating its rationality into terms of historical practice. The conclusion? "Liberation of inherent possibilities" no longer adequately expresses the historical alternative.

The enchained possibilities of advanced industrial societies are: development of the productive forces on an enlarged scale, extension of the conquest of nature, growing satisfaction of needs for a growing number of people, creation of new needs and faculties. But these possibilities are gradually being realized through means and institutions which cancel their liberating potential, and this process affects not only the means but also the ends. The instruments of productivity and progress, organized into a totalitarian system, determine not only the actual but also the possible utilizations.

At its most advanced stage, domination functions as administration, and in the overdeveloped areas of mass consumption, the administered life becomes the good life of the whole, in the defense of which the opposites are united. This is the pure form of domination. Conversely, its negation appears to be the pure form of negation. All content seems reduced to the one abstract demand for the end of domination—the only truly revolutionary exigency, and the event that would validate the achievements of industrial civilization. In the face of its efficient denial by the established System, this negation appears in the politically impotent form of the "absolute refusal"—a refusal which seems the more unreasonable the more the established System develops its productivity and alleviates the burden of life. In the words of Maurice Blanchot:

> Ce que nous refusons n'est pas sans valeur ni sans importance. C'est bien à cause de cela que le refus est nécessaire. Il y a une raison que nous n'accepterons plus, il y a une apparence de sagesse qui nous fait horreur, il y a une offre d'accord et de conciliation que nous n'entendrons pas. Une rupture s'est produite. Nous avons été ramenés à cette franchise qui ne tolère plus la complicité.[3]

But if the abstract character of the refusal is the result of total reification, then the concrete ground for refusal must still exist, for reification is an illusion. By the same token, the unification of opposites in the medium of technological rationality must be, *in all its reality,* an illusory unification, which eliminates neither the contradiction between the growing productivity and its repressive use, nor the vital need for solving the contradiction.

But the struggle for the solution has outgrown the traditional forms. The totalitarian tendencies of the one-dimensional society render the traditional ways and means of protest ineffective —perhaps even dangerous because they preserve the illusion of popular sovereignty. This illusion contains some truth: "the people," previously the ferment of social change, have "moved up" to become the ferment of social cohesion. Here rather than in the redistribution of wealth and equalization of classes is the new stratification characteristic of advanced industrial society.

However, underneath the conservative popular base is the substratum of the outcasts and outsiders, the exploited and persecuted of other races and other colors, the unemployed and the unemployable. They exist outside the democratic process; their life is the most immediate and the most real need for ending intolerable conditions and institutions. Thus their opposition is revolutionary even if their consciousness is not. Their opposition hits the System from without and is therefore not

[3] "What we refuse is not without value or importance. Precisely because of that, the refusal is necessary. There is a reason which we no longer accept, there is an appearance of wisdom which horrifies us, there is a plea for agreement and conciliation which we will no longer heed. A break has occurred. We have been reduced to that frankness which no longer tolerates complicity." "Le Refus," in *Le 14 Juillet,* No. 2, Paris, October 1958.

deflected by the System; it is an elementary force which violates the rules of the game and, in doing so, reveals it as a rigged game. When they get together and go out into the streets, without arms, without protection, in order to ask for the most primitive civil rights, they know that they face dogs, stones, and bombs, jail, concentration camps, even death. Their force is behind every political demonstration for the victims of law and order. The fact that they start refusing to play the game may be the fact which marks the beginning of the end of a period.

Nothing indicates that it will be a good end. The economic and technical capabilities of the established societies are sufficiently vast to allow for adjustments and concessions to the underdog, and their armed forces sufficiently trained and equipped to take care of emergency situations. However, the specter is there again, inside and outside the frontiers of the advanced societies. The facile historical parallel with the barbarians threatening the empire of civilization prejudges the issue; the second period of barbarism may well be the continued empire of civilization itself. But the chance is that, in this period, the historical extremes may meet again: the most advanced consciousness of humanity, and its most exploited force. It is nothing but a chance. The critical theory of society possesses no concepts which could bridge the gap between the present and its future; holding no promise and showing no success, it remains negative. Thus it wants to remain loyal to those who, without hope, have given and give their life to the Great Refusal.

At the beginning of the fascist era, Walter Benjamin wrote:

> *Nur um der Hoffnungslosen willen ist uns die Hoffnung gegeben.*
> It is only for the sake of those without hope that hope is given to us.

from Strategy For Labor

ANDRÉ GORZ

Especially after the Hungarian crisis of 1956 and the subsequent moral collapse of the French Communist Party, one of the major sources of advanced critical theory and analysis has been the informal circle of philosophers and generalists centering loosely around Jean-Paul Sartre's Les Temps Modernes. *If it has hardly been "New Leftist" in its self-conception, this group has nonetheless been very much post-CP in both theory and practice and has been the most important single educator of the current generation of French student activists.*

Gorz was writing Strategy for Labor[1] *when* One-Dimensional Man *appeared; the similarity of his and Marcuse's concerns will be obvious, a convergence no doubt owing less to any direct influence than to each writer's access to a vigorous Hegelian tradition. Gorz's critique differs from Marcuse's in being somewhat more concrete (though no less general) and perhaps also more* Marxist. *That is, Gorz seems more inclined than Marcuse to understand a need for political motion as implying its possibility. He suggests here that social rather than strictly economic issues may be the key to a revived labor radicalism.*

WORK IS NO LONGER only the production of merchandise objects; labor power is no longer subject only to the inertia of things; the worker is no longer only the instrument of a society attempting to organize its survival. Work, labor power, and worker tend to unite in the persons who produce themselves while producing a world. And this production takes place not only in the work situation but just as much in the schools,

[1] Boston: Beacon Press, 1967.

cafés, athletic fields; on voyages; in theaters, concerts, newspapers, books, expositions; in towns, neighborhoods, discussion and action groups—in short, wherever individuals enter into relationships with one another and produce the universe of human relationships.

More and more, this production tends to be an integral part not only of the production of man but of the necessarily wider reproduction of labor power itself. The international and intercontinental development of trade, the division of labor on an ever larger economic scale, the tendency toward regional and national specialization, the rapidity of communications, place every productive activity through the interplay of ever more numerous intermediaries into relationship with the entire world, and tend in practice to unify it.

It is impossible to produce artichokes in the León region or citrus fruits in Sicily without taking into account the activities of other producers, not only in León and Sicily, but in the French Midi, in Spain, and in Algeria. It is impossible to produce turbines in Grenoble without knowing what is being done in Milan, Ljubliana, in the Ruhr, and in Scotland. And this knowledge is part of the "labor power" not only of the commercial director or of the president of a cooperative, but also of every engineer, technician, supervisor, and, through the mediation of the latter, of every worker and every member of the cooperative. It is impossible in a modern production unit, even of medium size, to be on top of one's job without becoming familiar with world history in the process. And it is impossible to be ignorant of political, scientific, technical, socio-economic, and cultural evolution in the largest sense, or else one will lose the ability to enter into relationships with others, however close, or of suffering that absolute oppression which consists of knowing that one does not know what others know.

That is why cultural activity is an integral part of the necessarily broad reproduction of labor power, that is, of the ability of individuals to cooperate in a given common task. That also is why cultural activity is a *need.* And that, finally, is why the reduction of the "work" week remains a fundamental demand, together with the multiplication of cultural facilities and their self-management by the workers. The time necessary for the reproduction of labor power is not the same in 1964 as it was in 1904, for any kind of worker; just as it has never been the same for a concert pianist and for a piano tuner. The increase in free time is not an increase in idle time, but an increase in the socially productive time which is objectively and subjectively necessary for the production of human individuals and a human world.

Confronted by this necessity, it is true, neocapitalist civilization has set up a gigantic apparatus of repression: an apparatus in the service of mystification, the perpetuation of ignorance, the destruction of culture, the conditioning of reflexes, and the transformation of free time into passive, empty time devoted to sterile diversions which a gentle terror summons every individual to perform. The need for culture must be deflected by corrupting it even as far as the consciousness it has of itself; it must be demeaned by offering it trashy objects, and by greeting cultural creation and its agents with derision in the name of primitivism and mass ethics.

Mass culture, a by-product of commercial propaganda, has as implicit content a mass ethic: playing on, maintaining, and flattering ignorance, it encourages the ignorant to resent those who "know," persuades them that the latter despise them, and encourages or provokes their contempt. This abject demagogy, one of whose elements—contempt for "intellectuals" (a term which has become an insult not only in the United States) and for culture—can be found in all fascist movements, professes no respect for exceptional individuals except insofar as their superiority can be accounted for by what they *are*, not by what they *do:* athletes, beauty queens, princely personages. This is because the superiority of *being*, physical or hereditary, can be taken as a product of the nature—of the soil, the race, the nation—from which all individuals derive, and can thus reflect to them a natural bond of community with the hero, their own vicarious aristocracy, their original identity, reproclaimed in chauvinism.

This demogogy of leveling and of the least common denominator begins as business and ends as politics: in order to sell newspapers, radio time, or advertising space, one begins by flattering superstition and lulling reason, by emphasizing myths rather than facts, sensational rather than significant things; one prefabricates individuality in order to sell some of it to individuals whose own individuality one has destroyed (and which one destroys further by this forced sale), and one ends up preferring *and selling,* with the same commercial techniques, the "personality" of a Leader, a Chief, a paternal Dictator possessed of magic powers.

This gentle totalitarianism of monopoly civilization is a consequence as much as a cause. It is a cause insofar as the sales technique of "affluent" capitalism is a technique of manipulation and of domination which aims deliberately at the psychological implantation in public life of the power of production and commerce, and the destruction of the forces which challenge it. It is a cause also insofar as it aims to destroy the concrete and autonomous communication between individuals, and their human relationships; insofar as it aims to conceal from the agents of praxis that the universe which they produce is in truth and in fact their own product. But this mystification, obviously, is possible only because it proceeds on a field which already favors it: because the destruction of the universe of human relationships, the uprooting of culture, the specialization and mutilation of individuals are already in advanced stages. This process originated in the backwardness which the "spontaneous" priorities of monopoly expansion imposed on the cultural and practical levels.

The insufficiency and then the degradation and industrialization of education; the repression of autonomous cultural activity by the militarization of industrial labor; the lack of collective cultural facilities; the rationing of free time; the more or less deliberate dispersion of workers in different locations (that is, the impossibility for them of communicating or meeting together after work, the obligation of living where they do not work and working where they do not live)—all this tends to create individuals who are isolated and beaten down, powerless because of their dispersion and their ignorance of the mechanisms which were born from their collective labor.

And it is among these underdeveloped and "mutilated" individuals (deliberately mutilated insofar as this made their exploitation easier and as their human development was considered an "unproductive expense") that monopoly capitalism, in order to perpetuate its domination, continues to repress and deflect the need for culture, to exploit and to flatter the feeling of powerlessness and of ignorance.

This is a particularly odious aspect of the subordination of individuals to production. But we have already seen that this subordination tends to become an obstacle for production itself; and that insofar as the latter requires workers who have a comprehensive vision of the productive cycle, of socio-economic processes, and of the production process itself, a contradiction arises between the industrialization of culture and the culture of the industrial societies.

TECHNOCRACY

From then on, a double movement begins. At the bottom, in the technologically most advanced industries—as well as in the professionally qualified sectors of the small and medium peasantry—the workers move toward self-management (cooperative and regional, in the peasants' case) of the means of production and of local and regional life, a management for which they have the necessary competence. *Technological* power has already slipped away from the bourgeoisie (the owners) on this level, and their economic power is compromised by an inevitable process of financial concentration.

At the summit during this time the bourgeoisie sees its power limited by technocrats, specialists in coordination, planning, and synthesis, tasks which the local economic agents, no matter how powerful they may be, are not able to perform. A narrow stratum of specialists is thus given sole responsibility for the task of centralizing and synthesizing—indispensable to the functioning of the over-all System—a task for which the economic agents, whoever they may be, generally have neither the time, nor the competence, nor the information necessary. Totalitarian and dictatorial in the large sense, the technocratic apparatus has become the answer to a real necessity mainly *because of* a cultural Malthusianism which deprives individuals (including the majority of the bourgeoisie itself) of the competence necessary for self-management and democracy on all levels.[2] The decadence of political democracy, which technocracy likes to attribute to the senility of the parties and to the backwardness of political ideologies relative to economic realities, has therefore in fact some deeper reasons: it derives from the incapacity—which is in turn due to cultural and educa-

[2] The necessity for technocratic dictatorship (or centralization of real power) does not arise, in my opinion, from the need for central coordination and direction of decision-making centers. The Yugoslavian system of self-management, which found itself, as was to be expected, faced with the problem of coordinating and integrating decentralized management units, has undertaken a solution which does not reinforce the central power: the 1963 Yugoslavian constitution assigns the task of coordination to specialized federal Assemblies made up of the representatives of self-management bodies of the various sectors (industries, culture and education, health, administration). The technocrats of the national Plan are controlled by these specialized Assemblies, by the federal Parliament, and by a Senate; and the right of self-management of all enterprises (including schools, hospitals, administration, etc.) is reinforced.

tional backwardness—of individuals, organized or not (the owners, political "elites," the bourgeoisie as a class, organized workers), to perform for themselves the management of social production and of society, on whatever level—local, regional, national; the industrial branch, the sector, the city.

Technocratic power, therefore, arises much less as a new form of the direct domination of monopoly capital and more as a contradictory and mediated form of this power. While its members are most often of bourgeois origin, technocracy is not generally the errand boy of the monopolies and does not necessarily wield power as their representative. It is rather the mediator between the particular and contradictory interests of the capitalists on the one hand, the general interest of capitalism on the other, and finally the general interest of society.

The power of the technocracy cannot simply be identified with the direct, totaliarian power of monopoly capital, even though it also is a totaliarian power and even though this power is exercised *in fact* for the benefit of monopoly capital. Technocrats are much more than the trustees or the representatives of the power of the bourgeoisie as a class; they are rather a "caste": because they alone are specialized in the tasks of coordination and synthesis, they cannot accomplish these tasks without having—and without demanding, by virtue of their work, as an inherent requirement of their work—autonomy with regard to all interests, including the various interests of capitalist groups.

By its very function, technocracy tends therefore to locate itself "above the classes," to deny the necessity for class struggle, to set itself up as mediator and referee and in so doing to enter into contradiction with the classes. The famous "depoliticization" of the masses which technocracy pretends to take note of is not a fact it observes; it is rather the end it pursues, the result it wants to obtain—and does obtain in a very limited degree. *"Depoliticization" is the ideology of technocracy itself.* The so-called "neutrality" of the State is the ideology which justifies the power and the domination which technocracy is led to claim for itself by the logic of its situation.

The conflict of technocracy with the working classes as well as with the bourgeoisie is always profoundly ambiguous: this caste refuses from the outset to make decisions on the political terrain. Objectively progressive (or "on the Left") in its conflicts with the monopolies, technocracy is subjectively conservative ("on the Right") in its conflicts with the working class.

Attempting to eliminate in advance the question of power, which it thinks can be held only by professional managers, it tries to keep a clear conscience in the midst of the contradictory criticisms to which it is exposed. Toward the monopolies it internalizes the conservatism of which the Left accuses it by showing that the rationalization measures which it proposes consolidate and protect the capitalist system. Toward the labor movement it boasts of its conflicts with the monopolies in order to underscore its objectively progressive role.

This double game is obviously a mystification: to pretend to keep a balance between a bourgeoisie which is in power and a working class which is not is necessarily to play into the hands of the former. Technocracy is conservative ideologically (subjectively) to the very degree that its objective progressivism serves it as an alibi in its efforts to consolidate the existing System, to arbitrate its conflicts, and to absorb the anticapitalist forces.

It shares this conservatism with all technicians insofar as they are empiricists. Conductor of an apparatus which interests him only for its smooth and efficient functioning, the technician cares a great deal more for the instrument than for the ends it serves. He lives from the beginning in a ready-made rationality with predetermined purposes which his work and his education do not lead him to question. The only truth, for him, is smooth functioning; and he sees value only in immediately applicable propositions. The rest is utopia.

However, this attitude is essentially fragile. The role of arbitrator and of neutral manager above classes and parties, dedicated to a rationality which transcends them—this role which technocracy attributes to itself is tenable only on three conditions:

1. That there exists no alternative to the type of rationality of the existing society, or that this alternative never be made sufficiently explicit to appear as a requirement already on the way to fulfillment, to unmask the present System. For this System is a combination of choices which anticipate certain solutions, purposes, and a certain model of life to the detriment of other choices, other purposes, a different model whose superior rationality would burst apart the irrationality of the present rationality.

2. That the incompetence of the anticapitalist forces be evident, that their inability to manage the economy and the State without catastrophe strike the eye. Only this incompetence, this

glaring inability and the absence of an anticapitalist alternative which is sufficiently worked out and coherent, can justify and confirm technocracy in its "vocation" of serving capitalism.

3. That the labor movement, on the other hand, be strong enough to counterbalance the pressure exercised by monopoly capital on the State, that is to say, on technocracy itself. Only a strong labor movement can prevent technocracy from becoming the servant of monopoly capital, the manager of a society in bondage, the accomplice of the repressions and cultural devastations of a capitalism without counterbalance.

To the degree to which the incompetence of the labor movement and the absence of a coherent anticapitalist perspective are real, technocracy will thus deploy its forces with the aim of attracting into its camp and integrating into the institutions of the capitalist State all the labor organizations which are susceptible to such a maneuver without, however, destroying the labor movement as a "loyal" opposition (or "countervailing power") to the power of monopoly capital.

If, on the other hand, the labor movement does not retreat into a defensive position but instead begins vigorously to work out an anticapitalist alternative with strategically scaled and economically coherent objectives, then it will destroy the ideology which justifies technocracy; it will force technocracy to choose between the monopolies and the working-class movement, and will win over a more than negligible portion of this "caste" to its side. This will be the case not only because the socialist movement can no longer appear to the technocrats as a simple protest movement, capable of destroying the apparatus of production but not of managing it for other ends; but also because a minority among the technocrats work for monopoly capital not out of conviction but because they find no other outlet for their competence, because they believe they can follow a policy of the "lesser evil," and because they see no real road to socialism.

These technocrats are in the same position as that vast sector of lower- and middle-class groups who "sympathize" with socialism but are in practice skeptical. They will not make a choice until they can see intermediate objectives, that is, mediations, which will make them see socialism not as something beyond the present society, separated from it by an unbreachable wall, but like the real horizon of the internal exigencies of this society—as a horizon toward which the progression of realizable intermediate objectives indicates a practicable way. Only the possibility of such a way will force this vague mass of "sympathizers" to make a choice which in the recent past it has all too often been spared.

Besides, the cooperation of technocrats is indispensable to the labor movement for the specification (but not the definition) of certain strategic objectives, of an economically coherent antimonopolist alternative.[3] The fact is that the labor movement, in order to take power and to manage the State, needs specialized managers. But this requirement must not in any way imply that the socialist State can or should maintain the dictatorial and totalitarian character of the capitalist State, nor that socialism can, likewise, preserve for technocracy the monopoly of management, coordination, and organization of social relationships.

THE CRISIS OF CAPITALIST VALUES

The formation of a technocracy as instrument and agent of the totalitarian and repressive power of the State arises in all advanced industrialized societies, whether capitalist or socialist, because it is impossible for organized workers to manage their production and exchange by themselves. But this impossibility is not inherent in the complexity of social production and exchange. This impossibility, as we have already emphasized, is provoked—and in certain respects deliberately created—by cultural underdevelopment, by the mutilation of individuals in their work and even in their professional education, by the overexploitation of labor power, i.e., the deprivation of free time and of cultural facilities, and finally by the absence or the deliberate liquidation of institutions and organs of democratic control.

This formidable repression has been justified up to now in the name of efficiency, of the need for an ever more specialized division of labor, with the aim of a rapidly increasing productivity and production of wealth. But with the advent of automation, this rationalizing and specializing tendency now

[3] The definition of objectives cannot be carried out except by the labor movement itself because these objectives must make social *needs* explicit, needs whose satisfaction requires structural reforms, that is to say, a modification in the relationship of powers. Once these objectives are defined, the collaboration of technicians is essential for determining how they may be made economically coherent, how soon they may be implemented, and therefore, in a limited way, which of them has priority. For no matter how wide-sweeping structural reforms may be, not everything can be done at once; some things must have precedence over others.

reaches its limit: it must be reversed if advanced industria
civilization is to be something other than a barbaric system o
waste and stupefaction. On the level of production itself, thi
tendency collides with a technological evolution which tend
to re-establish the value of the many-sided worker and of auton
omous praxis. The replacement of laborers and of semiskille
workers who are tied down to their solitary work spot, by skille
teams who regulate their own cooperation themselves and wh
are conscious of their technical power and of their inde
pendence, creates a crisis within hierarchy inside *and outsid*
the company.

The demand for self-management which arises out of pro
ductive praxis cannot be contained within the factory walls, th
laboratories, and research bureaus. Men who cannot be ordere
around in their work cannot indefinitely be ordered around i
their life as citizens, nor can they submit to the rigid decision
of central administrations.

The contemporary transition from mechanization to automa
tion will bring about a crisis in the organization of work and th
techniques of domination founded on it. The notion of indi
vidual output and even of labor-time tends to fall by the way
side; the borderline between productive activity and leisur
becomes confused; manual and intellectual work tend to g
together and to cause the rebirth of a humanism of work whic
had been destroyed by Taylorism.[4] But this humanism of wor
is itself only a transitional form: automation will cause it i
turn to disappear, as it destroyed it for the technicians of th
nuclear plant at Marcoule, thus creating a crisis in the whol
system of "values" of capitalist ideology. Already the latter de
nies the "values" of efficiency and of maximum output by pro
claiming the "values" of affluent consumption and of comfort
"Its sweeping rationality, which propels efficiency and growth
is itself irrational . . . Here, the social controls exact the over
whelming need for the production and consumption of waste
the need for stupefying work where it is no longer a real neces
sity; the need for modes of relaxation which soothe and prolon
this stupefaction; the need for maintaining such deceptive lib

[4] Frederick Winslow Taylor (1856–1915), an American engineer wh
was generally credited with pioneering the time-motion study of factor
work. Taylor's method consisted of dividing each manual operation int
a series of standard motion-components. He then eliminated "unes
sential" motions and so finally shaped the work process into the serie
of infinitely repeated simple tasks which are the essence of moder
nonautomated assembly-line manufacturing. [Translators' note.]

erties as free competition at administered prices, a free press which censors itself, free choice between brands and gadgets . . . Advanced industrial society is approaching the stage where continued progress would demand the radical subversion of the prevailing direction and organization of progress."[5]

For capitalist civilization, efficiency, productivity, and output have always been the supreme "values"; these "values" now reveal themselves in their true light: as a religion of *means*. They could find their justification in the midst of acute scarcity by making possible an intense accumulation of the means of overcoming scarcity. In the midst of disappearing scarcity, they become a religion of waste and of factitious opulence. But these two value systems—the one which requires the worker to become subhuman in his work, and the one which requires him to consume superfluous goods—cannot long coexist. They could coexist only if dehumanization in work were strong enough to make the workers unfit for any but subhuman and passive leisure and consumption. Such is no longer the case.

When an individual discovers himself as a praxis subject in his work it is no longer possible to make him consume and destroy superfluous wealth at the price of the essential element, his free disposal of himself. The creation of consumer wealth no longer needs to be bought at that price in the midst of disappearing scarcity. There is too glaring a disparity between the goods which "affluent" capitalism offers to individuals, and the possibilities which, in exchange, it denies to them by its pursuit of an ever greater efficiency, by the division of tasks and the centralization of power. "Thus, economic freedom would mean freedom *from* the economy—from being controlled by economic forces and relationships; freedom from the daily struggle for existence, from earning a living. Political freedom would mean liberation of the individuals *from* politics over which they have no effective control. Similarly, intellectual freedom would mean the restoration of individual thought now absorbed by mass communication and indoctrination, abolition of 'public opinion' together with its makers. The unrealistic sound of these propositions is indicative, not of their utopian character, but of the strength of the forces which prevent their realization."[6]

It also reveals the strength and the nature of the means that

[5] Herbert Marcuse, *One-Dimensional Man* (Boston: Beacon Press, 1964), pp. xiii, 7, 16.

[6] *Ibid.*, p. 4.

will have to be applied to break this opposition. The only humanism which can succeed the humanism of work is the humanism of free activity and of self-management at all levels. It presupposes that individuals, instead of seeing themselves and being seen as means of society and of production, be seen and see themselves as ends, that no longer the time at work, but free time becomes the standard of wealth. As Marx wrote:

> But to the degree that big industry develops, the creation of real wealth comes to depend less on labor-time and on the quantity of labor expended, and more on the power of the instruments brought into play . . . whose powerful effectiveness itself has no relation to the direct labor-time necessary to produce them, but depends rather on the general level of science and the progress of technology, or on the application of this science to production . . . Real wealth is manifest rather . . . in the monstrous disproportion between expended labor-time and its product, and equally in the qualitative disproportion between work, reduced to a pure abstraction, and the power of the productive process which it supervises. Work appears less as a part of the productive process, for man relates to the productive process rather as supervisor and regulator. (*What is true for machinery also holds true for the combination of human activity and the development of human relationships* [emphasis added —A. G.].) It is no longer the worker who inserts a modified natural object [i.e., a tool—A. G.] between himself and the object; he rather inserts the process of nature, transformed by him into an industrial process, as a link between him and inorganic nature, whose master he becomes. He stands at the side of the productive process, instead of being its chief agent. In this transformation, the great fundamental pillar of production and of wealth is neither the direct labor which man performs, nor the time he works, but *the appropriation of his own productive force in general* [emphasis added—A. G.], his understanding of nature and his mastery over nature in his existence as a social being—in a word, the development of the social individual . . . As soon as labor, in its direct form, has ceased to be the great source of wealth, labor-time ceases and must cease to be its measure, and exchange value the measure of use value. The *surplus labor of the masses* has ceased to be the precondition of the development of collective wealth, and the *idleness of the few* for the development of the general powers of human thought . . . The free development of individuals, and therefore not the reduction of necessary labor-time to create surplus labor, but in general the reduction to a minimum of necessary labor-time in the society [becomes the goal of production—A. G.], which then corresponds to the artistic, scientific, etc. development of individuals in the time which has become

> free and with the means that have been created for all. Capital is its own contradiction in this process, for it seeks to reduce labor-time to a minimum, while at the same time postulating labor time as the sole measure and source of wealth. *It therefore reduces necessary labor-time, in order to increase superfluous labor-time; in an increasing measure, therefore, it posits superfluous labor-time as the precondition—a question of life and death—of the necessary* [emphasis added—A. G.]. Thus, on the one hand, it enlists all the powers of science and nature, as well as of social organization and social intercourse, in order to make the creation of wealth (relatively) independent of labor-time expended. On the other hand, it wants to measure the gigantic social forces created in this way by means of labor-time, and to restrict these forces within the limits necessary to preserve already-created value as value. Productive power and social relationships—which are different sides of the development of the social individual—appear to capital only as means, and are only means to allow it to produce on its restricted base. But in fact these are the material preconditions to blow this base to pieces . . .
>
> The measure of wealth is then not labor-time at all, but disposable time.[7]

It is neither utopian nor premature to wage a struggle in this perspective. Automation will be a reality in the industrialized societies before the end of the century. At least one generation will be necessary to rid individuals of the idea that they are the tools of their tools, to accustom them to a liberty which will be within their reach, and of which the sociologists only demonstrate that it "is frightening," without demonstrating at the same time that this fright is due to the emptiness with which the dictatorship of efficiency and profit has filled the men it mutilates.

"The ultimate cause of the degradation of leisure is to be found in the degradation of *work* and of *society*";[8] in the subordination of the State to the interests of capital, in the destruction of the organs and institutions of democracy, by-passed by the fundamental decisions of those who wield power in the economy, free of control by elected assemblies. As the technicians who presently die of boredom in Marcoule, Lacq, and elsewhere—administered with a very bureaucratic and distant efficiency by officials who are equally bored—become the predominant reality, the path of liberation will inevitably proceed

[7] *Grundrisse der Kritik der Politischen Oekonomie* (Berlin: Dietz, 1953), pp. 592–594, 596. [Translated from the German by Martin A. Nicolaus.]

[8] Ernest Mandel, *Traité d'Economie Marxiste* (Julliard, ed.), II, p. 363.

through the individuals' conquest of the right to "administer" themselves in their work, their company, their community, their leisure, their home, their cultural and social services.

But when that day comes it may well be too late already if the preparations for this conquest are not begun now. The despecialization, generalization, and the autonomous management of higher education, the decommercialization of the media and of culture, the decentralization and multiplication of centers of democratic decision-making, the enlargement of local, provincial, and regional autonomies, the multiplication of self-managed cultural centers and installations are all fundamental demands from now on.

THE CULTURAL BATTLE

"To be sure," writes Herbert Marcuse, "labor must precede the reduction of labor, and industrialization must precede the development of human needs and satisfactions. But as all freedom depends on the conquest of alien necessity, the realization of freedom depends on the *techniques* of this conquest."[9] The means determine the end, and when the end is the "all-sided development of the individual," the means cannot be left to chance.

The *de facto* dictatorship of organized capitalism can no longer be combatted in the advanced industrial countries in the name of an opposed dictatorship or a dictatorship which differs only in details and color scheme. It is impossible to fight against it only on the economic and political fields. The dictatorship of capital is exercised not only on the production and distribution of wealth, but with equal force on the manner of producing, on the model of consumption, and on the manner of consuming, the manner of working, thinking, living. As much as over the workers, the factories, and the State, this dictatorship rules over the society's vision of the future, its ideology, its priorities and goals; over the way in which people experience and learn about themselves, their potentials, their relations with other people and with the rest of the world. This dictatorship is economic, political, cultural, and psychological at the same time: it is total.

That is why it is right to fight it as a whole, on all levels, in the name of an over-all alternative. A battle which is not from the beginning waged on the cultural, "ideological," and theoretical fields as well as on the *main* battleground, would be in

[9] *Op. cit.*, p. 18.

vain—as vain as a battle fought in the name of an over-all alternative but without knowing how to embody it in mediations, without knowing how to link it to immediate struggles and needs.

The cultural battle for a new conception of man, of life, education, work, and civilization, is the precondition for the success of all the other battles for socialism because it establishes their meaning. But the precondition for waging this battle is a labor movement which has abandoned its cult of conformity and all schematicism, which has re-established research and theoretical creativity with full rights and autonomy, which lets all disputes develop freely, which does not subordinate theory to ephemeral tactical opportunities. Never has the workers' movement had so great a need of theorists, and never in France has it been so poor in them, abandoning immense fields of potentially creative research to empiricist sociologists, abandoning with the same blow to neocapitalism the task of forging an ideology of consolidation and justification for the ever growing strata of non-manual workers.

If Marxism—as the humanism of praxis and of free human development—wanted to play a losing game, it would go about it no differently. In fact, it has everything to gain by occupying itself with all problems and by enriching itself, insofar as these problems have concrete substance, with the currents and researches which proceed in its margins.

> The deepening contradiction between monopolist development and the most profound human ideological and professional requirements of the intermediate social strata, cannot ripen except through the mediation of the elites, of the avant-garde which are capable of interpreting the deepest demands, the most permanent interests of these social groups . . . The contents which the proletariat can directly express are not really sufficient to constitute a positive critique of the capitalist system . . . Power will not be achieved by the proletariat without the lasting alliance of the social and political forces which can adhere to a revolutionary solution only insofar as they can see it as a well-defined positive whole. The ideals of communist society, its content, its institutions, and values, cannot therefore remain a vague promise for the future (if they ever could), but must become, even in the form of successive approximations, a decisive preliminary element of the struggle for power.[10]

[10] Lucio Magri, *Les Temps Modernes*, September–October 1962, pp. 616, 619.

The Western labor movement cannot wait for the positive model of the society that is to be constructed to be furnished to it from outside. Certainly one can speculate that automation will bring all the capitalist societies to the point of crisis; it will destroy the quantitative criteria of efficiency on which these societies are based; automation will make it clear that the rational utilization of machines (fixed capital) according to the exigencies of maximum profitability cannot be achieved except at the price of an irrational utilization of men, of their time and their abilities, to the detriment of their human exigencies. One may further speculate that automation will be imposed on the capitalist societies by the advanced socialist societies, for whom there are no economic and ideological obstacles (although there are bureaucratic ones) to its application.

But this kind of speculation would simply defer the problem a generation or more while permitting the continued existence of the risk that capitalism, in order to maintain its criteria of rationality, will defend itself against the social and political consequences of automation by the organization of waste and destruction on a global scale. It is not possible to wait until a ready-made model is furnished by the socialist societies, which are barely emerging from decades of forced accumulation. They are not very far advanced in the theoretical investigation of the purposes and the model of life. All investigations to that purpose in the "Western" socialist movement will be for them a positive contribution.

Contradiction and Overdetermination

LOUIS ALTHUSSER

First Jean-Paul Sartre submits to Marxism (conditionally) in the name of existentialism. Then, in the name of structuralism, the anthropologist Claude Levi-Strauss resumes the attack on Marxism in an extended debate with Sartre. Whereupon the phenomenologist Louis Althusser produces a Structuralist Marxism. The French are clearly superior at this.

"Contradiction and Overdetermination" is the most difficult essay in this collection, partly just because Hegelian styles of thought, ways of posing questions, are not familiar to Americans, whose philosophical sense is more likely to have been shaped by a generally empiricist outlook. Its difficulty does not diminish its importance, however, for the question Althusser is posing is central to the Marxist view of the world. Very much simplified: is it the general contradictions of the objective economic structure which determine events, or are they determined by the special textural realities of a society—its public ideologies, institutions, superstitions, customs, etc? The conventional Marxist view is that the former produce the latter and are always determinant in the final analysis. Althusser's response is that there is no final analysis except that which remains, by definition, on the other side of history—and that Marx and Engels never argued otherwise.

IN AN ARTICLE devoted to the young Marx,[1] I have already stressed the ambiguity of the idea of "inverting Hegel." It seemed to me that, strictly speaking, this expression suited Feuerbach perfectly; the latter did, indeed, "turn speculative

[1] "Sur le Jeune Marx," in *Pour Marx* (Paris, 1965), pp. 45–83.

philosophy back onto its feet," but the only result was to arrive with implacable logic in an idealist *anthropology*. But the expression cannot be applied to Marx, at least not to the Marx who had grown out of this "anthropological" phase. I could go further, and suggest that in the well-known passage: "With Hegel the dialectic is standing on its head. It must be turned right side up again, if you would discover the rational kernel within the mystical shell,"[2] this "turning right side up again" is merely gestural, even metaphorical, and it raises as many questions as it answers.

How should we really understand its use in this quotation? It is no longer a matter of a general "inversion" of Hegel, i.e., the inversion of speculative philosophy as such. From *The German Ideology* onward we know that such an undertaking would be meaningless. Anyone who claims purely and simply to have inverted speculative philosophy (to derive, for exam-

[2] Karl Marx: *Das Kapital*, Post-script to the second edition. This is a literal translation of the German original. Here is a translation of the crucial passages: "In principle *(der Grundlage nach)* my dialectical method is not only distinct from Hegel's but its direct opposite. For Hegel, the process of thought, which he goes so far as to turn into an autonomous subject under the name of the Idea, is the demiurge of the real, which only represents *(bildet)* its external phenomena. For me, on the contrary, the ideal is nothing but the material transposed and translated in man's head. The mystificatory *(mystifirende)* side of the Hegelian dialectic I criticized about thirty years ago while it was still fashionable . . . I then declared myself openly a disciple of that great thinker, and, in my chapter of the theory of value I went so far as to flirt *(ich kokettirt . . . mit)* here and there with his peculiar mode of expression. The mystification the dialectic suffered at Hegel's hands does not remove him from his place as the first to expose *(darstellen)* consciously and in depth its general forms of movement. With him it is standing on its head. It must be turned right side up again if you would discover the rational kernel *(Kern)* within the mystical shell *(mystische Hulle)*.

"In its mystified form the dialectic was a German fashion because it seemed to transfigure the given *(das Bestehende)*. In its rational image *(Gestalt)* it is a scandal and abomination for the bourgeoisie . . . As it includes in the understanding of the given (*Bestehende*) the simultaneous understanding of its negation and necessary destruction, as it conceives any mature *(gewordne)* form as in motion and thus equally in its ephemeral aspect it allows nothing to impose on it, and is in essence critical and revolutionary."

[Althusser here makes several criticisms of French translations of *Das Kapital*, particularly those of Roy and Molitor. These are not applicable to this passage in the English translation by Moore and Aveling (Moscow 1961) except for the use of "the present" for "*das Bestehende*" (the given)—but elsewhere this translation leaves much to be desired—Translator's note.]

ple, materialism) can never be more than philosophy's Proudhon, its unconscious prisoner, just as Proudhon was the prisoner of bourgeois economics. We are now concerned with the *dialectic*, and the dialectic alone. It might be thought that when Marx writes that we must "discover the rational kernel within the mystical shell" he means that the "rational kernel" is the dialectic itself, while the "mystical shell" is speculative philosophy. Engels's time-honored distinction between *method* and *system* implies precisely this.[3] The shell, the mystical wrapping (speculative philosophy), should be tossed aside and the precious kernel, the dialectic, retained. But in the same sentence Marx claims that this shelling of the kernel and the inversion of the dialectic are one and the same thing. How can an extraction be an inversion? Or in other words, what is "inverted" during this extraction?

Let us look a little closer. As soon as the dialectic is removed from its idealistic shell, it becomes "the direct opposite of the Hegelian dialectic." Does this mean that for Marx, far from dealing with Hegel's sublimated, inverted world, it is applied to the real world? This is certainly the sense in which Hegel was "the first consciously to expose its general forms of movement in depth." We could therefore take his dialectic from him and apply it to life rather than to the Idea. The inversion would then be an inversion of the sense of the dialectic. But such an inversion in sense would in fact leave the dialectic untouched.

THE KERNEL AND THE SHELL

Taking young Marx as an example, in the article referred to above, I suggested that to take over the dialectic in rigorous Hegelian form could only expose us to dangerous ambiguities, for it is impossible, given the principles of a Marxist interpretation of *any* ideological phenomenon, to conceive of the place of the dialectic in Hegel's system as that of a kernel in a nut.[4]

[3] *Feuerbach and the End of Classical German Philosophy* in Marx–Engels: *Selected Works* II, 360–402 (2 volume edition).

[4] On the kernel, see Hegel: Introduction to the *Philosophy of History;* great men "must be named heroes insofar as they have drawn their goals and vocations not only from the tranquil ordered stream of events sanctioned by the reigning system, but from a source whose content is hidden and has not yet attained actual existence, in the still subterranean internal spirit *which knocks for admittance to the external world, and breaks its way in, because it is not the almond which suits this kernel.*" A curious variant on the long history of the kernel, the pulp, and the almond. Here the kernel plays the part of an eggshell

It is inconceivable that the essence of the dialectic in Hegel's work should not be contaminated by Hegelian ideology, or, since such a "contamination" presupposes the fiction of a pure pre-"contamination" dialectic, that the Hegelian dialectic could cease to be Hegelian and become Marxist by a simple, miraculous "extraction."

Even in the rapidly written lines of the postscript to the second edition of *Das Kapital* Marx saw this difficulty clearly. By the accumulation of metaphors, he not only hints at something more than he says, but elsewhere he puts it clearly enough, though our translators have half sneaked it away.

A close reading of the German text shows clearly enough that the *mystical shell* is by no means (as some of Engel's later commentaries would lead one to think)[5] speculative philosophy,

---

containing the almond; the kernel is outside and the almond inside. The almond (the new principle) finally bursts the old kernel which no longer suits it (it was the kernel of the old almond); it wants a kernel of *its own:* new political and social forms, etc. This reference should be borne in mind whenever the problem of the Hegelian dialectic of history arises.

[5] Cf. Engels *Feuerbach, op. cit.* Perhaps we should not take too literally all the formulations of a text on the one hand destined for wide popular diffusion, and therefore, as Engels himself admits, somewhat schematic, and on the other set down by a man who forty years previously lived through the great intellectual adventure of the discovery of historical materialism, and himself passed through the *philosophical* forms of consciousness whose broad history he is writing. The essay does, in fact, contain a noteworthy critique of Feuerbach (Engels sees that for him "nature and man remain mere words," p. 384) and a good sketch of the relations between Marxism and Hegelianism. For example, Engels demonstrates Hegel's extraordinary critical virtue as compared with Kant (this I think particularly important), and correctly declares that "in its Hegelian form this (dialectical) method was unusable," p. 386. Further, and basic: the development of philosophy is not philosophical; it was the "practical necessities of its fight" in religion and politics that forced the neoHegelians to oppose Hegel's "system" (p. 367); it is the progress of science and industry which overturns philosophies (p. 372). Also the recognition of the profound influence of Feuerbach on *The Holy Family* (p. 368), etc. But the same essay contains formulations which, if taken literally, can only lead to dead ends. For example, the theme of the "inversion" is taken so seriously that Engels draws the logical conclusion that "ultimately, the Hegelian system represents merely a *materialism* idealistically *turned upside down* in method and content" (p. 372). If the inversion of Hegel into Marx is well-founded, it follows that Hegel must already have been a previously inverted materialism; two negations make an affirmation. Later (p. 387), we discover that the Hegelian dialectic was unusable in its Hegelian form precisely because it stands on its head (on the idea, not the real):

or its "world-conception," or its "system," i.e., an element we can regard as external to its method, but refers directly to the dialectic itself. Marx goes so far as to talk of "the mystification the dialectic suffered at Hegel's hands," of its "mystificatory side," its "mystified form" (*mystificirte Form*), and of the rational figure (*rationelle Gestalt*) of his own dialectic. It would be difficult to indicate more clearly that the mystical shell is nothing but the mystified form of the dialectic itself: that is, not a relatively external element of the dialectic (e.g., the "system") but an *internal* element, *consubstantial with the Hegelian dialectic.* It is not enough, therefore, to disengage it from its *first wrapping* (the system) to free it. It must also be freed from a second, almost inseparable skin, Hegelian in principle. This extraction cannot be painless; in appearance an unpeeling, it is really a *demystification,* an operation transforming what is extracted.

EXTRACTION, INVERSION, OR STRUCTURE?

To conclude, in its approximation, this metaphorical expression —the inversion of the dialectic—does not raise the problem of the nature of the objects to which a single method should be applied (the world of the Idea for Hegel—the real world for Marx), but rather the problem of the *nature of the dialectic* itself, that is, the problem of *its specific structures;* not the problem of the inversion of the "sense" of the dialectic, but that of the *transformation of its structures.* It is hardly worth pointing out that, in the first case, the application of a method, the exteriority of the dialectic to its possible objects poses a predialectical question, a question without any strict meaning for

---

"Thereby the dialectic of concepts itself became merely the conscious reflex of the dialectical motion of the real world and thus the dialectical of Hegel was placed upon its head; or rather, turned off its head, on which it was standing, and placed upon its feet." Obviously these are approximate formulations only, but their very approximation indicates a difficulty. Also noteworthy is a singular affirmation of the necessity for all philosophers to construct a system: (Hegel "was compelled to make a system and, in accordance with traditional requirements, a system of philosophy must conclude with some sort of absolute truth." p. 363), a necessity which "springs from an imperishable desire of the human mind—the desire to overcome all contradictions" (p. 365); and another statement that explains the limitations of Feuerbach's materialism by his life in the country and his consequent rustication in isolation (p. 375).

Marx. The second problem, on the other hand, raises a real question to which it is hardly likely that Marx and his disciples should not have given a concrete answer in theory or in practice.

Let us say, to end this overextended textual exposition, that if the Marxist dialectic is in principle the opposite of the Hegelian dialectic, if it is rational and not mystical-mystified-mystificatory, this radical distinction must be manifest in its essence, that is, in its determinations and specific structures. To be clear, this means that fundamental structures of the Hegelian dialectic such as negation, the negation of the negation, the identity of opposites, "sublation," the transformation of quantity into quality, contradiction, etc., have for Marx (insofar as he uses them, and he uses by no means all of them) a structure different from that which they have for Hegel. It also means that these structural differences can be demonstrated, described, determined, and thought. And if it is possible, it is therefore necessary, I would go so far as to say vital, for Marxism. We cannot go on reiterating indefinitely approximations such as the difference between system and method, the inversion of philosophy or dialectic, the extraction of the "rational kernel," etc., and let these formulae think for us, confining ourselves to the magic of a number of completely devalued words for the understanding of Marx's work. I say vital, for I am convinced that Marxism in its philosophical development is at present hanging back from this task.[6]

THE RUSSIAN REVOLUTION

As someone must take the first step, I shall brave the perils of a brief discussion of the Marxist concept of contradiction in a particular case: the Leninist thesis of "the weakest link."

Lenin gave this metaphor, above all, a practical meaning.

[6] Mao Tse-tung's pamphlet *On Contradiction* (1937) contains a whole series of analyses in which the Marxist conception of contradiction appears in a quite un-Hegelian light. Its essential concepts may be sought in vain in Hegel: principle and secondary contradiction; principle and secondary aspect of the contradiction; antagonistic and nonantagonist contradiction; law of uneven development—the contradiction. However, Mao's essay, inspired by his struggle against dogmatism in the Chinese Party, remains generally on a descriptive level, and is consequently abstract in certain respects. Descriptive: his concepts correspond to concrete experience. In part abstract: the concepts, though new, and rich in promise, are presented as specifications of the dialectic in general, rather than as necessary implications of the Marxist conception of society and history.

A chain is as strong as its weakest link. Anyone who wants to control a given situation will look out for a weak point, in case it should render the whole system vulnerable. On the other hand, anyone who wants to attack it, even if the odds are apparently against him, need only discover this one weakness to make all its power precarious. So far there is nothing new here for the readers of Machiavelli or Vauban, who were as expert in the arts of the defense as of the destruction of a position, and who judged armor by its faults. But this is where we should pay attention: if it is obvious that the theory of the weakest link guided Lenin in his theory of the revolutionary party (faultlessly united in consciousness and organization to avoid adverse exposure and to destroy the enemy), it was also the inspiration for his reflections on the revolution itself. How was the revolution possible in Russia, why was it victorious there? It was possible in Russia for a reason which transcended Russia: because with the unleashing of imperialist war humanity entered into an *objectively revolutionary* situation.[7] Imperialism tore off the "peaceful" mask of the old capitalism. The concentration of industrial monopolies, their subordination to financial monopolies, increased the exploitation of the workers and of the colonies. Competition between the monopolies made the war inevitable. But this same war, which dragged vast masses, even colonial peoples from whom troops were drawn, into limitless suffering, drove its cannon-fodder not only into massacre, but also into history. Everywhere the experience, the horrors of war were confirmation of a whole century's protest against capitalist exploitation; a focusing-point too, for hand-in-hand with this shattering exposure went the effective means of action. But though this effect was felt throughout the greater part of the European popular masses (revolution in Germany and Hungary, mutinies and mass strikes in France and Italy, the soviets of Turin) *only in Russia,* precisely the "*most backward*" country in Europe, *did it produce a triumphant revolution.*

Why this paradoxical exception? For this basic reason: in the "system of imperialist states"[8] Russia represented the weak-

[7] Lenin: *Farewell Letter to Swiss Workers* (April 8th, 1917). "It was the *objective conditions* created by the imperialist war that brought the *whole* of humanity to an impasse, that placed it in a dilemma: either allow the destruction of more millions of lives and utterly ruin European civilization, or hand over power in *all* the civilized countries to the revolutionary proletariat, carry through the socialist revolution." *Collected Works,* XXIII, 370–371.

[8] Lenin: *Report of the Central Committee to the 8th Congress of the RCP(B), Collected Works,* XXIX, 153.

est point. The Great War had, of course, precipitated and aggravated this weakness, but it had not by itself created it. Already, even in defeat, the 1905 Revolution had demonstrated the weakness of Tsarist Russia. This weakness was the product of this special feature: the accumulation and exacerbation of all the historical contradictions then possible; contradictions of a regime of feudal exploitation at the dawn of the twentieth century, attempting to control as threats to it mounted, with the aid of a deceitful priesthood, an enormous mass of "ignorant"[9] peasants (circumstances which dictated a singular association of the peasants' revolt with the workers' revolution);[10] contradictions of large-scale capitalist and imperialist exploitation in the major cities and their suburbs, in the mining regions, oilfields, etc.; contradictions of colonial exploitation and wars imposed on whole peoples: the gigantic contradiction between the stage of development of capitalist methods of production (particularly in respect to proletarian concentration: the largest factory in the world at the time was the Putilov Works at Petrograd, with forty thousand workers and auxiliaries) and the medieval state of the country. Again, the exacerbation of class struggles in the whole country, not only between exploiter and exploited, but even within the ruling classes themselves (the great feudal proprietors supporting autocratic, militaristic, police Tsarism; the small aristocracy constantly fomenting plots; haute bourgeoisie and liberal bourgeoisie opposed to the Tsar; the petits bourgeoisie oscillating between conformism and anarchistic "leftism"). The detailed course of events added other "exceptional"[11] circumstances, incomprehensible outside this tangle of contradictions inside and outside Russia. There was for example, the "advanced" nature of the Russian revolutionary elite, exiled by Tsarist repression; in exile it becme "cultivated," it absorbed the whole heritage (above all, Marxism) of the political experience of the Western European working classes; this was particularly true of the formation of the Bolshevik Party, far ahead of any Western "Socialist" party in consciousness and organization.[12] There was the "dress rehearsal" for the Revolution in 1905, which, in common with most serious crises, set class relations sharply

[9] Lenin.

[10] Lenin: *Left-Wing Communism, an Infantile Disorder, Selected Works* III, 412–35.

[11] Lenin: *Our Revolution* in *Selected Works* III, 821.

[12] Lenin: *Left-Wing Communism, an Infantile Disorder, Selected Works* III, 379.

into relief and made possible the discovery of a new form of mass political organization: *soviets*.[13] Last, but not least, there was the unexpected respite the exhausted imperialist nations allowed the Bolsheviks for them to make their opening in history, the involuntary but effective support of the Anglo-French bourgeoisie; at the decisive moment, wishing to be rid of the Tsar, they did everything to help the Revolution.[14] In brief, as precisely these details show, the privileged situation of Russia with respect to the *possible* revolution was a matter of *an accumulation and an exacerbation of historical contradictions* that would have been incomprehensible in any country which was not, as Russia was, at the same time at least a century behind the imperialist world, *and at the highest point of its development.*

THE WEAKEST LINK

All this can be found throughout Lenin's work,[15] and Stalin summarized it in particularly clear terms in his speeches of April 1924.[16] The unevenness of capitalist development led, via the 1914–18 war, to the Russian Revolution. In the revolutionary situation facing the whole of humanity Russia was the weakest link in the chain of imperialist states. It had accumulated the largest sum of historical contradictions then possible; for it was at the same time the most backward and the most advanced nation, a gigantic contradiction which its divided ruling classes could neither avoid nor solve. In other words, Russia was overdue with its bourgeois revolution at the birth of its proletarian revolution; pregnant with two revolutions, at the birth of the first it could not withhold the second. This exceptional situation was "insoluble" (for the ruling classes)[17] and Lenin was correct to see in it the *objective conditions* of a

[13] Lenin: *The Third International and its Place in History, Collected Works,* XXIX, 311.

[14] Lenin: *Report to the Petrograd City Conference of the RSDRP(B), Collected Works,* XXIV, 141.

[15] See particularly *Left-Wing Communism, op. cit.,* pp. 379; 412, 435–436; 439; 444–445. *The Third International, op. cit.,* pp. 310. *Our Revolution, op. cit.,* pp. 820ff. *Letters from Afar,* No. 1, *Selected Works* II, p. 31ff. Lenin's remarkable theory of the conditions for a revolution (*Left-Wing Communism,* pp. 434–435; 444–446) deals thoroughly with the decisive effect of Russia's specific situation.

[16] Stalin: *The Foundations of Leninism,* Problems of Leninism (11th edition) pp. 13–93, particularly pp. 15–18, 29–32, 71–73. Despite their "pedagogical" dryness, these pieces are in many ways excellent.

[17] Lenin: *Our Revolution, op. cit.,* p. 821.

Russian revolution, and to forge its *subjective conditions,* the means of a decisive assault on this weak link in the imperialist chain, in a Communist Party that was a chain without weak links.

What else did Marx and Engels mean when they declared that history always progresses by its bad side?[18] This obviously means the worst side for the rulers, but without stretching its sense unduly we can interpret the bad side as that for those who expect the reverse from history. For example, the German Social-Democrats of the end of the nineteenth century imagined they would shortly be promoted to socialist triumph by virtue of belonging to the most powerful capitalist state, then undergoing rapid economic expansion, just as they were undergoing rapid electoral expansion (such coincidences occur). They obviously saw history as progressing through the other side, the "good" side, the side with the greatest economic development, the greatest growth, with its contradiction reduced to the purest form (that between Capital and Labor), so they forgot that all this was taking place in a Germany armed with a powerful State machine, endowed with a bourgeoisie which had long ago given up its political revolution in exchange for Bismarck's (and later Wilhelm's) military, bureaucratic, and police protection, in exchange for the super-profits of capitalist and colonialist exploitation, endowed too with a chauvinist and reactionary petits bourgeoisie. They forgot that, in fact, this simple quintessence of a contradiction was quite simply abstract: the real contradiction was so much one with its "circumstances" that it was only discernible, identifiable, and manipulable *through and with them.*

What is the essence of this practical experience and the reflections it inspired in Lenin? It should be pointed out immediately that this was not Lenin's sole illuminating experience. Before 1917 there was 1905, before 1905 the great historical deceptions of Germany and England, before that the Commune, even earlier the German failure of 1848–49. En route, these experiences provoked more or less direct reflections (Engels: *Revolution and Counterrevolution in Germany;* Marx: *The Class Struggles in France; The Civil War in France; The Eighteenth Brumaire; The Critique of the Gotha Programme;* Engels: *The Critique of the Erfurt Programme;* etc.), and had been related to even earlier revolutionary experience: the bourgeois revolutions of England and France.

[18] *The Poverty of Philosophy,* p. 121.

OVERDETERMINATION

How else should we summarize these practical experiences and theoretical commentaries other than by saying that the whole Marxist revolutionary experience shows that, if the general contradiction (it has already been specified: the contradiction between forces of production and relations of production, essentially embodied in the contradiction between two antagonistic classes) is sufficient to define the situation when revolution is the order of the day, it cannot of its own simple, direct power provoke a "revolutionary situation," nor *a fortiori* a situation of revolutionary rupture and triumph of the revolution. If this contradiction is to become active in the strongest sense, to become a ruptural principle, there must be an accumulation of circumstances and currents so that whatever their origin and sense (and many of them will *necessarily* be strangely foreign to the revolution, or even its "direct opponents" in origin and sense), they *fuse* into a *ruptural unit:* the immense majority of the popular masses grouped in an assault on a regime which its ruling classes are unable to defend.[19] Such a situation presupposes not only the fusion of the two basic conditions into a "single national crisis" but each condition considered (abstractly) by itself presupposes the fusion of an accumulation of contradictions. How else could the class-divided masses (proletarians, peasants, petits bourgeois) throw themselves together into a general assault on the existing regime? And how else could the ruling classes (aristocrats, big bourgeois, industrial bourgeois, finance bourgeois, etc.), who have learned through long experience and sure instinct to fix among themselves, despite their class differences, a holy alliance against the exploited, find themselves reduced to impotence, divided at the decisive moment, with neither new political solutions nor new political leaders, deprived of foreign class support, disarmed in the very fortress of their State machine, and suddenly over-

[19] For the whole of this passage, see (1) Lenin: *Left-Wing Communism, op. cit.*, pp. 430, 444–445; particularly: "Only when the *'lower classes' do not want* the old way, and when the *'upper classes' cannot carry on in the old way*—only then can revolution triumph." p. 430. (2) Lenin: *Letters from Afar,* No. 1, *op. cit.*, pp. 35–36, notably: "That the revolution succeeded so quickly . . . is only due to the fact that, as a result of an extremely unique historical situation, *absolutely dissimilar currents, absolutely heterogeneous* class interests, *absolutely contrary* political and social strivings have merged . . . in a strikingly 'harmonious' manner . . . " p. 35 (Lenin's emphasis).

whelmed by the people they had so long suppressed by exploitation, violence, and deceit? If, as in this situation, a vast accumulation of "contradictions" come into play in the same court, some of which are radically heterogeneous—of different origins, different sense, different *levels* and *points* of application—but which nevertheless group themselves into a ruptural unity, we can no longer talk of the sole, unique power of the general "contradiction."

Of course, the basic contradiction dominating the period (when the revolution is "the order of the day") is active in all these contradictions and even in their fusion. But, strictly speaking, it cannot be claimed that these contradictions and their fusion are merely the *pure phenomena* of the general contradiction. The circumstances and currents constituting it are more than its phenomena pure and simple. They derive from the relations of production, which are, of course, one of the *terms* of the contradiction, but at the same time its *conditions of existence;* from the superstructures, instances deriving from it, but with their own consistency and efficacy; from the international conjuncture itself, which intervenes as a determination with a specific role to play.[20] This means that if the differences constituting each of the instances in play (manifested in the accumulation discussed by Lenin) group themselves into a real unity, they are not dissipated as pure phenomena in the internal unity of a simple contradiction. The unity they constitute in this fusion into a revolutionary rupture,[21] is constituted by their own essence and efficacy, by what they are according to the specific modalities of their action. In constituting this unity, they reconstitute and consummate their basic animating unity, but at the same time they also bring out its *nature*: the contradiction is inseparable from the total structure of the social body in which it is found, inseparable from its formal conditions of existence, even from the instances it governs; it is radically affected by them, determining and determined in one and the same movement by the various *levels*

[20] Lenin goes so far as to include among the causes of the success of the Soviet Revolution the natural wealth of the country and its geographical extent, the shelter of the Revolution in its necessary military and political "retreats."

[21] The crisis situation, as Lenin often remarked, has a *revelatory* role for the structure and dynamic of the social formation living through it. What is said of a revolutionary situation can therefore be referred cautiously to the social formation in a situation prior to the revolutionary crisis.

and *instances* of the social formation it animates; it might be called *in principle overdetermined.*[22]

I am not particularly taken by this term *overdetermination* (borrowed from other disciplines), but I use it in the absence of anything better, both as an index and as a problem, and also because it enables us to see clearly why we are dealing with something quite different from the Hegelian contradiction.

HEGEL AND MARX

In fact, a Hegelian contradiction is never really overdetermined, even when it has all the appearances of being so. For example, in the *Phenomenology of Mind,* which describes the experiences of consciousness and the dialectic which culminates in Absolute Knowledge, contradiction does not appear to be simple, but on the contrary very complex. Strictly speaking, only the first contradiction—between sensuous consciousness and its knowledge—can be called simple. The further we progress in the dialectic of its production, the richer becomes consciousness, the more complex its contradiction. However, it can be shown that this complexity is not the complexity of an *effective overdetermination,* but the complexity of a cumulative *interiorization* which is only apparently an overdetermination. In fact, at each moment of its becoming, consciousness lives and experiences its own essence (the essence corresponding to its stage of development) through all the echoes of the essences it has previously been, and through the allusive presence of the corresponding historical forms. Hegel, therefore, argues that any consciousness has a suppressed-conserved past even in its present, and a world (the world whose consciousness it could be, but which is marginal in the *Phenomenology,* its presence virtual and latent), and that therefore it also has as its past the worlds of its surpassed essences. But these past images of consciousness and these latent worlds (corresponding to the images) never affect present consciousness as effective determinations different from itself: these images and worlds concern it only *as echoes* (memories, phantoms of its historicity) of what has become, that is, *as anticipations of or allusions to itself*. Because the past is never more than the internal essence of the future it contains, this presence of the past is the presence to consciousness of con-

[22] Cf. Mao's development of the theme of the distinction between *antagonistic* (explosive, revolutionary) contradictions and *nonantagonistic* contradications *(On Contradiction),* etc.

sciousness itself, *and no true external determination.* A circle of circles, consciousness has only one center, which solely determines it; it would need circles with another center than itself—*eccentric circles*—for it to be affected at its center by their action, in short for its essence to be overdetermined by them. But this is not the case.

This truth emerges even more clearly from the *Philosophy of History*. Here again we encounter an apparent overdetermination: are not all historical societies constituted of an infinity of concrete determinations, from political laws to religion via customs, habits, financial, commercial, and economic regimes, the educational system, the arts, philosophy, etc.? However, none of these determinations is essentially outside the others, not only because together they constitute an original, organic totality, but above all because this totality is *reflected in a unique internal principle*, which is the truth of all those concrete determinations. Thus Rome: its mighty history, its institutions, its crises and ventures are nothing but the temporal manifestation of the internal principle of the abstract juridical personality, and its destruction. Of course, this internal principle contains as echoes the principle of each of the historical formations it has sublated, but as its own echoes—this is why it has only one center, the center of all the past worlds conserved in its memory; this is why it is *simple*. And the contradiction appears in this very simplicity: in Rome, the Stoic consciousness as consciousness of the contradiction is inherent in the concept of the abstract juridical personality, which aims for the concrete world of subjectivity, but misses it. This is the contradiction that will bring down Rome and generate its future: the image of subjectivity in medieval Christianity. All Rome's complexity fails to overdetermine the contradiction in the simple Roman principle, which is merely the internal essence of this infinite historical wealth.

We have only to ask *why* Hegel conceived the phenomena of historical mutation in terms of this simple concept of contradiction to reach precisely *the* essential question. The simplicity of the Hegelian contradiction is made possible only by the simplicity of the internal principle constituting the essence of any historical period. If it is possible in principle to reduce the totality, the infinite diversity, of a historically given society (Greece, Rome, The Holy Roman Empire, England, etc.) to a simple internal principle, this very simplicity can be reflected in the contradiction to which it thereby acquires a right. Must we be even plainer? This reduction itself (Hegel derived the idea from Montesquieu), the reduction of *all* the elements that make up the concrete life of a historical epoch (economic, social, political, and legal institutions, customs, morals, art, religion, philosophy, and even historical *events:* wars, battles, defeats, etc.) to *one* principle of internal unity, is only possible on the absolute condition of taking the whole concrete life of a people for the exteriorization-alienation of an internal spiritual principle, which can never definitely be anything but the most abstract form of self-consciousness of that epoch: its religious or philosophical consciousness, that is, its ideology.

I think we can now see how the "mystical shell" affects and contaminates the "kernel"—for the simplicity of the Hegelian contradiction is never more than a reflection of the simplicity of this internal principle of a people, that is, not its material reality, but its most abstract ideology. It is also why Hegel could represent Universal History from the Ancient Orient to the present day as "dialectical," that is, moved by the simple play of a principle of *simple* contradiction. It is why there is never for him any really basic rupture, no actual end to any real history—nor any radical beginning. It is why his philosophy of history is garnished with uniformly "dialectical" mutations. This stupefying conception is only defensible from the Spirit's topmost peak. From that vantage point, what does it matter if a people die if it has embodied the determinate principle of a moment of the Idea (which has plenty more to come), if it has cast it off to add it to that Self-Memory which is History, thereby delivering it to such and such another people (even if their historical relation is very tenuous) who, reflecting it in their substance, will find in it the promise of their own internal principle, as if by chance the logically consecutive moment of the Idea, etc., etc. It must be clear that all these arbitrary decisions (shot through with insights of genius) are not just confined miraculously to Hegel's world-conception, to his "system," but are reflected in the structure of his work, even the structures of his dialectic, particularly in the "contradiction" whose task is the magical movement of the concrete contents of a historical epoch onwards to its ideological Goal.

Thus the Marxist "inversion" of the Hegelian dialectic is something quite different from an extraction pure and simple. If we clearly perceive the intimate and close relation that the Hegelian structure of the dialectic has with Hegel's world-conception, the latter cannot simply be cast aside without obliging us to alter profoundly the structures of that dialectic. If not, whether we will it or no, we shall drag along with us, 150 years after Hegel's death, and 100 years after Marx's, the shreds of the famous "mystical wrapping."

THE EXCEPTION AND THE RULE

Let us return to Lenin and thence to Marx. If it is true, as Leninist practice and reflection prove, that the revolutionary situation in Russia was precisely a result of the intense over-determination of the basic class contradiction, we should perhaps ask what is exceptional in this exceptional situation and if, like all exceptions, this one does not clarify a rule—is not, unbeknownst, *the rule itself*. For, after all, *are we not always in exceptional situations*? The failure of the 1849 revolution in Germany was an exception, the failure in Paris in 1871 was an exception, the German Social-Democratic failure of the beginning of the twentieth century in producing the chauvinism of 1914 was an exception, the success of 1917 was an exception . . . exceptions, but *with respect to what*? Nothing but the *abstract* idea, which is nonetheless comforting and reassuring, of a pure, simple, dialectical schema, which in its very simplicity seems to have retained the memory (or rediscovered the allure) of the Hegelian model and its faith in the resolving power of the abstract contradiction as such: particularly the beautiful contradiction between Capital and Labor. I do not deny that the simplicity of this purified schema answered to certain subjective necessities for the mobilization of the masses; after all, we know perfectly well that utopian forms of socialism also played their historical part, and played it well because they appealed to the masses within the limits of their consciousness and to lead them forward, here, above all, is where they must be seized. It will soon be necessary to do what Marx and Engels did for utopian socialism, but this time for those still schematic-utopian forms of mass consciousness influenced by Marxism (even the consciousness of certain of its theoreticians) in the first stage of its history: a real historical study of the conditions and forms of that consciousness.[23] In fact, we find that all the

[23] In 1890 Engels wrote (in a letter to J. Bloch, September 21, 1890): "Marx and I are ourselves partly to blame for the fact that the younger people sometimes lay more stress on the economic side than is due to it. We had to emphasize the main principle vis-à-vis our adversaries, who denied it, and we had not always the time, the place, or the opportunity to allow the other elements involved in the interaction to come into their rights." (*Selected Works* II, 490).

In the control of this proposed research, I would like to quote the notes Gramsci devoted to the mechanistic-fatalistic temptation in the

important historical and political articles by Marx and Engels during this period give us precisely the material for a preliminary reflection on these so-called exceptions. They reveal the basic notion that *the contradiction between Capital and Labor is never simple, but always specified by the historically concrete forms and circumstances in which it is exercised.* It is specified by the forms of the superstructure (the State, the dominant ideology, religion, politically organized movements, etc.); specified by the internal and external historical situation which determines it as on the one hand a function of the *national past* (completed or "relapsed" bourgeois revolution, feudal exploitation eliminated wholly, partially, or not at all, local customs, specific national traditions, even the particular style of political struggles and behavior, etc. . .), and on the other as functions of the *existing world* context (what domi-

---

history of nineteenth-century Marxism: "the determinist, fatalist element has been an immediate ideological 'aroma' of the philosophy of praxis, a form of religion and a stimulant (but like a drug) necessitated and historically justified by the 'subordinate' character of certain social strata. When one does not have the initiative in the struggle and the struggle itself is ultimately identified with a series of defeats, mechanical determinism becomes a formidable power of moral resistance, of cohesion, and of patient and obstinate perseverance. 'I am defeated for the moment but the nature of things is on my side in the long run,' etc. Real will is disguised as an act of faith, a sure rationality of history, a primitive and empirical form of impassioned finalism which appears as a substitute for the predestination, providence, etc. of the confessional religions. We must insist on the fact that even in such cases there exists in reality a strong active will . . . We must stress the fact that fatalism has only been a cover by the weak for an active and real will. This is why it is always necessary to show the futility of mechanical determinism, which, explicable as a naive philosophy of the masses, becomes a cause of passivity, of imbecile self-sufficiency, when it is made into a reflexive and coherent philosophy on the part of the intellectuals . . ." This opposition (intellectuals-masses) might appear strange from the pen of a Marxist theoretician. But it should be realized that Gramsci's concept of the *intellectual* is infinitely greater than ours, that it is not defined by the idea intellectuals have of themselves, but by their social role as *organizers* and (more or less subordinate) *leaders*. In this sense he wrote: "The affirmation that all the members of a political party should be considered intellectuals lends itself to jokes and caricature. But on reflection nothing could be more accurate. There must be a distinction of levels, with a party having more or less of the higher or lower level, but this is not what matters: what does matter is their function, which is to direct and to organize, that is, it is educational, which means intellectual." (Antonio Gramsci: *Opere* II, *Il Materialismo Storico*, pp. 13–14; The Modern Prince, pp. 69–70. *Opere* III, *Gli Intellettuali*, p. 12).

nates it: competition of capitalist nations, or "imperialist internationalism" or competition within imperialism, etc.), many of these phenomena deriving from the "law of uneven development" in Lenin's sense.

What can this mean but that the apparently simple contradiction is *always overdetermined*? The exception thus discovers in itself the rule, the rule of rules, and the old exceptions must be regarded as methodologically simple examples of the *new rule*. To extend the analysis to all phenomena using this rule, I should like to suggest that an "overdetermined contradiction" may either be overdetermined in the sense of a historical inhibition, a real block for the contradiction (for example, Wilhelmine Germany), or in the sense of a revolutionary rupture[24] (Russia in 1917), but in neither condition is it ever found in the pure state. Purity itself would be the exception, but I know of no example to quote.

CONCEPTION OF HISTORY

But if every contradiction appears in historical practice and in Marxist historical experience as an overdetermined contradiction; if this overdetermination constitutes the *specificity* of the Marxist contradiction as opposed to the Hegelian contradiction; if the simplicity of the Hegelian dialectic is inseparable from his world-conception, particularly the conception of history it reflects, we must ask what is the content, the *raison d'être* of the overdetermination of the Marxist contradiction, and how can the Marxist conception of society be reflected in this overdetermination. This is a crucial question, for it is obvious that if we cannot demonstrate the *necessary link* uniting the particular structure of contradiction according to Marx to his conception of society and history; if this overdetermination is not based on the concepts of the Marxist theory of history, the category is up in the air. For however accurate and verified it may be in political practice, we have only so far used it descriptively, that is contingently, and like all descriptions it is still at the mercy of the earliest or latest philosophical theory.

But this raises the ghost of the Hegelian model again—not

[24] Cf. Engels (Letter to Schmidt, October 27, 1890, *op. cit.*, II, 493): "The reaction of the state power upon economic development can be one of three kinds: it can run in the same direction, and then development is more rapid; it can oppose the line of development, in which case nowadays state power in every great people will go to pieces in the long run . . ." This demonstrates the character of the two limit positions.

of its abstract model of contradiction, but of the concrete model of his *conception of history* reflected in the contradiction. If we are to prove that the specific structure of the Marxist contradiction is based on Marx's conception of history, we must first ensure that this conception is not itself a mere "inversion" of the Hegelian conception. It is true that we could argue as a first approximation that Marx inverted the Hegelian conception of history. This can be quickly illustrated. The whole Hegelian conception is dominated by the dialectic of the internal principle of each society; as Marx said twenty times, Hegel explains the material life, the concrete history of peoples by a dialectic of consciousness (the self-consciousness of a people; its ideology). For Marx, on the other hand, the material life of men explains their history; their consciousness, their ideologies are then merely phenomena of their material life. This opposition certainly has all the appearances of an "inversion."

To take it to an extreme caricature: what do we find in Hegel? A conception of society which takes over the achievements of eighteenth-century political theory and political economy, and considers any society (any modern society of course; but the present reveals what was once only a promise) as constituted of two societies: the society of needs, or *civil society*, and the political society or state and everything embodied in the state: religion, philosophy; in short, the self-consciousness of an epoch. For Hegel, material life (civil society, that is, the economy) is merely a ruse of reason. Apparently autonomous, it is obedient to a law outside itself: its own goal, its condition of possibility, the State, that is spiritual life. So we have therefore a way of inverting Hegel which would apparently give us Marx. It is simply *to invert the relation of the terms (and thus to retain them)*; civil society and state, economy and politics-ideology—to transform the essence into phenomena and the phenomena into an essence, or if you prefer, to make the ruse of reason work backwards. While for Hegel the politico-ideological was the essence of the economic, for Marx the economic is the essence of the politico-ideological. Politics and ideology are therefore merely pure phenomena of the economic, which is their truth. For Hegel's pure principle of consciousness (of the self-consciousness of an epoch), for the simple internal principle which he conceived as the principle of the intelligibility of all the determination of a historical period, we have substituted another simple principle, its opposite: material life, the economy—a simple principle which in turn becomes the sole principle of the universal intelligibility of all the determinations of a historical people.[25] Is this a caricature? If we take Marx's famous comments on the hand-mill, the water-mill, and the steam-mill literally or out of context, this is their meaning. The logical consequence of this is the *exact mirror image of the Hegelian dialectic*—the only difference being that it is no longer a question of deriving the successive moments from the Idea, but from the Economy, on the basis of the same internal contradiction. This attempt results in the radical reduction of the dialectic of history to the dialectic generator of the successive modes of production, that is, in the last analysis, of the different production techniques. There are names for these deviations in the history of Marxism: *economism* and even *technologism.*

But these terms have only to be spoken to evoke the memory of the theoretical and practical struggles of Marx and his disciples against these "deviations." And how many peremptory attacks on economism there are to counterbalance that well-thumbed piece on the steam engine! Let us abandon this caricature, not to hide behind official condemnation, but to examine the authentic principles at work in those condemnations and in Marx's real thought.

THE STATE AND CIVIL SOCIETY

For all its apparent rigor, the fiction of the inversion is now clearly untenable. We know that Marx did not retain the terms of the Hegelian model of society and invert them. He substituted other, distantly related terms for them. Further, he overhauled the relation which had previously dominated the terms. For Marx, both terms and relation changed in nature and sense.

Firstly, *the terms* are not the same.

Of course, Marx still talks of "civil society" (especially in *The German Ideology*) but as an allusion to the past, to denote the site of his discoveries, not to reutilize the concept. The formation of this concept requires close examination. Beneath the abstract forms of the political philosophy of the eighteenth century and the more concrete forms of its political economy we discover, not a true theory of economic history, nor even a true economic theory, but a situation and description of economic behavior, in short a sort of philosophico-economic phenomenology. What is remarkable in this undertaking, as much in its philosophers (Locke, Helvetius, etc.) as in its economists

[25] Of course, as with all "inversions" this retains the terms of the Hegelian conception: *civil society* and *the State.*

(Turgot, Smith, etc.), is that this description of civil society acts as if it were the description (and foundation) of what Hegel, aptly summarizing its spirit, called "the world of needs": a world, in its internal essence, in immediate relation to the relations of individuals defined by their particular wishes, personal interests, in short, their needs. We know that Marx's whole conception of political economy is based on the critique of this presupposition (the *homo oeconomicus* and its moral or legal abstraction, the "Man" of philosophy); how then could he make use of a concept which is its direct product? Neither this (abstract) description of economic behavior nor its supposed basis in the mythical *homo oeconomicus* interested Marx—his concern was rather the "anatomy" of this world, and the dialectic of the mutations of this anatomy. Therefore the concept of "civil society"—the world of individual economic behavior and its ideological origin—disappears from Marx's work. He understands abstract economic reality (which Smith, for example, rediscovers in the laws of the market as a result of his search for a foundation) as the effect of a deeper, more concrete reality: the mode of production of a determinate social formation. Thus for the first time individual economic behavior (which was the pretext for economico-philosophic phenomenology) is measured according to its conditions of existence. The degree of development of the forces of production, the state of the *relations of production:* these are the basic Marxist concepts. Civil society may well have indicated the *place* of the new concepts, but it did not contribute to their matter. But where in Hegel would you find this matter?

As far as the State is concerned, it is quite easy to show that it has a quite different content for Marx from that it had for Hegel. Not just because the State can no longer be the "reality of the Idea," but primarily because it is systematically considered as an *instrument of coercion* in the hands of the ruling, exploiting class. Beneath the description and sublimation of attributes of the State, Marx finds here also a new concept, foreshadowed in the eighteenth century (Longuet, Rousseau, etc.), taken up by Hegel in his *Philosophy of Right* (which made it into a phenomenon of the ruse of reason which triumphs in the State: the opposition of wealth and poverty), and abundantly used by the historians of the 1830's: the concept of social class, in direct relation with the relations of production. The intervention of this new concept and its relationship with one of the basic concepts of the economic structure transforms the *essence of the state* from top to toe, for the latter is no longer above human groups, but at the service of the ruling class; it is no longer its mission to consummate itself in art, religion, and philosophy, but to set them at the service of the ruling class, or rather to force them to base themselves on ideas and themes which it renders dominant; it therefore ceases to be the truth of civil society to become, not the truth of some other thing, nor even of the economy, but the means of action and domination of a social class, etc.

But *the relations themselves* change as well as *the terms*.

We should not think that this means a new technical distribution of roles imposed by the multiplication of new terms. How are these new terms arranged? On the one hand the *infrastructure* (the economic base: the forms of production and relations of production); on the other the *superstructure* (the State and all legal, political, and ideological forms). We have seen that one could attempt to maintain *a Hegelian relation* (the relation Hegel imposed between civil society and the State) between these two groups of categories: the relation between an essence and phenomena, sublimated in the concept of the "truth of . . ." For Hegel the state is the "truth of" civil society, which thanks to the action of the ruse of reason is merely its own phenomenon consummated in civil society. For a Marx thus relegated to the rank of a Hobbes or a Locke, civil society would be nothing but the truth of its phenomenon, the State, which an economic ruse of reason had then put at the service of a class: the ruling class. Unfortunately for this neat schema this is not Marx. For him this tacit identity (phenomenon-essence-truth-of . . .) of the economic and political disappears in favor of a new conception of the relation of determinant instances in the infrastructure-superstructure complex which constitutes the essence of any social formation. Of course these specific relations between infrastructure and superstructure still need theoretical elaboration and research. However, Marx has at least given us the two ends of the chain and has told us to find out what goes on between them: on the one hand *determination in the last instance by the (economic) mode of production;* on the other *the relative autonomy of the superstructures and their specific efficacy.* This clearly breaks with the Hegelian principle of explanation by self-consciousness (ideology), but also with the Hegelian theme of phenomenon-essence-truth-of. We are definitely concerned with a new relationship between new terms.

Listen, again, to Engels in 1890, taking the young "economists" to task for not having understood that this was a *new relationship.*[26] Production is the determinant factor, but only "in the last instance": "more than this neither Marx nor I have ever asserted. Hence if somebody twists this into saying that the economic element is the *only* determining one, he transforms that proposition into a meaningless, abstract, empty phrase." And for explanation: "The economic situation is the basis, but the various elements of the superstructure—the political forms of the class struggle and its results; to wit, constitutions established by the victorious class after a successful battle, etc., juridical forms, and then even the reflexes of all these actual struggles in the brains of the participants, political, juristic, philosophical theories, religious views and their further development into systems of dogmas—also exercise their influence upon the course of the historical struggles, and in many cases preponderate in determining their *form* . . ." The word "form" must be taken in its strongest sense, as quite different from merely "formal." As Engels also says: "The Prussian state also arose and developed from historical, ultimately economic causes. But it could scarcely be maintained without pedantry that among the many small states of North Germany, Brandenberg was specifically determined by economic necessity to become the great power embodying the economic, linguistic, and, after the Reformation, also the religious difference between North and South, and not by other elements as well (above all by the entanglement with Poland, owing to the possession of Prussia, and hence with international political relations—which were indeed also decisive in the formation of the Austrian dynastic power)." [27]

BASE AND SUPERSTRUCTURE

Here, then, are the two ends of the chain: the economy is determinant, but *in the last instance*; Engels is prepared to say, in the long run, the run of history. But history blazes its trail through the multiform world of the superstructure, from local tradition[28] to international circumstance. Leaving aside the

[26] Letter from Engels to J. Bloch, September 21, 1890 (Marx–Engels: *Selected Works*, II, 488–489).

[27] Engels adds: "Marx hardly wrote anything in which this theory did not play a part. But especially *The Eighteenth Brumaire of Louis Bonaparte* is a most excellent example of its application. There are also many allusions in *Captial.*" (p. 489). He also cites *Anti-Dühring* and *Ludwig Feuerbach.*

[28] Engels: "Political conditions . . . and even the traditions which haunt human minds also play a part." (*Ibid.*, p. 488).

theoretical solution Engels proposes for the problem of the relation between determination *in the last instance*—the economic—those determinations imposed by the superstructures, national traditions, and international events, it is sufficient to hang on to what should be called the *accumulations of effective determinations* (deriving from the superstructures and special national and international circumstances) *on the determination in the last instance by the economic.* It seems to me that this clarifies the expression: *overdetermined contradiction,* which I am proposing, *this* specifically because the existence of overdetermination is no longer a fact pure and simple, for in its essentials we have related it to its foundations, even if our exposition has so far been merely gestural. This *overdetermination* is inevitable and conceivable as soon as the real existence of the forms of the superstructure and of the national and international conjuncture is recognized—an existence largely specific and autonomous, and therefore irreducible to a pure *phenomenon.* We must carry this through to its conclusion and say that this overdetermination does not just refer to apparently unique or aberrant historical situations (Germany, for example), but is universal; the economic dialectic is never active *in the pure state;* in history, those instances—the superstructures, etc.—are never seen to step aside when their work is done or, when the time comes, as his pure phenomena, to scatter before His Majesty the Economy as he strides along the royal road of the Dialectic. From the first moment to the last the lonely hour of the "last instance" never comes.

In short, the idea of a pure and simple nonoverdetermined contradiction is, as Engels said of the economist turn of phrase, "meaningless, abstract, senseless." That it can act as a pedagogical model, or rather that it served as a polemical and pedagogic instrument at a certain point in history does not fix its destiny for all time. After all, pedagogic systems often change historically. It is time to make the effort to raise pedagogy to the level of circumstances, that is, of historical needs. But we must all be able to see that this pedagogical effort *presupposes* another purely theoretical effort. For if Marx has given us the general principle and some concrete examples (*The Eighteenth Brumaire, The Civil War in France,* etc.), if all political practice in the history of socialist and communist movements constitutes an inexhaustible reservoir of concrete "experiential protocol," it has to be said that the theory of the specific influence of the superstructures and other circumstances largely remains to be elaborated; and before the theory of their influence or simultaneously (for by formulating their influence their *essence* is attained) there must be elaboration of the theory of the particular essence of the specific elements of the superstructure. Like the map of Africa before the great explorations, this theory remains a realm sketched in outline, with its great mountain chains and rivers, often unknown in detail beyond a few well-known regions. Who has attempted to follow up the explorations of Marx and Engels? I can only think of Gramsci.[29] But this task is indispensable if we are to be able even to set out propositions more precise than these approximations on the character of the overdetermination of the Marxist contradictions, based primarily on the existence and nature of the superstructures.

SURVIVALS AND PHANTOMS

Allow me one last example. Marxist political practice is constantly coming up against that reality known as "survivals." There can be no doubt that these survivals exist; they cling tenaciously to life. Lenin struggles with them inside the Russian Party before the revolution. It does not have to be pointed out that from then till now they have been the source of constant difficulties, struggles, and commentaries. What is a "survival"? What is its theoretical status? Is it essentially social or psychological? Can it be reduced to the survival of certain economic *structures* which the Revolution was unable to destroy with its first decrees: for example, the small-scale production (primarily peasant production in Russia) which so preoccupied Lenin? Or does it refer as much to *other structures*, political, ideological structures, etc.: customs, habits, even traditions such as the "national tradition" with its specific traits? The term "survival" is constantly invoked, but it is still virtually unknown, insofar as it has only been a *name* and not a *con-*

[29] Lukács' essays, which are limited to the history of literature and philosophy, seem to me to be contaminated with a guilty Hegelianism, as if Lukács wanted to absolve through Hegel his upbringing by Simmel and Dilthey. Gramsci is of another stature. The jottings and developments in the *Prison Notebooks* touch on all the basic problems of Italian and European history: economic, social, political, and cultural. There are some completely original and in some cases genial insights into our problem. Also, as always with true discoveries, there are *new concepts*, for example, *hegemony:* a remarkable example of a theoretical solution in outline to the problems of the interpenetration of the economic and political. Unfortunately, at least as far as France is concerned, who has taken up and followed through Gramsci's theoretical effort?

cept. The concept it deserves (and has fairly won) must be more than a vague Hegelianism such as "sublation"—the maintenance-of-what-has-been-negated-in-its-very-negation (that is the negation of the negation). If we return to Hegel for a second we can see that the survival of the past as the sublated (*aufgehoben*) can simply be reduced to the modality of a *memory,* which, further, is merely the inverse of (that is, the same thing as) an *anticipation.* Just as at the dawn of human history the first stammering of the Oriental Spirit—joyous captive of the giants of the sky, the sea, and the desert, and then of its stone bestiary—already betrayed the unconscious presage of the future achievements of the Absolute Spirit, so in each instant of time the past survives in the form of a memory of what it has been—that is, as the whispered promise of the present. That is why *the past is never opaque or an obstacle* It must always be digestible as it has been *predigested.* Rome lived happily in a world impregnated by Greece: "sublated" Greece survived as objective memories: its reproduced temples its assimilated religion, its reworked philosophy. Without knowing it, as at last it died to bring forth its Roman future, it was already Rome, so it never shackled Rome in Rome. That is why the present can feed on the shades of the past, or project them before it, just as the great effigies of Roman virtue opened the road to revolution and terror for the Jacobins. The past is never anything more than the present and only recalls that law of interiority which is the destiny of the whole future of humanity

This is enough to show that, though the word is still meaningful, Marx's conception of "sublation" has nothing to do with this dialectic of historical comfort; his past was no shade, not even an objective shade—it is a terribly positive and active structured reality, just as cold, hunger, and the night are for his poor worker. How, then, are these survivals conceived? As a determined number of *realities,* whether superstructures ideologies, national traditions, or the customs and spirit of a people, etc. As the overdetermination of any contradiction and of any constitutive element of a society, which means: (1) that a revolution of the infrastructure does not *ipso facto* modify the existing superstructures and particularly the ideologies at one blow (as it would if the economic were the sole determinant factor), for they have sufficient of their own consistency to survive beyond their immediate life context, even to recreate to secrete substitute conditions of existence temporarily; (2) that the new society produced by the revolution may itself ensure the survival and reactivation of older elements through both the forms of its superstructures and specific (national and international) circumstances. Such a reactivation is totally inconceivable for a dialectic deprived of overdetermination. I shall not evade the most burning issue: it seems to me that either the whole logic of sublation must be rejected, or we must give up any attempt to explain how the proud and generous Russian people bore Stalin's crimes and repression with such resignation; how the Bolshevik Party could tolerate them; and how a communist leader could order them. But there is obviously much *theoretical* effort needed here as elsewhere. By this I mean more than the historical work which has priority—precisely because of this priority, priority is given to one essential of any Marxist historical study: rigor; *a rigorous conception of Marxist concepts, their implications and their development; a rigorous conception and research into their essential subject-matter, that is, into what distinguishes them once and for all from their phantoms.*

One phantom is more especially crucial than any other today: the shade of Hegel. To drive this phantom back into the night we need *a little more light* on Marx, or what is the same thing, *a little more Marxist light on Hegel himself*. We can then escape from the ambiguities and confusions of the "inversion."

The Unknown Marx

MARTIN NICOLAUS

The early and even current new-working-class theorizing typically implied a departure from Marx. Based on a close reading of a relatively neglected Marxian text, the Grundrisse*, Nicolaus's essay suggests that it is perhaps an unwitting* return *to Marx—to an aspect of Marx's thought, that is, which had lain relatively neglected or unnoticed until the postwar period.*

The recovery of this text should explode most of the familiar images with which mainstream Marxism has depicted the famously forthcoming breakdown of capitalism. The revolutionary worker whom we had expected to arrive tomorrow in a tattered blue collar, worn out with overwork or starving from joblessness, may instead arrive the day after tomorrow in a lab smock. "When one considers," writes Nicolaus, "the requirements that must be met, in Marx's view, before the capitalist order is ripe for overthrow, one comes to wonder whether the failure of previous revolutionary movements in Europe and the United States is not imputable simply to prematurity."

Nicolaus's scholarly essay may quite likely be the American New Left's most important single contribution to Marxist thought. Its implications are clearly immense.

When he assessed his intellectual career in 1859, Karl Marx condemned to deserved obscurity all of his previous works but four. *The Poverty of Philosophy* (1847) first set forth the decisive points of his scientific views, although in polemical form, he wrote; and he implied that the same description applied to the *Manifesto of the Communist Party* (1848), a *Speech on Free Trade* of the same year, and an unfinished series of newspaper articles entitled *Wage-Labor and Capital*, published in

1849. He made no mention of the *Economic-Philosophical Manuscripts* (1844), *The Holy Family*, and the *Theses on Feuerbach* (1845), and he referred to the manuscript of *The German Ideology* (1846) without naming its title as a work which he and Engels gladly abandoned to the mice.[1] Three years before his death, when he received inquiries regarding the eventual publication of his complete works, he is reported to have answered dryly, "They would first have to be written."[2]

Marx, then, viewed most of the early works which have so aroused the enthusiasm of contemporary interpreters with scepticism bordering on rejection, and was painfully conscious toward the end of his life that the works which he had presented or was ready to present to the public were mere fragments.

THE PUBLICATION OF THE "GRUNDRISSE"

Only once in his life did he speak with a tone of achievement and a sense of accomplishment about one of his works. Only once did he announce that he had written something which not only encompassed the whole of his views, but also presented them in a scientific manner. That occasion was in the *Preface* to the *Critique of Political Economy* (1859), a work which also remained merely a fragment, due to difficulties with its publisher. Only two chapters of the *Critique* reached the public, but their content, while of importance, hardly justified the claims implicitly made for them in their *Preface*. The *Preface* outlines a whole world-view, a set of scientific doctrines which explains the movement of history in its sociological, political, and economic dimensions, and demonstrates how and why the present organization of society must collapse from the strain of its internal conflicts, to be replaced by a higher order of civilization. The published chapters, however, demonstrate no such breadth, nor is the ultimate emergence of a new order clearly derivable from their content. They deal, rather, with

[1] Cf. The *Preface* of the *Critique of Political Economy*. With one exception, I have used the *Werke* edition of Marx's and Engels's writings, published by Dietz, Berlin, from 1962 to 1967; but I have quoted the English titles and supplied my own translations. The *Preface* appears in *Werke* Vol. 13, pp. 7–11. An English translation can be found in Marx–Engels *Selected Works*, Vol. I, pp. 361–365.

[2] Quoted in Maximilien Rubel: *Karl Marx, Essai de Biographie Intellectuelle* (Paris: Marcel Rivière, 1957), p. 10.

fairly technical economic questions, and promise a long, arduous road with no clearly visible goal. What, then, was Marx talking about in the *Preface*? Was he making claims for theories he had not yet constructed, for ideas he had not yet written down?

Until 1939, this question remained largely a mystery. The bold generalizations made in the *Preface* could be traced back to equally bold but equally general statements in *The Poverty of Philosophy* and in the *Manifesto;* the volumes of *Capital* contain some echoes, again polemical and general. But it was difficult, if not impossible, to derive from the extant portions of *Capital* the answers to the most important question which the *Preface* announces as theoretically solved, namely the question of how and why the capitalist social order will break down. Thus Rosa Luxemburg wrote her *Accumulation of Capital* (1912) precisely for the purpose of filling this most important gap in Marx's unfinished writings,[3] thereby throwing gasoline on a fiery intraparty dispute which still flickers today. Why the manuscript on the basis of which Marx wrote the *Preface* of 1859 remained buried until the outbreak of World War II remains a mystery still; but in any case, in 1939 the Marx-Engels-Lenin Institute in Moscow brought out of its files and published an enormous volume containing Marx's economic manuscripts from the years 1857–58. A second volume followed two years later; and in 1953 the Dietz publishing house in Berlin republished the two volumes in one. Entitled by the editors *Grundrisse der Kritik der Politischen Oekonomie (Rohentwurf)*—Fundamental Traits of the Critique of Political Economy (Rough Draft)—and published together with important extracts from Marx's notebooks of 1850–51, this work at long last permits an examination of the material of which the generalizations in the *Preface* are the distillate.[4]

The *Grundrisse* has not been ignored since its publication, but neither has it been appreciated for its full importance. Assessed initially as interesting material for a reconstruction of the genesis of *Capital,* the work long vegetated in the Marxologists' underground.[5] Eric Hobsbawm introduced a fraction of it,

[3] Cf. Paul Sweezy: *The Theory of Capitalist Development* (New York: Monthly Review Press, 1942), p. 202.

[4] Marx: *Grundrisse der Kritik der Politischen Oekonomie (Rohentwurf)* (Berlin: Dietz, 1953), and Europäische Verlagsanstalt, Frankfurt. Hereafter cited as *Grundrisse.* Excerpts published in a Rowohlt paperback, Marx: *Texte zu Methode und Praxis* III, hereafter cited as R.

[5] Maxmilien Rubel: "Contribution à l'histoire de la genèse du 'Capital' ", in *Revue d'Historie éconòmique et sociale,* II (1950), p. 168.

chiefly the historical passages, as *Pre-Capitalist Economic Formations* in 1965.[6] Of late, isolated excerpts have appeared in the works of André Gorz and Herbert Marcuse.[7] Together, these seem to have sharpened the appetite of a growing body of intellectuals, in the amorphous New Left especially, for a closer look at this hitherto unknown but obviously important work. A French translation of the first part of the whole has finally appeared this year, but readers who remain imprisoned within the English language will have to wait.[8] No definite plans for an English translation have been made public.

All the same, the work is of epochal significance. The fruits of fifteen years of economic research, the best years of Marx's life, are contained in these pages. Marx considered it not only a work which overthrew the central doctrines of all previous political economy, but also the first truly scientific statement of the revolutionary cause.[9] Although he could not know it at the time, it was to be the only work in which his theory of capitalism from the origins to the breakdown was sketched out in its entirety. However obscure and fractured, the *Grundrisse* may be said to be the only truly complete work on political economy that Marx ever wrote.

MARX'S FOCUS ON THE MARKET

The *Grundrisse* is a summit at the end of a long and difficult climb. Marx had published the first of what he considered his scientific works, the *Poverty of Philosophy,* a decade before; and he did not publish the first volume of *Capital* until a decade after. To understand the significance of the *Grundrisse,* it will be necessary to survey briefly the economic writings which preceded it.

Immediately after the completion of his critique of Hegel's philosophy of law, in which he had concluded that the anatomy of society was not to be found in philosophy, Marx began to read the political economists. In this project he was preceded

[6] Lawrence and Wishart, London, and International Publishers, New York.

[7] André Gorz: *Strategy for Labor* (Boston: Beacon Press, 1967), pp. 128–30; Herbert Marcuse: *One-Dimensional Man* (Boston: Beacon Press, 1964), pp. 35–36.

[8] Karl Marx: *Les Fondements de la Critique de l'Economie Politique (Grundrisse),* 2 vols. (Paris: Editions Anthropos, 1967).

[9] *Grundrisse,* p. xiii; cf. also Marx to Engels, January 14th, 1858: "I am getting some nice developments. For instance, I have thrown over the whole doctrine of profit as it has existed up to now." *Selected Correspondence,* London and New York, 1942, p. 102.

and no doubt also guided by the young Engels, who had published his *Umrisse zu einer Kritik der Nationalökonomie* in Marx's and Ruge's *Deutsch-Französische Jahrbücher* for the same year, 1844. Engels argued in this article that the development of the bourgeois economy for the last century, as well as the development of the economic theory which corresponded to it, could be summarized as one long, continuous, and increasingly outrageous affront to all fundamental principles of morality and decency; and that if a rationally ordered, moral economic system were not immediately installed, then a monstrous social revolution must and ought to occur shortly. The brunt of Engels's attack was directed at what he considered the fundamental principle of the bourgeois economy, namely the institution of the *market.* All moral bonds in society have been overthrown by the conversion of human values into exchange-values; all ethical principles overthrown by the principles of competition; and all hitherto existing laws, even the laws which regulate the birth and death of human beings, have been usurped by the laws of supply and demand. Humanity itself has become a market commodity.[10]

With one significant difference, this line of reasoning was taken up and developed by Marx throughout his economic writings from 1844 to 1849. The difference is that (as is plain from his 1844 *Manuscripts*) Marx immediately rejected the one-sided moralism of Engels's critique to replace it with a dialectical basis. He threw out the categorical imperatives which lurked beneath the surface of Engels's paper. Competition and the market, he wrote, were not so much an affront to morality as rather a fragmentation and surrender of the developmental potentialities inherent in the human species. Within the society based on private property, the products of human labor belong not to the laborer for his own enjoyment; rather, they become the property of alien persons and are used by them to oppress him. The clearest symptom of this fact, Marx wrote, is that the laborer does not produce the things most useful to him, but instead the things which will fetch the highest exchange-value for their private owner. Thus the process of material creation becomes fractured into segments, and the product itself becomes fractured into use-value and exchange-value, of which the latter alone is important. "The consideration of *division of labor* and *exchange* is of the greatest interest, since they are the *perceptible, alienated* expression of human *activity*

[10] Engels: "Umrisse zu einer Kritik der Nationalökonomie," W1:499–524, and as an appendix to Marx: *Economic-Philosophical Manuscripts*, trans. Milligan, London and New York.

and *capacities*. . . ."[11] In sum, from an entirely different philosophical starting point, Marx arrived at the same critical perspective as Engels, namely that the crux of bourgeois society was to be found in competition, supply and demand, the market; that is, in its system of *exchange*.

The notion of alienation (as an economic category) also contained within it the seeds of a different insight, but one which did not rise to prominence until the *Grundrisse*, as will be seen. Meanwhile, however, Marx continued along with the majority of his radical intellectual acquaintances to sharpen his attack on the sovereignty of competition. His polemic against Proudhon (*The Poverty of Philosophy*) reveals him in sharp disagreement with that self-declared luminary on almost every point of economics and philosophy, including especially every issue relating to the institutions of exchange and competition in bourgeois society, except one: that competition is basic.[12] If the bourgeoisie abolishes competition to replace it with monopoly, it thereby only sharpens the competition among workers. In the *Manifesto* Marx writes: "The essential condition for the existence, and for the sway of the bourgeois class, is the formation and augmentation of capital; the condition for capital is wage-labor. Wage-labor rests exclusively on competition between the laborers."[13] From which Marx concludes that if the workers can, by forming associations, eliminate the competition among themselves, then "the very foundation on which the bourgeoisie produces and appropriates products" will be cut out from under its feet. In Marx's *Speech on Free Trade*, the same theme recurs: if industrial development slumps, workers will be thrown out of jobs and their wages must fall; if industry grows, the workers will enjoy a momentary up-swing, only to be cast down again when machinery replaces them.[14] Here as in *Wage-Labor and Capital*, Marx's "law" that wages must always tend toward the absolute minimum necessary to keep the worker barely alive is derived straight-forwardly from the principles of supply and demand, with the additional assumptions that the supply of the labor commodity must always tend to exceed demand.[15] We find here occasional hints of insight that other

[11] The 1844 Manuscripts are only to be published in a supplementary volume of the *Werke* edition. The reference here is from the Bottomore translation in Marx: *Early Writings*, London, 1963, p. 187.

[12] W4: 161 and *Poverty of Philosophy*, London and New York, p. 149.

[13] W4: 474 and Marx-Engels: *Selected Works*, I, p. 45.

[14] W4: 455 and *Poverty of Philosophy*, pp. 215–16.

[15] W6: 397–423 and *Selected Works*, I, pp. 79–105; see also W6: 535–56.

processes are at work also, but the only systematically worked out doctrines are those which analytically derive the future course of capitalist development and the role of the working class within it from the competitive mechanism, from the expected shape of the market for the commodity, labor. The economics of commodity exchange and of money formed Marx's chief study.

FROM COMPETITION TO PRODUCTION

The first and most important thing that needs to be made clear about the place which the *Grundrisse* occupied in Marx's intellectual development is that it represents a critique of all these earlier ideas. "Critique" does not mean "rejection," rather, in this case, it means penetration to a deeper level. The great advance which the *Grundrisse* represents in Marx's thinking lies in its rejection, on grounds of superficiality, of the thesis that the market-mechanism is a motivating, causal, or fundamental factor; and in its recognition that the market is merely a device to coordinate the various individual moments of a process far more fundamental than exchange. While Marx's earlier economics had centered around the movement of *competition,* in the *Grundrisse* he analyzes systematically, and for the first time in his work, the economics of *production.*

Before we examine the text more closely, a few examples may be in order for the sake of gaining an overview.

1. The most obvious and easily traceable difference between pre- and post-1850 economic theory in Marx is a shift in terminology. Before, Marx consistently refers to the commodity which the worker offers for sale as "labor," and makes explicit that this commodity is exactly like any other commodity. If one sees bourgeois society exclusively as a system of markets, this definition is true enough. In the *Grundrisse* and thereafter, however, Marx arrives at the view that labor is not a commodity like any other, that labor in fact is unique, and that the commodity which the worker sells must be called "labor-power." In later re-editions of the earlier economic works, Marx and Engels duly alter the terminology to correspond to the new view, and in various prefaces state their reasons for so doing, and the importance of the change.[16]

2. In the earlier economic writings, the course of capitalist development is derived analytically, as noted, from the pro-

[16] See notably Engels' preface to the 1891 re-edition of *Wage-Labor and Capital,* W6: 593–99 and *Selected Works,* I, pp. 70–78.

jected motion of supply and demand. Compare this with Marx's flat statement at several occasions in *Capital* that the mechanisms of competition "show everything backward"[17] and that analytic deductions made from supply and demand alone are superficial, in fact, contradictory to the hidden but essential core-processes of capitalist production and accumulation. The intellectual foundations for these later statements in *Capital* are laid in the *Grundrisse*.

3. Finally, a general overview of the analytic progress which the *Grundrisse* represents can be gained by tracing Marx's attitude toward Ricardo, especially toward Ricardo's theory of the surplus. At the time of his first encounter with Ricardo and the surplus in 1844, Marx noted only that the emphasis Ricardo lays on the surplus proves that profit, not human beings are the chief concern of bourgeois economics, and that this theory is the ultimate proof of the infamy to which political economy has sunk.[18] In the *Poverty of Philosophy* (1847), Ricardo is treated with somewhat more respect, and Marx quotes at length from the English socialist Bray, who uses the Ricardian surplus-theory to prove the exploitation of the working class. Yet Marx quotes Bray not in order to emphasize the fundamental importance of this theory, but merely to criticize certain deductions derived from it.[19] Likewise, in *Wage-Labor and Capital,* Marx simply states the Ricardian thesis that the product of labor is worth more than the reproduction of the laborer, but without analyzing it further.[20] He is clearly aware at this point of the *existence* of a surplus, but he is clearly not conscious of the enormous implications for economic theory of this fact; the theory, in short, is not central to his analysis, but coexists passively together with, and in the shadow of, the dominant supply-and-demand analysis. When he began his economic studies all over again from the beginning in 1850, however, Marx plunged directly into Ricardo and spent at least the next two years absorbing Ricardo in detail. His notebooks and excerpts from this period, which are appended to the text of the *Grundrisse* by the editors, show that Ricardo's surplus theory then began to reveal its implications for Marx, and that he concentrated his attention upon it.[21] Finally, in the *Grundrisse* it-

[17] *Capital* III, W25: 219. English translation, London and New York, 1962, p. 205.

[18] Quoted in Rubel: *Biographie Intellectuelle,* p. 119.

[19] W4: 98–105 and *Poverty of Philosophy,* pp. 69–79.

[20] W6: 409–410 and *Selected Works,* I, pp. 91–92.

[21] See *Grundrisse,* pp. 787–92, 829.

self, although Marx criticizes Ricardo at several points, he treats him with a great amount of respect and calls him the "economist *par excellence* of production."[22] This gradual shift of attitude corresponds to, and reflects, Marx's growing awareness of the importance of the theory of surplus-value, on which Marx begins to base his entire theory of capitalist accumulation in the *Grundrisse*.

Like any exercise in comparative statics, these before/after examples may give rise to the mistaken idea that the application of Ricardian concepts changed Marx overnight from a supply-demand theorist into a surplus-value accumulationist. The change, to be sure, was much more gradual; there are elements of the surplus theory, as we have said, scattered in the early works, and the later works by no means assert the unimportance of the competitive mechanism, quite the contrary. These subtleties should not obscure the fact that a qualitative breakthrough beyond the surface of market-based analysis took place, and that this breakthrough is the chief analytic problem with which the *Grundrisse* is concerned.

THE SOCIAL BOND OF MONEY

Although gnomic in detail, the larger structure of the *Grundrisse* text moves consistently toward the solution of clearly defined problems. After a brilliant, unfinished Introduction—which cannot detain us here—the work consists of two chapters, the first dealing with money and the second, much longer, with capital. The latter is subdivided into three parts, dealing respectively with production, circulation, and the transformation of surplus-value into profits. The problems and issues with which the text deals, however, are not so narrowly economic as the chapter headings might imply. Here as elsewhere, but perhaps more clearly here than elsewhere, Marx's "economics" is also and at the same time "sociology" and "politics." The first chapter immediately makes this clear.

On one level, the chapter on money is a polemic against the monetary-reform scheme then newly proposed by Alfred Darimon, a follower of Proudhon and therefore a bitter opponent of Marx. On a somewhat less superficial level, it is merely a treatise on money, and can be read as the first draft of Marx's developed monetary theory as it appears in the *Critique*. Its most important aspect, however, is its sociological and political critique of a society in which money is the predominant me-

[22] *Grundrisse*, p. 18 and R: 20.

dium of exchange. Under what historical circumstances can money become the abstraction of exchange-values, and exchange-values become the abstraction of all forms of exchange? What social preconditions must exist in order that money may function as a nexus between individuals engaged in exchange-relations? What are the social and political consequences of this form of the exchange-relation? What larger forms of social organization correspond to this molecular constellation of individuals engaged in private transactions? These are the problems with which Marx is concerned, just as Sombart, Weber, Simmel, and Tönnies about a half-century later investigated the effects of money-exchange on societal bonds. Marx writes:

> The convertibility of all products and activities into exchange-values presupposes the dissolution of all fixed personal (historic) relations of dependence in production, and presupposes the universal dependence of all producers on one another. The production of every individual is dependent on that of all the others, and the conversion of his product into articles for his consumption has become dependent on the consumption of all others. Prices *per se* are old; exchange, likewise; but the growing determination of prices by production cost and the increasing role of exchange among all relations of production are things which first develop, and continue to develop more fully, within bourgeois society, the society of free competition. Relegated by Adam Smith in true eighteenth-century fashion to the prehistoric period, these developments are in truth the product of history.
>
> This reciprocal dependence can be seen in the ever-present need to exchange, and the fact that exchange-value is the universal medium. The economists express this as follows: everyone pursues his private interest and only his private interest, and thus without knowing or willing it, everyone serves the private interests of all, the general interests. The point here is not that, in following his private interests, everyone attains the totality of private interests, namely the collective interest. One could as well conclude from this abstract slogan that everyone reciprocally blocks the interests of the others, so that, instead of a general affirmation, this war of all against all produces a general negation. The point is rather that private interest is itself already a socially determined interest, which can be attained only within certain socially ordained conditions and with socially given means, and which is therefore dependent on the reproduction of these conditions and means. It is the interest of a private person; but its content and the form and means of its realization are set by social conditions independently of the individual.
>
> This universal reciprocal dependence of individuals who

> are [otherwise] indifferent to one another forms their social bond. This social bond is expressed in *exchange-value* . . . An individual exercises power over the actions of others, he lays a claim to social wealth, insofar as he possesses *exchange-value, money.* He carries his social power and his bond with society in his pocket . . .
>
> Every individual possesses social power in the form of an object, a thing. Take away from this thing its social power, and this power over persons must be invested in persons.
>
> Relations of personal dependence . . . are the first forms of social organization, in which human productive powers are but little developed, and only in isolated points. Personal independence, based on dependence on *things,* is the second great form, which for the first time allows the development of a system of universal social exchange, universal relations, universal needs, and universal wealth. Free individuality, based on the universal development of individuals and on their joint mastery over their communal, social, productive powers and wealth, is the third stage. The second creates the preconditions of the third.[23]

Here we see the interpenetration of economic, social, and political categories clearly developed. Whatever Marx may have had to say about the specific fluctuations of monetary value, or about the effects of metallism or paper currency, is of minor importance to his system of ideas compared to the fundamental thesis, here expressed, that money is an object which expresses a certain type of historically produced relationship among human beings. Money is a *social bond;* that is, it links together and reciprocally governs the most diverse activities of otherwise isolated individuals. He who possesses this objectified social bond can dominate the activities of others; he represents the social bond *per se* and can thus act in the capacity of the representative of the generality, the collectivity, to govern the activities of individuals within the society.

THE EQUAL EXCHANGE THAT REPRODUCES INEQUALITY

So far, Marx's analysis of money formulates more sharply and more clearly the ideas about alienated exchange developed by him in the *Manuscripts* of 1844. In a brief transitional section which introduces the chapter on capital, however, Marx progresses a significant step beyond the earlier analysis. He no longer stops short at this point to bewail the alienation of indi-

[23] *Ibid.,* pp. 74–76 and R: 36–38.

viduals from each other and from themselves, which are results of bourgeois exchange-relations, but goes on to inspect this form of social relationships in historical and political perspective. Basic here is the comparison of bourgeois relations with feudal relations. After all, the revolutionary rise of the bourgeoisie did bring with it the political emancipation of the individual from the bonds of statutory domination, and did change the polity from a closed chain of inborn privilege and serfdom into an open market place of freely-contracting adults. No longer is the worker bound for life to his overlord, nor are there statutes to impress from the laboring classes a steadily growing secular tithe. The merchant who sells and the housewife who buys loaves of bread; the entrepreneur who buys and the worker who sells hours of labor—all are free persons freely engaged in the free exchange of equivalents. This is a line of argument which the socialists of Marx's time, at least in his estimation, could not systematically refute. While the socialists damned the competitive society, the market relation, and the cash nexus, the bourgeois ideologists were only too happy to reply by praising these very conditions as the basis of political freedom.[24]

> In these simple forms of the money-relation, all the immanent contradictions of bourgeois society appear extinguished, and that is why bourgeois democrats take refuge within them . . . to justify the existing economic relationships. In truth, so long as a commodity or labor is seen only as an exchange-value, and the relations between them are seen only as exchange-relations, as equilibration of these exchange-values, then the individuals, the subjects between whom this process takes place, are merely partners in exchange. There is absolutely no formal difference between them . . . Each subject is a partner in exchange; that is, each has the same relation to the other as the other has to it. Thus, as subjects of exchange, their relationship is one of *equality*. It is impossible to find a trace of distinction, much less of contradiction among them, not even a mere difference. Furthermore, the commodities which they exchange are, as exchange-values, equivalents; or at least count as equivalents. (There could at most be subjective error in their reciprocal appraisal, and insofar as one individual gained an advantage over another, *this would not be in the nature of the social function which brings them together*, for this function is identical for both, and within it they are equal. It would rather be the result of natural cleverness, persuasion, etc., in short, a result of

[24] "The analysis of what free competition really is, is the only rational answer to its glorification by the middle-class prophets or its damnation by the socialists." *Ibid.*, p. 545 and R: 198.

> the purely individual superiority of one individual over another . . .) Thus if one individual accumulates wealth and the other does not, neither is doing it at the expense of the other . . . If one becomes poorer and the other richer, it is of their own free will, and proceeds in no way out of the economic relation, the economic situation in which they meet.[25]

The argument which Marx is here putting into the mouth of an imaginary bourgeois antagonist is a telling one. For if it is true that the laborer, in selling labor, and the capitalist, in paying wages, are engaged in the reciprocal exchange of commodities having equal value—i.e., if their exchange is an exchange of equivalents—then the capitalist class structure is only coincidentally related to the capitalist economic system. The rich get richer not because of any inherent, structural necessity, but only by the accident of superior judgment and persuasiveness. Nor is the historic existence of the capitalist class economically accounted for by saying that the worker does not receive full value in exchange for his labor. If that were the case, if the capitalist paid the laborer less than an equivalent for his labor, then the capitalist could gain only to the extent that the laborer lost, but no more. The capitalist as buyer and the worker as seller of labor could disadvantage one another only to the degree that two nations engaged in foreign trade can; if one consistently pays the other less than full value, one can grow richer and the other poorer, but the total wealth of both together can be no greater at the end than at the beginning of their intercourse (or so the mercantilists believed). It is evident that such a process could not continue for long or on a large scale; soon the disadvantaged party must become extinct. The problem which must be solved is: how can it be that the worker does receive the full exchange-value for his commodity, and nevertheless there exists a surplus from which the capitalist class lives? How is it that the worker is *not* cheated *in* the wage-contract, and is nevertheless exploited? What is the source of surplus-value? That is the question to which Marx addresses himself in the first hundred pages of the chapter on capital.

THE EMERGENCE OF SURPLUS-VALUE

After a systematic review of earlier forms of capital (merchant capital or money capital), and after placing the problem in proper historical focus, Marx summarizes the analysis by con-

[25] *Ibid.*, pp. 153, 158 and R: 47, 53.

densing the process of capitalist production into two fundamental components, two basic elements:

> 1. The laborer gives his commodity, labor, which has a use-value and a price like all other commodities, and receives in exchange a certain sum of exchange-values, a certain sum of money from the capitalist.
> 2. The capitalist exchanges labor itself, labor as value-creating activity, as productive labor; that is, he exchanges the productive force which maintains and multiplies capital, and thereby becomes the productive and reproductive force of capital, a force belonging to capital itself.[26]

On inspection, the first exchange-process appears plainly comprehensible; Marx says simply that the laborer gives labor and receives wages in exchange. But the second process does not appear to be an exchange at all; even its grammar is one-sided, asymmetrical. That is precisely the point, Marx writes. In an ordinary exchange transaction, what each of the parties does with the commodity each receives is irrelevant to the structure of the transaction itself. The seller does not care whether the buyer uses the commodity acquired for productive purposes or not; that is his private affair and has no economic relevance for the process of exchange pure and simple. In the specific case of the "exchange" between labor and wages, however, the use to which the buyer of labor puts his purchase is of the utmost importance to him not only in his private capacity, but in his capacity as *homo oeconomicus*. The capitalist gives wages (exchange-value) for the use of labor (for its use-value) only in order to convert this use-value into further exchange-value.

> Here . . . the use-value of the thing received in exchange appears as a specific economic relation, and the specific use to which the thing bought is put forms the ultimate purpose of both processes [1 & 2 above]. Thus, the exchange between labor and capital is already formally different from ordinary exchange; they are two different processes . . . In the exchange between labor and capital, the first act is an exchange and can be classified entirely as ordinary circulation; the second process is qualitatively different from exchange, and to have called it exchange at all was a misuse. This process is the direct opposite of exchange; it is an essentially different category.[27]

After several digressions, Marx then examines this "essentially different category" at length. Approaching the question via

[26] *Ibid.*, p. 185.
[27] *Ibid.*, pp. 185–86.

the distinction between the use-value and the exchange-value of the labor commodity, he notes that the exchange-value of labor is determined by the value of the goods and services necessary to maintain and to reproduce the laborer. Insofar as the capitalist pays the laborer wages high enough to permit the worker to continue to live and to work, he has paid the full value of labor and the exchange-relation defined in the wage contract is a relation of equivalence. The capitalist has paid the full and fair exchange-value of the commodity. But what he has, in fact, purchased is a certain number of hours of control and disposition over the worker's productive activity, over his ability to create, his capacity to labor. Here Marx introduces for the first time the shift in terminology which corresponds to his discovery of the "essentially different category." What the worker sells is not "labor" but *labor-power (Arbeitskraft);* not a commodity like any other, but a commodity which is unique.[28] Labor alone has the capacity to create values where none existed before, or to create greater values than those which it requires to sustain itself. Labor alone, in short, is capable of creating *surplus-value*. The capitalist purchases control over this creative power, and commands this power to engage in the production of commodities for exchange during a specified number of hours. The worker's surrender of control over his creative power is called by Marx exploitation.

This is not the occasion to review in detail Marx's theory of surplus-value, of which the ideas here formulated are the cornerstone. Suffice it to say that Marx here begins not only to solve the problem of how exploitation can occur despite the fact that the wage-contract is an exchange of equivalents, but begins also the essential scientific task of quantification. Exploitation is for Marx a process verifiable in specific empirical variables which are at least in principle subject to precise measurement along the economic dimension. The variables which Marx would have us measure, however, are not those which are usually cited in critical reviews of his theory. Exploitation does not consist in the disproportion between the income of the working class and the income of the capitalist class; these variables measure only the disproportion between wages and profits. Since profits are only a fraction of surplus-value as a whole, such an index would capture only a fraction of Marx's meaning. Nor is exploitation fully measured in the ratio of

[28] Cf. *ibid.*, pp. 193–194 and R: 66. For "control" and "disposition" see pp. 193, 195, 201, 215, etc., or R: 66, 67, 73, 89, etc.

wages as a percentage of GNP; this index measures only the *rate* of exploitation in a given year. Perhaps more clearly than elsewhere, Marx states in the *Grundrisse* that the worker's *impoverishment* is to be measured in the power of the entire world which he constructs to capitalist specifications: "He inevitably impoverishes himself . . . because the creative power of his labor establishes itself in opposition to him, as the alien power of capital . . . Thus all the progress of civilization, or, in other words, every increase in the productive power of society, if you want, in the productive power of labor itself—such as results from science, invention, division and organization of labor, improved communications, creation of the world market, machinery, and so on—does not enrich the worker, but capital, and thus increases the power that dominates labor.[29]

An index of exploitation and impoverishment which accurately captures the variables to which Marx was referring, therefore, would have to array on one side the net property holdings of the working class, and on the other side the value of the entire capital stock of all the factories, utilities, infrastructural investments, institutions, and military establishments which are under the control of the capitalist class and serve its policy aims. Not only the economic value, but also the political power and social influence of these established assets would have to be included in the equation. Only a statistic of this kind would be adequate to test whether or not Marx's prediction of increasing exploitation and increasing impoverishment had been validated by the course of capitalist development.

WHAT IS THE FUNDAMENTAL CONTRADICTION?

The various steps by which Marx builds his fundamental insight that capitalist production involves a category radically different from mere commodity exchange into the fully fledged theory of capitalist accumulation which he later presents in *Capital* need not arrest us here. Exploitation proceeds "behind the back of the exchange-process"; that is the basic insight which marks his penetration beyond the critique of bourgeois society as a market society. We may proceed now to examine to what extent the text of the *Grundrisse* justifies the sweeping claims made for Marx's new scientific achievements in his 1859

[29] *Ibid.*, pp. 214, 215 and R: 88, 89.

Preface. In particular we will be interested in knowing whether the *Grundrisse* provides further elucidation of the famous passage in the *Preface* about *revolution:* "At a certain stage of their development, the material forces of production in society come into conflict with the existing relations of production, or—what is only a legal expression of the same thing—with the property relations within which they had been at work before. From forms which developed the forces of production, these relations now turn into their fetters. Then comes the period of social revolution."[30]

While there are echoes of this passage in some of the earlier works as well as on one occasion in *Capital*,[31] they remain on a level of generality so high as to be virtually useless. Above all, it is never made clear exactly what is meant to be included under the rubric of "forces of production" or "relations of production." Are we to understand "material forces of production" as meaning merely the technological apparatus, and "relations of production" as the political-legal system? In other words, is the phrase "material forces" only another way of saying "infrastructure" and does "relations" mean "superstructure"? What precisely do these terms refer to?

The basic clue for the deciphering of what Marx had in mind with the phrase "relations of production"—to begin with this half of the dichotomy—is already provided in the *Preface* itself. Marx writes that legal-political forms such as property relations are not these "relations of production" in themselves, but are merely an *expression* of these relations. From this starting point, the text of the *Grundrisse* can be seen as an extensive and detailed commentary on the nature of these "relations." For what else is the chapter on money? Here Marx demonstrates, as we have seen, that money in bourgeois society is no mere natural object, but rather the objectified form of the basic *social relation* within which capitalist production takes place. Money is the social bond which links the otherwise isolated producers and consumers within capitalist society together, and which forms the starting and ending points of the process of accumulation. The social relation which lies at the basis of all capitalist legal and political relations, and of which the latter are mere expressions—as Marx shows in the chapter on money—is the exchange-relation. It is the social imperative

[30] W13: 9 and *Selected Works,* I, p. 363.

[31] W4: 181 and *Poverty of Philosophy,* p. 174; *Manifesto,* W4: 467 and *Selected Works,* I, p. 39; *Capital* I, W23: 791 and *Capital* I, London and New York, p. 763.

that neither production nor consumption can take place without the mediation of exchange-value; or, in other words, that the capitalist must not only extract surplus-value but must also realize surplus-value by converting the surplus product into money, and that the individual must not only have a need for consumer goods, but must also possess the money to purchase them. Far from being immutable natural laws, these twin imperatives are characterized by Marx as historically produced social relations specific to the capitalist form of production.

As for the other side of the dichotomy, it is easy to be misled by the word "material" in the phrase "material forces of production." Indeed, the German original *(materielle Produktivkrafte)* could as well be translated as "forces of material production," and it is clear in any case that the term "material" for Marx did not refer merely to the physical attributes of mass, volume, and location. A machine is always a material thing, but whether it is utilized in a productive capacity, whether or not it becomes a force of production, depends on the social organization of the productive process, as Marx goes to great lengths to point out in the *Grundrisse*.[32] The forces of production are themselves a social and historical product, and the productive process is a social process for Marx. It is necessary to emphasize this point in order to make clear that the important role which Marx assigns to the development of the material production forces under capitalism does not make Marx a technological determinist. Quite the opposite is the case; it is not technology which compels the capitalist to accumulate, but the necessity to accumulate which compels him to develop the powers of technology. The basis of the process of accumulation, of the process through which the forces of production gain in power, is the extraction of surplus-value from labor-power. The force of production is the force of exploitation.

It is apparent, then, that the dichotomy formulated by Marx in the *Preface* is identical to the dichotomy between the two distinct processes which Marx identifies as basic to capitalist production in the *Grundrisse:* on the one hand, production consists of an act of exchange, and on the other, it consists of an act which is the opposite of exchange. On the one hand, production is an ordinary exchange of equivalents, on the other, it is a forcible appropriation of the worker's world-creating power. It is a social system in which the worker, as seller, and the capitalist, as purchaser, are juridically equal and free

[32] *Grundrisse*, pp. 169, 216, 579, etc., and R: 89–90.

contracting parties; and it is at the same time a social system of slavery and exploitation. At the beginning and at the end of the productive process lies the social imperative of exchange-values, yet from beginning to end the productive process must yield surplus-values. The exchange of equivalents is the fundamental social relation of production, yet the extraction of nonequivalents is the fundamental force of production. This contradiction, inherent in the process of capitalist production, is the source of the conflicts which Marx expected to bring about the period of social revolution.

THE ROAD TO REVOLUTION

The problem of precisely how this contradiction can be expected to lead to the breakdown of the capitalist system is one which has plagued students of Marx for at least half a century. The volumes of *Capital* provide no very clear answer. This deficiency is at the root of the "breakdown controversy" which agitated German Social-Democracy and which continues intermittently to flare even today. Veritable rivers of ink have been spent in an effort to fill up this gap in Marx's theoretical system. Yet this gap is present not because the problem was insoluble for Marx, not because he saw no answer, but because the conclusions he had reached in the *Grundrisse* lay buried and inaccessible to scholars until twenty years after World War I. *Capital* is a work which proceeds slowly and carefully from pure forms of economic relationships step by step toward a closer approximation of economic-historic reality; nothing is prejudged and no new theories are introduced until the basis for them has been prepared. At that rate, it is easily conceivable that several more volumes of *Capital* would have been necessary before Marx could catch up with the point he had reached in the outline of his system in the *Grundrisse*. *Capital* is painfully unfinished, like a mystery novel which ends before the plot is unraveled. But the *Grundrisse* contains the author's plot-outline as a whole.

From the very beginning, the economics of the *Grundrisse* are more ambitious and more directly relevant to the problem of the capitalist breakdown than the economics of the extant portions of *Capital*. In the latter work, Marx relegates the relationship between persons and commodities (the utility relation) to a realm with which he is not then concerned, and he accepts the level of consumer needs which prevails in the economic system as a historical given which receives little further analysis.[33] In general, he takes consumption for granted, and concentrates his investigation on the how, instead of on the whether, of surplus realization. In the *Grundrisse*, however, he begins with the general assertion that the process of production, historically considered, creates not only the object of consumption but also the consumer need and the style of consumption.[34] He specifically criticizes Ricardo for consigning the problem of utility to the extra-economic sphere, and states that the relation between the consumer and the commodity, because this relation is a product of production, belongs squarely within the proper purview of political economy.[35] That he is aware not only of the qualitative but also of the quantitative aspects of the problem of consumption is apparent from excerpts such as this: "Incidentally . . . although every capitalist demands that his workers should save, he means only *his own* workers, because they relate to him as workers; and by no means does this apply to the remainder of the workers, because these relate to him as consumers. In spite of all the pious talk of frugality he therefore searches for all possible ways of stimulating them to consume, by making his commodities more attractive, by filling their ears with babble about new needs *(neue Bedürfnisse ihnen anzuschwatzen)*. It is precisely this side of the relationship between capital and labor which is an essential civilizing force, and on which the historic justification—but also the contemporary power—of capital is based.[36]

These general remarks are then set aside with a reminder to himself that "this relationship of production and consumption must be developed later."[37] A hundred pages later on, the problem is taken up again. After a critique of Ricardo's neglect of the problem of consumption, and of Sismondi's utopian panaceas against overproduction, Marx formulates the inherent contradiction of capitalism as a "contradiction between production and realization" of surplus-value. "To begin with, there is a limit to production, not to production in general, but to production founded on capital . . . It suffices to show at this point that capital contains a *specific* barrier to production—which contradicts its general tendency to break all barriers to produc-

[33] *Capital* I, W23: 49–50 (Section One, Chapter One, page one).
[34] *Grundrisse*, pp. 13–18 and R: 14–18.
[35] *Ibid.*, pp. 178–179n., 226–27, 763.
[36] *Ibid.*, p. 198 and R: 71.
[37] *Ibid.*

tion—in order to expose the basis of *overproduction,* the fundamental contradiction of developed capitalism." As is apparent from the lines which follow immediately, Marx does not mean by "overproduction" simply "excess inventory"; rather, he means excess productive power more generally.

> These inherent limits necessarily coincide with the nature of capital, with its essential determinants. The necessary limits are:
> 1. *necessary labor* as limit to the exchange-value of living labor-power, of the wages of the industrial population;
> 2. *surplus-value* as limit to surplus labor-time; and, in relation to relative surplus labor-time, as limit to the development of the productive forces;
> 3. what is the same thing, the *transformation into money,* into exchange-value, as such, as a limit to production; or: exchange based on value, or value based on exchange, as limit to production. This is again
> 4. the same thing as *restriction of the production of use-values* by exchange-value; or: the fact that real wealth must take on a specific form distinct from itself, absolutely not identical with it, in order to become an object of production at all.[38]

While a proper analysis of the implications of these rather cryptic theses would require a book, it is immediately apparent that these four "limits" represent no more than different aspects of the contradiction between "forces of production" and "social relations of production." The task of maintaining the enormous powers of surplus-value extraction within the limits set by the necessity of converting this surplus-value into exchange-value becomes increasingly difficult as the capitalist system moves into its developed stages. In practical terms, these four limits could be formulated as four related, but mutually contradictory political-economic alternatives among which the capitalist system must choose, but cannot afford to choose: 1. Wages must be raised to increase effective demand; 2. Less surplus value must be extracted; 3. Products must be distributed without regard to effective demand; or 4. Products that cannot be sold must not be produced at all. The first and second alternatives result in a reduction of profit; the third is capitalistically impossible (except as a political stopgap); and the fourth means depression.

[38] *Ibid.,* pp. 318–19. A five-element model of a closed capitalist system, from which Marx deduces the impossibility of expanded reproduction due to the impossibility of realization, appears on pp. 336–47. More on realization on pp. 438–442 (R: 174–176) and elsewhere.

SURPLUS LABOR

What is most remarkable and ought most to be emphasized about Marx's theory of capitalist breakdown as we see it at this point is its great latitude and flexibility. Cataclysmic crises rising to a revolutionary crescendo are only one possible variant of the breakdown process; and indeed, Marx lays little stress on this type of crisis in the *Grundrisse*. For every possible tendency toward breakdown, Marx names a number of delaying tendencies; this list includes the development of monopoly, the conquest of the world market, and, significantly, Marx mentions the payment by capitalists to workers of "surplus wages."[39] All things considered, Marx's breakdown theory in the *Grundrisse* provides important amplification of the statement in the *Preface* that "no social order ever disappears before all the productive forces for which there is room in it have been developed."[40] When one considers the requirements that must be met, in Marx's view, before the capitalist order is ripe for overthrow, one comes to wonder whether the failure of previous revolutionary movements in Europe and the United States is not imputable simply to prematurity.

> The great historic role of capital is the creation of surplus labor, labor which is superfluous from the standpoint of mere use-value, mere subsistence. Its historic role is fulfilled as soon as (on the one hand) the level of needs has been developed to the degree where surplus labor in addition to necessary subsistence has itself become a general need which manifests itself in individual needs, and (on the other hand) when the strict discipline of capital has schooled successive generations in industriousness, and this quality has become their general property, and (finally) when the development of the productive powers of labor, which capital, with its unlimited urge to accumulate and to realize, has constantly spurred on, have ripened to the point where the possession and maintenance of social wealth require no more than a diminished amount of labor-time, where the laboring society relates to the process of its progressive reproduction and constantly greater reproduction in a scientific manner; where, that is, human labor which can be replaced by the labor of things has ceased.[41]

Noteworthy in this long sentence, among many other things, is the statement that the capitalist order is not ripe for revolu-

[39] *Ibid.*, p. 341.
[40] W13: 9 and *Selected Works,* I.
[41] *Grundrisse,* p. 231 and R: 91.

tion until the working class—far from being reduced to the level of ragged, miserable brutes—has expanded its consumption *above* the level of mere physical subsistence and includes the enjoyment of the fruits of surplus labor as a general necessity. Instead of the image of the starving proletarian slowly dying from an eighteen-hour day in a mine or a sweatshop, Marx here presents the well-fed proletarian, scientifically competent, to whom an eight-hour day would presumably appear as a mere waste of time. In another passage, Marx goes further; he envisages a capitalist productive apparatus more completely automated than that of any presently existing society, and writes that nevertheless, despite the virtual absence from such a social order of a "working class" as commonly defined, this economic organization must break down.

> To the degree that large-scale industry develops, the creation of real wealth comes to depend less on labor-time and on the quantity of labor expended, and more on the power of the instruments which are set in motion during labor-time, and whose powerful effectiveness itself is not related to the labor-time immediately expended in their production, but depends rather on the general state of science and the progress of technology . . . Large industry reveals that real wealth manifests itself rather in the monstrous disproportion between expended labor-time and its product, as well as in the qualitative disproportion between labor, reduced to a pure abstraction, and the power of the productive process which it supervises. Labor no longer appears as an integral element of the productive process; rather, man acts as supervisor and regulator of the productive process itself . . . He stands at the side of the productive process, instead of being its chief actor. With this transformation, the cornerstone of production and wealth is neither the labor which man directly expends, nor the time he spends at work, but rather the appropriation of his own collective productive power, his understanding of nature and his mastery over nature, exercised by him as a social body—in short, it is the development of the social individual. The theft of other people's labor-time, on which contemporary wealth rests, appears as a miserable basis compared to this new one created by large-scale industry itself. As soon as labor in its direct form has ceased to be the great wellspring of wealth, labor-time ceases and must cease to be its measure, and therefore exchange-value the measure of use-value . . . With that, the system of production based on exchange-value collapses . . . Capital is its own contradiction-in-process, for its urge is to reduce labor-time to a minimum, while at the same time it maintains that labor-time is the only measure and source of wealth. Thus it reduces labor-time in its necessary form in order to aug-

> ment it in its superfluous form; thus superfluous labor increasingly becomes a precondition—a question of life or death—for necessary labor. So on the one side it animates all the powers of science and nature, or social coordination and intercourse, in order to make the creation of wealth (relatively) independent of the labor-time expended on it. On the other side it wants to use labor-time as a measure for the gigantic social powers created in this way, and to restrain them as values. Productive forces and social relations—both of which are different sides of the development of the social individual—appear to capital only as means, and only means to produce on its limited basis. In fact, however, these are the material conditions to blow this basis sky-high.[42]

This passage and similar ones in the *Grundrisse* demonstrate once again, if further proof were needed, that the applicability of the Marxian theory is not limited to nineteenth-century industrial conditions. It would be a paltry theory indeed which predicted the breakdown of the capitalist order only when that order consisted of child labor, sweatshops, famine, chronic malnutrition, pestilence, and all the other scourges of its primitive stages. No genius and little science are required to reveal the contradictions of such a condition. Marx, however, proceeds by imagining the strongest possible case in favor of the capitalist system, by granting the system the full development of all the powers inherent in it—and then exposing the contradictions which must lead to its collapse.

THE UNKNOWN PIVOT

The gradual emergence of the *Grundrisse* out of obscurity into the consciousness of students and followers of Marx should have a most stimulating influence. This work explodes in many ways the mental set, the static framework of formulae and slogans to which much of Marxism has been reduced after a century of neglect, ninety years of social democracy, eighty years of "dialectical materialism," and seventy years of revisionism. To put it more pithily, the *Grundrisse* blows the mind. A number of conclusions seem inescapable.

First, this work will make it impossible or at least hopelessly frustrating to dichotomize the work of Marx into "young" and "old," into "philosophical" and "economic" elements. Hegel-enthusiasts and partisans of Ricardo will find the work equally stimulating or, conversely, equally frustrating, for the *Grund-*

[42] *Ibid.*, pp. 592–94 and R: 209–211.

risse is so to speak the pineal gland through which these two great antecedents of Marx engage in reciprocal osmosis. It contains passages which formulate Ricardian ideas with Hegelian language and Hegelian ideas with Ricardian language; the intercourse between them is direct and fruitful. Although we have not here examined this point in detail, a reader of the *Grundrisse* will find a direct line of continuity going back to many of the ideas of the 1844 *Manuscripts,* and from the perspective of the *Grundrisse* it will not be clear whether the earlier manuscripts were indeed a work of philosophy at all, or whether they were not simply a fusion of economic and philosophical thoughtways for which there is no modern precedent. Likewise, from the perspective of the *Grundrisse,* the often apparently "technical" obscurities of *Capital* will reveal their broader meaning. Between the mature Marx and the young Marx the *Grundrisse* is the missing link.

On the other hand, the fact that Marx makes a number of fresh discoveries and advances in the course of the *Grundrisse* must make students and followers of Marx more sensitive to the economic deficiencies of the earlier works. The *Grundrisse* contains the graphic record of Marx's discovery and systematization of the theory of surplus-value, about which his theory of capitalist breakdown is constructed. If it was not already clear, a reading of this work makes it clear that the theory of surplus-value was not a functional element of the economic model on which the *Manifesto* is based. Marx was aware, in 1848, of the *existence* of a surplus; but certainly he was not aware of the *importance* of this element. There is evidence of Marx's awareness of the Ricardian theory of the surplus in other early economic writings (the *Poverty of Philosophy* and *Wage-Labor and Capital*), but these works equally demonstrate that the surplus-value theory had *not* become a functional part of the economic model on which Marx based his predictions. Marx's early theory of wages and of profits, for example, is clearly a function of a supply-demand model of the economic system; and it will be necessary to re-examine this early theorizing critically in the light of the later surplus-value model. In at least one important problem-area, the question of class polarization, it can be demonstrated that the prophecy of the *Manifesto* is explicitly contradicted by Marx on the basis of his theory of surplus-value in a later work.[43] How many other such discrepancies exist, and

[43] Cf. Martin Nicolaus: "Hegelian Choreography and the Capitalist Dialectic: Proletariat and Middle Class in Marx," in *Studies on the Left* VII: 1, Jan.–Feb., 1967, pp. 22–49.

how many of them are traceable to the differences between the early market-model and the later surplus-value model, is a question which ought to be examined not only for its own sake, but also to clear up the confusion which often results when it is asked what precisely Marx had to say on the question of increasing impoverishment, for example.

It follows that the most important Marxian political manifesto remains to be written. Apart from the brief *Critique of the Gotha Programme* (1875) there exists no programmatic *political* statement which is based squarely on the theory of surplus-value, and which incorporates Marx's theory of capitalist breakdown as it appears in the *Grundrisse*. No grounds exist to reject the 1848 *Manifesto* as a whole; but there is every reason to submit all of its theses and views to critical re-examination in the light of Marx's own surplus-value theory. Many startling surprises might come to light, for example, if an edition of the *Manifesto* were published containing thorough and detailed annotations drawn from the later writings, point by point and line by line. Clearly the theory of surplus-value is crucial to Marx's thought; one can even say that with its ramifications it *is* Marx's theory. Yet how many "Marxist" political groupings and how many "Marxist" critics of Marx make the surplus-value theory the starting point of their analysis? The only major contemporary work in which the surplus-value plays the central role is Baran and Sweezy's *Monopoly Capital.*[44] Despite the deficiencies of that work, it points the way in the proper Marxian direction and forms the indispensable foundation for the type of analysis which must be made if Marx's theory of capitalism is to reassert its political relevance.

Unfortunately from several points of view, *Monopoly Capital* ends with the conclusion (or, perhaps more accurately, begins with the assumption) that domestic revolution within the advanced capitalist countries is not presently foreseeable. This argument can and must be confronted with Marx's thesis in the *Grundrisse* that all of the obstacles to revolution, such as those which Baran and Sweezy cite, namely monopoly, conquest of the world market, advanced technology, and a working class more prosperous than in the past, are only the preconditions which make revolution possible. Similarly, it cannot be said that Marx's vision of the central contradiction of capitalism, as he states it in the *Grundrisse*, has ever been thoroughly ex-

[44] Paul Baran and Paul Sweezy, *Monopoly Capital* (New York: Monthly Review Press, 1966).

plored and applied to an existing capitalist society; here *Monopoly Capital* falls short quite seriously. The results of such an analysis might also contain some surprising insights. In short, much work remains to be done.

That, we may conclude, is after all the most important conclusion to be drawn from the *Grundrisse*. Because this work underlines the deficiencies of the earlier economic writings and throws into sharp relief the fragmentary nature of *Capital*, it can serve as a powerful reminder that Marx was not a vendor of ready-made truths but a maker of tools. He himself did not complete the execution of the design. But the blueprints for his world-moving lever have at last been published. Now that Marx's unpolished masterwork has come to light, the construction of Marxism as a revolutionary social science which exposes even the most industrially advanced society at its roots has finally become a practical possibility.

from The May Day Manifesto

STUART HALL, RAYMOND WILLIAMS,
AND EDWARD THOMPSON

Rarely has a description of one political culture been so stunningly accurate a description of another. If England has a "new capitalism," American capitalism is still "newer." If England lays aside the "cockaded hat of the colonial governor" only to advance all the better her economic interests in the "ex-colonial world," it is the aggressive skill of the American multinational companies which has proved the superiority of the new modes of international exploitation. If England's two-party system becomes in effect a one-party system in which differences are restricted to the domain of fiscal technique, this is a hundred times truer of the American two-party system. (Whence, in part, the rise of Wallace populist fascism.) If the prosperity of radical democracy in England requires the transcending of electoral-parliamentary means, the argument holds a fortiori *for the United States.*

A bit more than half the full text of the May Day Manifesto *is excerpted below, including the beginning and the end. (A revised version was issued by Penguin too late for inclusion here.)*

For nearly eighty years, the international labor movement has taken May Day as a festival: an international celebration and commitment. On this May Day, 1967, as we look at our world, we see the familiar priorities of money and power, but now with one difference: that their agent, in Britain, is a Labour government. It is a strange paradox, which must be faced and understood. In an economic crisis, with the wages of millions of workers frozen, the wife of a Labour minister launches a Polaris nuclear submarine. While thousands of our people are without homes, while our schools are overcrowded and our health service is breaking under prolonged strain, a Labour cabinet orders what it calls a new generation of military planes, as if that, now, were the priority meaning of generation. In a hungry world, Britain appears east of Suez not as a friend but as what Labour politicians call a military presence: battleships, bombing planes, armed troops.

This is now the dangerous gap: between name and reality; between vision and power; between our human meanings and the deadening language of a false political system. In an increasingly educated society in which millions of people are capable of taking part in decisions, in which there is all the experience of a mature labor movement and a political democracy, in which there is a growing and vital confidence in our ability to run our lives, we are faced with something alien and thwarting: a manipulative politics, often openly aggressive and cynical, which has taken our meanings and changed them, taken our causes and used them; which seems our creation, yet now stands against us, as the agent of the priorities of money and power.

How has this happened? This is the only real question to ask, on this May Day, so that we can find ways of ending the danger and the insult that the political situation in Britain now increasingly represents. The sound of protest is rising again, in many parts of the country, and this is a critical moment. The years of radical campaigning, from Suez through Aldermaston to the early Sixties, made connections that still hold, groups that still function. The labor movement, in the unions and in the constituencies, has worked and struggled with a remarkable resilience. And it seemed, for a time, just a few years ago, that all this effort was coming together, into a new move forward. While the Tory illusion disintegrated, the Labour Party, under the new leadership of Harold Wilson, caught up, for a while, the sense of movement, the practical urgency of a change of direction. After the defensive years, we saw the hope and the possibility of a really new start. There was a notable quickening in the Labour Party itself, and the new radicals, campaigning for human alternatives to a nuclear strategy, to social poverty, and to cultural neglect, came, in majority, to work for a Labour government: never uncritically, but with a measured and seemingly reasonable hope.

After those years of shared effort, we are all, who worked for the Labour Party, in a new situation. For the sense of failure —a new kind of failure, in apparent victory—is implacably there, in every part of the Left. Not the crowing over failure;

not the temporary irritation; but a deeply concerned and serious recognition of a situation we had none of us wholly understood. The obstacles to progress, once so confidently named for our eager combined assault, may now, for the government, have become a platform. But, however plausible the rationalizations, however ingenious the passing reassurances, hardly anyone is deceived. A definition has failed, and we are looking for new definitions and directions.

At any time in the history of a people, such a moment is critical. For to recognize failure can be to live with failure: to move, as it would be easy to do, away from politics, and let the game, the sound, go on over our heads. There will always, it is true, be an irreducible nucleus of active resisters: the nonconformists, as has happened so often in Britain, losing their impetus to change the society but digging in, in their own circles, to maintain their positions. This minority is still large in Britain, by comparison with earlier periods: large enough, by any standards, to make certan that a living radicalism is maintained. Yet it seems to many of us, when all the pressures have been weighed, that now is not the moment for that kind of withdrawal. On the contrary, it is now, during the general failure, that it is time for a new, prolonged, and connected campaign.

What failed to happen, in the early Sixties, was a bringing together, into a general position, of the many kinds of new political and social response and analysis, around which local work had been done and local stands made. The consequence of this failure is now very apparent. While the positions were fragmentary, they could be taken, without real commitment, into the simple rhetoric of a new Britain. Now, as that rhetoric breaks, the fragments are thrown back at us: this issue against that. So a failure in one field—the persistence of poverty—can be referred to another—the economic crisis—and this in turn to another—the military expenditure—and this again to another—our foreign policy—and this back to the economic crisis, in an endless series of references and evasions. And then the character of the general crisis, within which these failures are symptoms, can never be grasped or understood or communicated. What we need is a description of the crisis as a whole, in which not only the present mistakes and illusions, but also the necessary and urgent changes, can be intelligently connected.

It is our basic case, in this manifesto, that the separate campaigns in which we have all been active, and the separate issues with which we have all been concerned, run back, in their essence, to a single political system and its alternatives. We believe that the system we now oppose can only survive by a willed separation of issues, and the resulting fragmentation of consciousness. Our own first position is that all the issues—industrial and political, international and domestic, economic and cultural, humanitarian and radical—are deeply connected; that what we oppose is a political, economic, and social system; that what we work for is a different whole society. The problems of whole men and women are now habitually relegated to specialized and disparate fields, where the society offers to manage or adjust them by this or that consideration or technique. Against this, we define socialism again as a humanism: a recognition of the social reality of man in all his activities, and of the consequent struggle for the direction of this reality by and for ordinary men and women.

THE NEW CAPITALISM

Both in this country and elsewhere in the world, capitalism has to adapt and change in order to survive. In Britain, the attempt to manage such an adaptation has been the main task of postwar governments—in a piecemeal form under successive Conservative governments, and now, with gathering force, under a Labour government. Their purpose has been to reshape an economy in relative decline, structurally imbalanced in relation to the outside world, backward in many sectors, paralyzed by a slow rate of growth, by inflation, recession, and balance of payments crises; and to create in its place a "new model" capitalism, based on organized, rapid expansion. An essential part of this strategy has been the containment and ultimate incorporation of the trade-union movement. An essential prerequisite is the redefinition of socialism itself, and the internal adaptation of the agencies for change—including the Labour Party—within some broad consensus. The current crisis is, then, a phase in the transition from one stage in capitalism to another. It is the crisis which occurs when a system, already beset by its own contradictions and suffering from prolonged entropy, nevertheless seeks to stabilize itself at a "higher" level.

New capitalism, though a development from free-market capitalism, is—in terms of its essential drives and its modes of operation and control—a distinct variant. It is an economic order dominated by private accumulation, where decisive economic power is wielded by the handful of very large industrial corporations in each sector. The scale of operation, the complex organization, the advanced techniques required to man and control such units, and their pervasive impact upon society at large, are so great that the allocation of resources and the pattern of demand can no longer be left to the play of the free market. Technological innovation, the need for long-term, self-financed investment and growth, the desire to predict and prestructure consumer demand—these factors have already substantially modified the mechanisms of free-market capitalism in practice. What is needed now, according to the controlling philosophy, is a further process of rationalization, such as would enable societies to go over consciously to an administered price system, wage negotiation within the framework of agreed norms, managed demand, and the efficient, effective transmission of orders from the top to the bottom of the "chain of command." This would represent, in effect, a major stabilization of the system. The free market, once the central image of capitalism, would be progressively by-passed for the sake of greater management and control, and the rewards of growth. It is this shift which makes some kind of planning imperative.

But planning in this sense does not mean what socialists have always understood—the subordination of private profit (and the directions which profit-maximization imposes on the whole society) to social priorities. The fact that the same word is used to mean different things is important, for it is by way of this linguistic sleight-of-hand that Labour has mystified and confused its supporters, taking up the allegiance of the labor movement to one concept of planning while attaching another meaning, another kind of content, to the word in practice. Planning now means better forecasting, better coordination of investment and expansion decisions, a more purposeful control over demand. This enables the more technologically equipped and organized units in the private sector to pursue their goals more efficiently, more "rationally." It also means more control over unions and over labor's power to bargain freely about wages. This involves another important transition. For in the course of this rationalization of capitalism, the gap between private industry and the State is narrowed. The State, indeed, comes to play a critical role. It makes itself responsible for the over-all management of the economy by fiscal means. It must tailor the production of trained manpower to the needs of the economic system—a calculation to which many important pages in the Robbins Report on Higher Education were devoted. In the political field, it must hold the ring within which the necessary bargains are struck between competing interests. It must manipulate the public consensus in favor of these bargains, and take on the task directly—as it did in the seamen's strike—of intervening to whip labor into line behind the norms. In relation to labor and the unions, it is the State which draws the unions into the consensus, identifies them with the planning decisions and the fixing of norms, and thereby wins their collusion with the system.

Workers, of course, can only be expected to cooperate with the System if they regularly gain a share of the goods being produced. The first promise held out is that the State will be in a better position to manage the inflation-recession cycles which have beset the postwar economy. The second promise is that a stable system will be more efficient and productive, and that, so long as it works, labor will win its share in return for cooperation. When productivity rises, it is suggested, labor shares in the benefits. On the other hand, when the economy slows down, labor cannot contract out since it has become a party to the bargain. This looks on the surface like a more rational way of guaranteeing rising standards of living: it is in fact a profound restructuring of the relationship between labor and capital. We saw above how the term "planning" has been maintained, but how its content has been redefined. The same can be said of the word "welfare." Market capitalism was for a long time the enemy of the welfare state. In Britain, the welfare state was introduced as a modification of capitalism. Like wage increases, it represented a measure of redistribution and egalitarianism, cutting into profits, imposing human needs and social priorities on the profit system. But in Western European states of the modern capitalist type since the war, a welfare state in some form has come to be seen as a necessary element in organized capitalism: as is well known, some of these continental welfare provisions are more comprehensive now than the British system.

There is one vital difference, however, between this aspect of a modern capitalist economy and socialist economic models. Rising prosperity—whether in the form of higher wages, increased welfare, or public spending—is not funded out of the redistribution of wealth from rich to poor. Redistribution would eat into the necessary mechanisms of private accumulation, internal reinvestment, and the high rewards to management on which the whole system rests. Rising prosperity must, therefore come out of the margin of increased growth and productivity. The existing distribution of wealth and power is taken as given New wage claims can only be met by negotiation, out of the surplus growth, and controlled by a framework of agreed norms The norms, however, are not the norms of social justice, human needs, or the claims for equality: they are arrived at by cal culating the percentage rise in productivity over a given period, and by bargaining at what proportion of that is the "necessary" return to capital, and what proportion is left over for wage increases and welfare costs. In effect, within this new system of bargaining, wage increases must be tied to productivity agreements (not to the claims of equality), and welfare becomes a supporting structure for modern capitalism (not an inroad into or a modification of the system). This is one of the crucial markers between the new capitalism and the old, and between organized capitalism and socialism. It means that the rising prosperity of the working class is indissolubly linked with the growth and fortunes of private industry, since only by means of the productivity of industry will there be any wage or welfare surplus at all to bargain for. A successful modern capitalist system is therefore one in which people may enjoy a measure of increased abundance and prosperity provided there is growing productivity; but it is by definition not an egalitarian system in terms of income, wealth, opportunity, authority, or power. There may be a leveling of social status; nevertheless, "open" capitalist societies, where stratification is not marked, are still closed systems of power. Market capitalism created the hostile conflict relations of a class society; organized capitalism, where successful, seeks to end these conflicts, not by changing the real relations of property and power, but by suppressing all the human considerations of community and equality in favor of the planned contentment of organized producers and consumers.

MODERNIZATION

In the early 1960's, there was an open crisis of confidence in British society. The simplest versions of affluence and opportunity, which had sustained the Conservative Party in the Fifties, were breaking down in the repeated confusion of stop-go economic policies. From the New Left there was already a socialist critique of the values of that kind of affluence, but now it was joined by a different set of arguments, which identified the weakness of British society as excessive deference to the past, with an out-of-date economic and political establishment. As the Macmillan government disintegrated, it was a matter of extreme importance which version of the crisis was adopted by the Labour Party. The urge for renewal of a general kind was indeed quite quickly taken up, and it seemed possible, for a time, that a very broad and strong front for radical change was in process of being created. What was actually happening in the leadership of the Labour Party can be seen now to be very different. As we compare the official rhetoric of the pre-1964 campaigns with the government's present performance, what comes across with most telling force is the continuous process of redefinition, the major shifts of emphasis, the progressive narrowing of horizon. Mr. Wilson himself led the Party in the pre-1964 period into a savage assault on Tory stop-go economic policies. He attacked the speculation in land, the housing scandal, the control by "aristocratic connections," "inherited wealth," and "speculative finance" over the commanding heights of British industry. Abroad, he scorned the "nostalgic illusions," the "nuclear posturings" of the Tory Party. He drew the connection himself between the economy, defense, and foreign policy, and the social services in 1964: "Yes, we can borrow, that's where thirteen years of Conservative rule have brought us. You can get into pawn, but don't then talk about an independent defense policy. If you borrow from some of the world's bankers you will quickly find you lose another kind of independence, because of the deflationary policies and the cuts on social services that will be imposed on a government that has got itself into that position."

In the ensuing months, however, the whole strategy disintegrated, the radical mood was dissipated, and quite new emphases asserted themselves. Labour's mission to "transform" British society narrowed to the more ambiguous call to "the nation" to build the "New Britain." Then the "New Britain" was itself redefined—first, in terms of "the scientific revolution," then in terms of "modernization." Many of the crucial shifts of emphasis and meaning took place within the context of that term, "modernization." But what did modernization mean? In the first place, it meant overcoming inefficiency—the cause to which all the weaknesses of the British economy were attributed. The British economy is indeed inefficient in many ways. But to abstract its deficiencies from the general character of British society was wilfully misleading. The problems of inefficiency cannot be detached, for instance, from problems of foreign policy, since some of the economy's heaviest burdens follow from the particular international policy which successive British governments continued to pursue. It cannot be separated from the gross inequalities in terms of opportunity and reward, the immense discrepancies in terms of power, authority, and control, between those who manage men and those who sell their labor. Neither can it be abstracted from the whole drive to consolidate a new capitalist economy which successive governments also pursued—a policy involving the emergence of larger private economic units, the control and absorption of the trade unions, the redefinition of the role of the State in economic activity. If we want to test the validity of modernization as an economic panacea, we have to see it in its real context: as not a program but a stratagem—part of the language and tactics of the new capitalist consolidation.

Modernization is, indeed, the "theology" of the new capitalism. It opens up a perspective of change—but at the same time it mystifies the process and sets limits to it. Attitudes, habits, techniques, practices must change; the system of economic and social power, however, remains unchanged. Modernization fatally short-circuits the formation of social goals—any discussion of long-term purposes is made to seem utopian in the down-to-earth, pragmatic climate which modernization generates. The discussion about "modernized Britain" is not about what sort of society, qualitatively, is being aimed at, but simply about how modernization is to be achieved. All programs and perspectives are treated instrumentally. As a model of social change, modernization crudely foreshortens the historical development of society. Modernization is the ideology of the never-ending present. The whole past belongs to "traditional" society, and modernization is a technical means for breaking with the past without creating a future. All is now: restless, visionless, faithless: human society diminished to a passing technique. No confrontations of power, values, or interests, no choice between competing priorities, are envisaged or encouraged. It is a technocratic model of society—conflict-free and politically neutral, dissolving genuine social conflicts and issues in the abstractions of "the scientific revolution," "consensus," "productivity." Modernization presumes that no group in the society will be called upon to bear the costs of the scientific revolution—as if all men have an equal chance in shaping the consensus, or as if, by some process of natural law, we all benefit equally from a rise in productivity. "Modernization" is thus a way of masking what the real costs would be of creating in Britain a truly modern society.

Second, "modernization" is identified with "planning." But the present Labour government's policies amount, in fact, to the continuation and consolidation of that form of capitalist planning whose foundations were laid by Mr. Maudling and Mr. Selwyn Lloyd in the final years of the Conservatives . . . The style of planning which Labour adopted is not even a means by which the economic drives of capitalism can be modified by some over-all framework of social priorities; it is "indicative" planning, the dovetailing and rationalization of business decisions and targets. Labour "planning" is thus actively furthering the transition—under way before Labour came to power, but now considerably advanced—from a market capitalist economy to an organized capitalism centered on long-term planning and prediction, with State intervention and control to sustain capitalist enterprise, the inclusion of public capital in the private monopoly field (North Sea Gas, for example), and the application of private commercial practices to the public sector (as in the liner trains dispute).

It is a striking historical irony that the consensus on which the new capitalism relies could be achieved in Britain only through the agency of a Labour government. One has only to watch the confused response of the trade-union leadership to the Incomes Policy, the wages freeze, and the establishment of some permanent system of control over wage negotiations to appreciate fully the role which Labour has played in the whole process. Participation in capitalist planning is held out as the model role for trade unions in a modern economy. The unions know that there is something badly skewed about this model, but they fall back defensively on the older definitions—free wage-bargaining between labor and capital. They are then vulnerable to the charge that they want a return to the very "free-for-all," the "wages scramble" which they have actively critized in the past. The whole weight of the consensus is then brought to bear, by government and the media, against them, making the recalcitrant unions appear backward-looking and old-fashioned in the heady atmosphere of modernization. Thus, over a period of time, and by means of a mixture of invitation, declarations of intent, cajoling, blackmail, and pressure, the government forces the union leadership to collude with the System. For this purpose, the economic crisis of 1966 proved a blessing in disguise, since the need for quick, tough action permitted the government to bring in measures which, in effect, represent the skeleton framework of new capitalist planning. Under the rubric of "emergency measures," Britain took a decisive step in the direction of the new capitalism.

MANAGED POLITICS

The political aim of the new capitalism, and the governments which sustain it, is clear. It is to muffle real conflict, to dissolve it into a false political consensus; to build, not a genuine and radical community of life and interest, but a bogus conviviality between every social group. Consensus politics, integral to the success of the new capitalism, is in its essence manipulative politics, the politics of man-management, and as such deeply undemocratic. Governments are still elected, M.P.'s assert the supremacy of the House of Commons. But the real business of government is the management of consensus between the most powerful and organized elites.

In a consensual society, the ruling elites can no longer impose their will by coercion: but neither will they see progress as a people organizing itself for effective participation in power and responsibility. Democracy, indeed, becomes a structure to be negotiated and maneuvered. The task of the leading politicians is to build around each issue by means of bargain and compromise a coalition of interest, and especially to associate the large units of power with its legislative program. Consensus politics thus becomes the politics of incremental action: it is not programmed for any large-scale structural change. It is the politics of pragmatism, of the successful maneuver within existing limits. Every administrative act is a kind of clever performance, an exercise of political public relations. Whether the maneuvers are made by a Tory or Labour government then hardly matters, since both accept the constraints of the status quo as a framework. Government, as the Prime Minister often reminds us, is simply the determination "to govern." The circle has been closed.

It has been closed in a very special way. There have always, in capitalist society, been separate sources of power, based on property and control, with which governments must negotiate. But the whole essence of the new capitalism is an increasing rationalization and coordination of just this structure. The states within the State, the high commands in each sector (the banks, the corporations, the federations of industrialists) . . . are given a new and more formal place in the political structure, and this, increasingly, is the actual machinery of decision-making: in their own fields, as always, but now also in a coordinated field. This political structure, which is to a decisive extent mirrored in the ownership and control of public communications, is then plausibly described as "the national interest." And it is not only that the national interest has then been defined so as to include the very specific and often damaging interests of the banks, the combines, the city. It is also that the elected element—the democratic process, which is still offered as ratifying—has been redefined, after its passage through the machines, as one interest among others: what is still, in an abstract way, called the public interest, but present now only as one—relatively weak and ill-organized—among several elements involved in effective decisions.

Under the present Labour government, then, we can watch the process of a whole monopoly-capitalist system seeking stabilization. The politics of the transitional period in which the old capitalism crystallizes into the new are primarily concerned with the management of political conflict and tension, dissolving old bonds and relationships as new ones emerge, until the new order is sufficiently stable. The perspective, however, is no short-term emergency adjustment to temporary problems. It is the establishment of a new status quo, indeed a whole new social order.

In this drive to organize and rationalize a stable new capitalism, both the individualist-liberal version of market capitalism and the community-egalitarian vision of socialism are surpassed, presented as technologically obsolete. The new model is made to seem inevitable, powered by the forces of technology, sustained by the drive for modernization. Until quite recently, this has been discussed as an abstract model. It is an abstract model no longer. It constitutes the real ground of politics, the true perspective of the Labour government. We can now see, in retrospect, some of the elements of this new system beginning to crystallize toward the end of the period of Conservative rule; but it has been converted into the living issues and textures of politics only within the period of the Labour government. For it is in the period of Labour rule that the emergent economic system has discovered its political counterpart and fashioned the sophisticated means of political control. The debates and divisions within socialism in the last decade can now be explained in this context. The strained exchanges between the "old" and the "new" Left in the Fifties can be seen as a crisis engendered by this emergent capitalism within socialism itself—the result of a faltering attempt to find a language in which the upheaval and transformation of capitalism—and with that, the restructuring of the Labour Party itself—could be correctly described.

To take the planning and modernization emphases of the government, then, in detachment from the capitalist realities in which they are rooted would be fatally to misread the nature of the crisis of British society. Such misreadings have already occurred, even among socialists: witness the belief that because an element of planning has entered our economic life, we are necessarily "stumbling into socialism." Yet this very error of judgment illustrates how the new capitalism dismantles older political ideas and values, confuses and fragments the labor movement. For the new capitalism, in the very process of "surpassing" socialism, in fact takes over many of the collectivist forms—though none of the content—of socialism. Thus socialists have always believed in planning—and now organized capitalism needs to plan. Socialists have opposed the free play of the market—and now organized capital transcends the market in its old form. Socialists have supported state intervention and control—but the new capitalism also believes in an active State. Socialists have supported a strong trade-union movement —and now organized capitalism needs a strong, centralized trade-union movement with which to bargain. It seems easy to turn around and say: we are making socialism, only we call it the "new Britain": the government and industry and the banks and the unions, all in it together. As a propaganda operation, this may succeed for a time, but it is of course ludicrous. What has happened is quite different. The Labour Party embodied the aspirations of the working people. Long before the present transition began, its leaders and intellectuals translated these aspirations into a narrow economism—expert planning—and a minimum welfare standard. This was already a critical redefinition, a reworking, with the whole element of the democratic recovery and exercise of power left out. In our own period, these aims and redefinitions came to coincide with the needs of capitalism, in its monopoly phase—thereby, in one movement, both confirming and transcending one part of the socialist case. The Labour leadership, already wedded to a very special and limiting concept of what socialism in practice would mean, saw in just this change its opportunity for power. It thus made a bid for the job of harnessing and managing the new system; but was then itself taken over, from outside and in. The Party and the government continue to operate under their old trade name, with all its accumulated goodwill and "consumer loyalty." It is simply the nature of the business which has changed.

A NEW INTERNATIONAL SYSTEM

This global system—which we call the new imperialism—is a complex structure, and only some of its features can be discussed here. The first and most significant development is the emergence of the international company. Throughout the 1950's and 60's, the large corporations in the United States, as well as Western European and Japanese economies, have been increasingly "internationalized." They have expanded at home —but also abroad, in the colonial and ex-colonial world, and, increasingly, through investment and the establishment of export and manufacturing subsidiaries, in one another's home territories. Nearly all investment is private, nearly all private investment is direct company investment, and a growing proportion of this is among the already developed industrial countries. More than half the private investment income flowing into both the United States and the United Kingdom comes from developed countries, and two-thirds of the outflow of capital goes to them. What we have today is a development of cross-investment, originating in the struggle for survival of the giant international combines: a struggle which is undertaken both within the developed countries of the world (at the expense of the developing countries) and in old traditional markets overseas. Only the international company has the capital resources, flexibility, access to research and development necessary for competition on this scale. This rapid internationalization of the private corporation has had a major impact on the pattern of world trade. It has squeezed the developing nations, with their single-crop or single-mineral economies; it has squeezed its smaller and less efficient rivals—notably in Britain. Further, it is these large international corporations which provide the institutional economic framework for national economies. It is their decision what shall be manufactured and exported in local subsidiaries, their decision how much of the profit on overseas operations should be repatriated, their decision where to hold liquid funds and where and when to transfer funds across foreign exchanges. It was not the gnomes of Zurich, but the giant international companies—many of them British—which made massive transfers out of sterling in November 1964 and again in June 1966. It is largely as a result of their pressure to export capital that both Britain and the United States have found themselves running large deficits in international payments. (Both countries have had to take steps to correct these deficits: the outcome, however, is a shortage in world liquidity). The large international companies are now the central institutions of the world economy. Their operations both undermine the position of the developing countries, and continually put national economies at risk.

These international concerns trade and invest heavily in the developed countries. But they are also deeply involved with the continued exploitation of the colonial and ex-colonial world. A relatively small proportion of British, United States, and Western European foreign investment now goes to the Third World, but this is a highly profitable investment sector. The pattern of this investment appears to be altering. The area of the small colonial enterprises and trading houses is declining, but the sector concerned with mining, electro-metallurgy, and industrial agriculture is growing. The much-publicized transformer industries set up as development industries in backward economies are, in fact, largely service industries to the great electrometallurgical and extractive concerns. To this, we must add the crucial foreign investment in oil, both in the Persian Gulf and elsewhere. The financial operations of these large concerns throughout the Third World represent an internationalization of economic colonialism in two senses. First, the large mining and metallurgical enterprises are financed by consortia in which banks and enterprises of all the imperialist countries participate—the United States, Britain, France, West Germany, etc. Second, the fields of operation cross the older lines laid down by traditional colonial spheres of influence. The whole area of the Third World is treated as a potential sphere of operation by these international units. Thus national colonialisms find themselves eliminated from the privileged positions they held in the nineteenth century, and are replaced by a more international economic operation geared exclusively to the needs of a world market. As far as a vulnerable but developed country like Britain is concerned, the impact of the system is critical. Flows outward—whether in the form of private investment or aid—affect the British national economy and its balance of payments and liquidity position; but what goes out in the context of a national situation (and is paid for, when the pressure is on, in terms of a national recession, unemployment on a national scale, a national squeeze), comes back in trading profits and very high returns on new investment into the hands of private investors and institutions—mainly international corporations and the City and finance houses.

A BRITISH INTEREST?

The return on British investment in the ex-colonial world may not be so large now as it was at the height of Empire. Certainly, equal weight must now be given, on the part of the modern corporation, to the penetration of markets in other developed countries—by exports, investment capital, and the establishment of subsidiary firms. It is a matter of controversy, even among socialist economists, how far, in terms of an ideal model, an industrial country like Britain still depends upon economic imperialism, even in its new form. Still, the return on investment with the Third World is lucrative, and a powerful sector of the British economy—partly for historical reasons—is deeply involved in it: the City, the foreign finance houses, firms like Unilever, the oil and mining corporations. Its importance to Britain can be seen in the fact that in 1964 and again in 1966, the government chose to sacrifice industrial growth at home to the interests of this sector—the defense of sterling, the maintenance of parity, the husbanding of foreign reserves, "confidence restoring" measures. The whole British way of life became identified—at untold cost—with the defense of sterling. Thus the international combines with a British interest, the banks, and the international capital market were able to exercise a decisive influence on national policy at a crucial turning-point, out of all proportion to their share of our total production and trade. There are in fact at this point important conflicts of interest between differently oriented sectors of British capitalism, which might, in certain circumstances, generate pressures for a different kind of solution—a sort of English Gaullism. This, too, would have its illusions and its limits, but the contradictions involved may have an important eventual effect on British politics. At present we can note only the subordination or containment of industrial-capitalist interests within the complicated structures of the domestic political and financial establishment, but also, and mainly, within the over-all pressures of an interlocking and international political and financial system.

This brings us to the increasing dominance of the United States in the evolution of the new imperialism. In the case of the United States, foreign investment in developed countries also accounts for a greater proportion than investment in the Third World, though once again the lucrative nature of the latter type of investment, as in the case of Latin America, should not be underestimated. Some American economists also point out that to gain a full measure of the economic involvement of the United States in foreign markets, the impact of military spending—the so-called "defense program"—must also be reckoned with. This raises another dimension of the new imperialism: the military global aspect. The significance of the industrial-military complex in the United States economy, and the contribution of defense contracts to the stability of the corporation, is a well-publicized and established fact. Defense expenditure is undertaken to service the United States' global role in "the defense of the West." But the "West" is not just a political idea, a way of life: it is a massive economic and political complex, engaged—as American governments see it—in a life-and-death struggle, at every level, with "international communism," centered in the Soviet Union and China, and with "wide-spread subversion" throughout the Third World. It is not necessary to argue that the United States' imperial role throughout the world can be wholly explained by reduction to economic factors. What does seem clear is that a parallelogram of forces, which include internal and external economic forces, the military program, political and ideological factors have acted, in the context of the Cold War, in such a way as to convert the West as a socio-economic system into an aggressive-defensive worldwide military presence.

It is in this sense that we have to look again at the ordinary belief that Britain's phase as an imperialist power has come to an end, in the twilight of the colonial era. Indeed, here, in this question, the overriding political questions of our time come together: the real relations between new capitalism and new imperialism; the true character of the Anglo-American political and military alliance; the actual position of Britain in the contemporary world.

THE END OF EMPIRE?

To most people in Britain, imperialism has its immediate images: the Union Jack, the cockaded hat of the colonial governor, the lonely district officer. Few people can now be nostalgic for these images: they so clearly belong to the past. It is a recurring theme in Labour Party pamphlets and speeches—how "we gave India independence," how "we" liquidated the Empire. Certainly, the old symbols have been dismantled: the flags hauled down, the minor royalty dancing with the new black prime minister, the new names on the atlas. And yet, if we look at Britain's relation to the Third World, we have to account both for change and renewal: politically, the colonial phase has been largely wound up, but there is still the vestigial role, dispensed with all the ambiguities of late colonialism, in Rhodesia and Aden. Economically, the operating staffs have been "Africanized"—but still, at every central point in our economic crisis, the imperial and international imperatives seem regularly to assert themselves as emphatic and determining. Militarily, Britain has recalled the occupying regiments from several quarters of the colonial globe; but still we have a "mission East of Suez," vital interests with our allies in the Middle East and Asia, defense responsibilities to India, frontiers on the Himalayas. The collapse of the old colonial empires is a major fact in the history of the world, and particularly in the history of Britain. But the revival of an imperial mission, of a global military system, in company with other Western powers, and especially the United States, is also a fact of history. What are the new and governing political, economic, military, and ideological structures of this new imperialism? What is the character of Britain's deep involvement with them? What is their meaning for the new nations of the Third World? So far as Britain is concerned, we can only speculate that the full liquidation of Empire never in fact took place. In economic terms, it is clear that where colonial governors left off, the new international companies and financial interests took over. Similarly, the political record is more complex and ambiguous than in the usual accounts. The story of how we "gave" the colonies their freedom comes to sound like that other story of how the rich and the privileged "gave" the rest of us the vote, the welfare state, full employment. This story looks different from the standpoint, say, of Kenya, Cyprus, Malaya, Guyana, Rhodesia, Aden. In many cases the process by which the Empire was "wound up" entailed armed revolution, civil war, prolonged civil disobedience. In other cases, freedom came in a hurry by political directive, almost before the national movement demanded it, while safe leaders and cadres still retained power. In between these extreme cases, there were many mixed examples: suppression of one wing of the national movement, handing of power to another; imprisonment of political and trade-union leaders; withdrawal under latent or mounting pressure; the creation of new and largely artificial political structures, such as federations, to bring independence in a particular way. The present complexity of the ex-colonial world is deeply related to this varied history. This is not a straight story of "liberation" by any means.

"UNDERDEVELOPMENT"

But now a new model comes into place to explain our relations with the ex-colonial countries. This model is not imperialism as we have described it above; it describes simply a physical, technical condition—the condition of "underdevelopment." This is, of course, just the kind of term the new capitalism would create (compare "underprivileged" and what it still calls the "underdog"). It has a special relevance as a way of looking at a country: not a poor people, but a poor tract of land, an "underdeveloped" land. Yet others, taking up the description, can see it as the duty of a developed country to help the underdeveloped countries, as it was the duty of the rich to help the poor. Into this model of what relations between the rich and poor countries are now like, much generous feeling is directed. And when it is realized, as is undoubtedly the case, that the gap between the rich and poor in the world is not closing but widening, and that with rapidly rising populations there is a profound danger of hunger and poverty disastrously increasing, still, within this model, we can only say that we must simply do more: give more aid, be more charitable. Much of the best feeling in Britain now is of just this kind.

Of course, the help must be given. But just as the labor movement developed as a better alternative than charity for ending poverty and inequality, so, in the problems of the poor nations, we need a different perspective, and we must begin by understanding the political and economic structures of the world we are trying to change. We are not linked to the Third World by "aid without strings," Oxfam, and Freedom-From-Hunger alone. We are linked also by the City of London, by sterling, by Unilever, by gold, by oil, by rubber, by uranium, by copper; by aircraft carriers, by expeditionary forces, by Polaris.

Consider "underdevelopment" as an idea. At its best it is meant to imply that the poor nations are rather like ourselves at an earlier stage of our own history. So they must be helped along until they also develop, or perhaps are developed by others, into our kind of economy and society. But, in its simplest form, this is really like saying that a poor man is someone who is on his way to being a rich man, but who is still at a relatively early stage on his development. In Victorian England, some people even believed this of the poor of their time. But very few poor men believed it. They saw wealth and poverty being created, as well as inherited, by the property and working relations of their society. In the same way, we have to ask of the poor countries: is this only an inherited, or is it also a created condition?

It is often inherited, from the familiar colonial period. Africa lost millions of its men to the slave trade. Oil, minerals, agricultural produce have been taken in great quantities, from the poor countries to the rich. In this process, during the colonial period, the economies concerned were developed and structured for this primary purpose: that is to say, in single-crop economies or in the mining and oil-extracting areas, they became directly dependent on the world market, through the colonial powers. At a later stage, in their own internal development and from the needs of the expanding economies of the colonial powers, they became also outlets for exports and for capital investment: their development, that is to say, was as satellite economies of the colonial powers. It will then be seen that when we say "underdevelopment" we are not making some simple mark along a single line: such development as there was took place in accordance with the needs of the occupying powers. The poor were not just poor in isolation; they were poor, in those precise ways, because there were rich in the world, and because the rich, through political and economic control, were determining the conditions of their lives.

We have then to ask how much was changed when these countries gained their political independence. They were still, obviously, dependent on the world market, because their whole economies had been built up for that main purpose. And this was in many ways a weak position, since it meant that prices could be determined by those in control of the world market in ways that could radically affect their whole national income. And, again, they needed capital, which for the most part could only come from overseas. On what terms would this capital be provided?

The working-out of these questions has been the political and economic history of the ex-colonial world. Two very different answers were possible. They could go on economically much as before, producing for the world market at prices fixed from outside, accepting imports from the industrial economies, again at prices fixed from outside, and accepting capital for development on terms and in ways convenient to its suppliers. Or, very differently, they could stop regarding their own economies as simply producers and consumers for others, take control of their own national resources, and develop them in accordance with their own needs, accepting foreign capital only within the context of that kind of national plan. The first course would lead to continued economic dependence, after political independence. But the second course would lead to immediate political and economic conflict with the foreign controllers of markets and capital. In the complexity and urgency of their actual poverty, no course was simple. But we must then consider our own position in the countries making the decisions about food and raw material prices and about investment. What, now, were our own priorities?

There have been some attempts to regulate trade and to provide capital on terms consistent with the development of the ex-colonial economies in their own peoples' interests. But what has mainly emerged is the system we are calling the new colonialism. The economic grip has been held, and has been described as assuring our own vital needs. Where a former colony has taken the quieter course, it has received investment and aid on terms which ensure its continued development as a satellite economy. Great efforts are made, in bargaining and in political maneuver, to maintain this situation. Instead of the flag and the cockaded hat, we have the commodity market and the international banker. It is not what has been popularly known as imperialism, but, to those experiencing it, it is still a decisive foreign control over the most critical matters in their lives. And then, if there is a political movement within the country to change priorities and end this dependence, it can be plausibly presented as subversive; to put it down is "peacemaking." A break for economic freedom by a government can be met with every kind of economic, political, and even military pressure, as at Suez. For us at home, reading of these events, decisive labels are attached to the contending parties: they are "pro-Western" and "moderate," or "extremist," "terrorist," and "communist." The new colonialism of the commodity markets, the mining corporations, the oil companies, and the financial syndicates becomes the new imperialism of the military presence, the peace-keeping force, the political maneuver.

POLITICAL MANAGERS OF THE WORLD

What was once a relatively specialized field of colonial management has become, in these ways, a whole and complicated global strategy. Within this strategy, economic, political, and military elements are so closely woven that they form an apparently seamless fabric. The investment programs of the giant corporations with a vested interest in the System are of course directly capitalist. But behind them there is another kind of investment, from different sources but sharing the same ideology. Heavy stress is laid, when capital is offered to an ex-colonial country, against schemes of nationalization, and for "free enterprise." Political developments in the receiving country must not "frighten investors away." Foreign corporations, with the ready technical know-how, must be allowed freedom to work. Political stability must be ensured: internally, to keep foreign plant and investments safe; strategically, to keep the country free from communist "subversion." Stable regimes are required—both the economic and the military strategies require them—even if they are military dictatorships or puppet regimes: order is preferable to the "chaos" which would be part of any radical change. The reference to chaos is of course hypocritical. Indonesia denouncing neocolonialism was a pariah: Indonesia after a massacre of its communists was suddenly a promising country, deserving a favorable mention from a British Foreign Secretary.

In certain circumstances, of course, political stability can be ensured by other means: by timely moderate reforms—some land reform, some improvement in health and housing conditions, some development in native terms. The limits of reform, however, are very strictly maintained. The Alliance for Progress is launched in Latin America: but groups which seek a more radical political solution are subverted and governments undermined; Cuba is beyond the pale. Where the economic climate and the political regimes are "favorable," the economies can be supported by infusions of economic aid. But it is characteristic that such schemes are financed out of the public revenue, and a great deal of it, which goes into the building of the infrastructure—roads, dams, power supply—also, incidentally, services and makes more profitable the ventures of private capital, though the actual cost of this kind of basic development is borne not by private capital but by public funds. But if moderate reforms are to be of lasting success, if aid is really to stimulate genuine economic growth, then new social forces must be released within the poor countries, and new programs set in motion which are to take these countries out of the safe orbits of the West. Old privileged groups may resist these changes, but these are just imperialism's best friends, the groups and classes within the new nations which precisely make them "safe" for democracy. When any such revolutionary momentum is generated, the bland face of "aid" is quickly replaced by the harsher face of political intervention and counter-subversion. The new nations, then, are forced to exist within this mystifying circle: aid for the safe, the trustworthy force; but a military presence for the revolutionary.

The exploitative military and economic relations between the new nations and the West thus confirm the exploiting situations within the new nations, and compound the very "backwardness" of the "backward countries." The peoples of the rich countries are exploited by the developers who claim to be acting on their behalf, and who are also exploiting the poor countries. But the peoples of the poor countries are also exploited within their own societies—by the many intermediate groups, the chiefs and sheiks, the local bourgeois and comprador classes, the indigenous landowners and producers for commodity markets, the local representatives of international concerns, local capitalist enterprises, and the political and military bureaucracies which exist to mediate and maintain the new colonial relationships. Between the imperial classes of the developed world and the exploiting classes of the underdeveloped world there exists a common economic, military, and political cause. Some of these bureaucracies and cadres are what we call the governments of the new states: their corruption and brutality can be justified as evidence of the inability of "backward" peoples to govern themselves properly, but their true role and character can only be understood within the complex of actual economic and political relations. The honest and patriotic governments are ceaselessly submitted to pressures, so that their survival is precarious. The resolute governments, determined to gain an economic independence to realize their political independence, are either broken or break from within under the strain. To the degree that they are successful, they are represented as our enemies.

This is the political and social reality of the relations between the rich and poor nations of the world. This is the reality we have to change. For we have only to look at the centers of violence in the contemporary world, all now precisely where the poor of the world are trying to win their independence, to know that it is not only exploitation we are seeking to end; it is also, in our time, the main cause and source of war.

THE COLD WAR

Socialists have traditionally seen war in the twentieth century as the conflict of rival imperialisms: for colonies, for trade, for spheres of influence. But this situation was already modified by the Russian revolution, and international politics, for a generation, came to be dominated by reactions to this new factor—the existence of a socialist state—and its associated movements. The Second World War, like the First, began in Europe, but it was already different in character. The old national and imperialist rivalries coexisted with the complicated process of political struggle between socialism and, on the one hand, liberal capitalism, and on the other hand, fascism. Before the war ended it was further complicated, in Asia, by an imperialist conflict of a new kind.

The making and remaking of alliances within this struggle during the war and postwar years have been deeply confusing. For socialists in Britain, the actual progress of Russian communism, under severe pressures—internally, in the rapid flight out of backwardness; externally, in the invasion and hostility of the old powers—was of a character to check all easy, utopian assumptions. Many features of this communism could not be recognized as anything but hostile to the socialist ideas nurtured in a more temperate historical experience. The remaking of the communist societies remains urgent, and, in expressing our opposition to their disciplinary and manipulative features, we are at the same time expressing a necessary solidarity with the growing volume of democratic criticism within these countries themselves. But it has been everywhere a matter of extreme difficulty to express this democratic opposition, clearly and strongly, without at the same time aligning ourselves with all those who are the enemies of socialism in any of its forms.

The Cold War was a bitterly divisive experience for these reasons. It was never possible for us to accept the propaganda version of the Soviet Union as an aggressive imperialist power; yet the fact that the charge was made in this way illustrated the complexity of the new politics: imperialism, now, was seen and offered as a natural enemy. Similarly, the previous apologists of the parties of order, of every kind of authoritarian regime here and elsewhere, expected us to join them because of Soviet authoritarianism; and yet, in declining, we had to insist, often against friends and comrades, that the authoritarianism was there and was brutal and insupportable. Millions of people, including many in the working-class movement, were then brought, if not to participation at least to acquiescence in the Cold War, on the understanding that it was an essentially defensive operation.

This had never been true, even from the beginning. For the popular resistance movements in occupied Europe during World War II, although communist-led, can be seen as agencies of Soviet imperialism only by the most grotesque historical distortion. They expressed an authentic popular movement, with authentic revolutionary aspirations, germane to those which brought Labour's own sweeping electorial victories in 1945. The case of Yugoslavia, during the worst years of Stalinism, was to show how far such indigenous and democratic impulses were beyond any imperialist control. And it was the repression of these popular movements—in Greece, in France, in Italy—and the reinstatement of the old interests and regimes (now under American military protection) which contributed as much to the origin of the Cold War as did the Stalinist repression of liberal, social-democratic, and (at length) communist opposition in Eastern Europe.

The Cold War had no single author. One page was written at Yalta, another at Fulton, yet another in Prague. It has always entailed a radical falsification of European culture, history, even elementary geography. There is no "West" confronting an "East": the lines of ideological argument, of cultural influence, and of political solidarities have always followed their own necessary logic across all arbitrary frontiers. We have never been able to see the Cold War as anything but an interregnum in European history, an unnatural parenthesis.

The parenthesis may at last be brought to an end. The Cold War, in its original character as a confrontation in Europe, has for several years now been changing its shape and source. We believe that, already confused by the Cold War and its tensions, the labor movement has been painfully slow to recognize the altered character of international relations. Under the nuclear arms race, the Cold War reached deadlock in Europe; it is now being fought elsewhere, on different issues and by different means, in ways that shed light back on the original confrontation. We believe that we were right, back in the Fifties, to identify nuclear weapons as the immediate and major danger to civilization and indeed human life. We were right to demand British withdrawal from a nuclear strategy and to offer this as a positive political and moral initiative. We had to choose, and had always needed to choose, even in the worst period of Stalinism, between rival world political orders which, in the sheer weight of their military power, made any unambiguous choice virtually unbearable. That was perhaps the instinct of the simple call for unilateral nuclear disarmament: to establish a human choice where no fully supportable political choice existed.

In the subsequent development of the Cold War, this situation has radically changed. The movement for nuclear disarmament, like the movement for colonial freedom or against world hunger, can become political in new ways. For while the dangerous deadlock has remained in Europe, the active conflict—for the reasons we explained in our study of the new imperialism—has moved to the formerly colonial world. The war in

Vietnam is an outstanding and brutal example of the political strategy of the new imperialism. Just because this is now an interlocking and international system, it has passed beyond the phase of simple pressure or intervention against a recalcitrant or revolutionary ex-colonial society, and successive imperialist powers can take up the fight. And then what is wrong in the Vietnam War is not only that it is pitiless and brutal, calling forth, as it must in every humane person, an answering cry for peace. It is also that it is a war consciously fought by the United States as part of an international struggle: an international test case.

The Cold War, that is to say, has moved outwards: from old metropolitan Europe to the newly awaking continents. In Asia, the United States has built up a chain of allies and satellite powers on China's peripheries—Japan, South Korea, Taiwan, the Philippines, Thailand, Saigon, Pakistan. Indonesia is rapidly moving toward inclusion; Indian neutralism became unviable after Nehru's death and the Sino-Indian border dispute. In Latin America—where the United States has for long enjoyed an unbroken economic hegemony—an inter-American military command has come into existence; and the security of this sphere of influence is maintained by aid programs, by direct political intervention, and by extensive counterrevolutionary training. In Africa, U.S. military aid and capital poured in as the older colonial powers pulled out: the first ideological military confrontation here was in the Congo.

The consolidation of this worldwide system of economic and military imperialism was completed as the old European colonial powers withdrew, and after a brief period of liberation. In that interregnum, a neutralist bloc of nations emerged, and the term "nonalignment" seemed to have a relatively stable and meaningful value. In fact, the West remained the final arbiter as to what kinds of nonalignment were acceptable and what kinds were not: the use of regular and irregular military contingents from NATO countries by Tshombe and Mobutu in the Congo was "acceptable"; the request by Lumumba to the Russians for help in the transport of his troops was not. Thus, in effective terms, the West established a definition of what types of political regimes, what kinds of economic reforms, what style of foreign relations were "safe for democracy" in the Third World, and took the means—by direct economic and military pressure, and by indirect subversion—to make those definitions operative. As a result, nonalignment has become progressively illusory. In some cases—Vietnam, Venezuela, the Dominican

Republic—the United States has intervened directly. But the new imperialism does not require everywhere a direct political and military presence, as the older style of colonialism did. A measure of local autonomy can be "permitted," especially where the regimes are "friendly" or "sympathetic," that is, "pro-West" in character (for a country does not need to have internal democracy in order to be "safe for democracy"). But these regimes are "neither in full control of their major economic resources nor domestically secure in their foreign policy options." As Conor Cruise O'Brien put it: "Instead of thinking of a nonaligned Third World, it would be more realistic to think in terms of a worldwide capitalist economy of which the supposedly nonaligned countries form an integral part and, considered as a whole, a profitable part." This economic relationship is maintained within the framework of a global system of military and strategic containment which operates as powerfully upon Third World countries as the colonial brigade of former days. In recent years, American policy has become more activist, with direct political pressure, the training of counterrevolutionary forces by the CIA, economic blackmail, and large-scale war as its common techniques. The choice for the Third World countries has become increasingly polarized, as their fragile independence is eroded by economic weakness vis-à-vis the developed countries, by internal stress and external pressure—either to be within the global orbit of imperialism or against it. The rapid toppling of regimes in the Third World, and the "emergence" of more pro-Western governments in recent months—in Brazil, the Congo, Algeria, Indonesia, Ghana, the Dominican Republic, and Guyana—suggest that this hard-line imperialism has not been unsuccessful.

It is impossible to believe that, confronted with this situation in a pure form, the Left could take any position other than outright opposition. But the confusion of the Cold War has been consciously continued, with the characteristic substitution of China for Russia as the main enemy: China, of course, because it is the contemporary example of a successful Asian revolution. And, further, the complicated and deeply rooted alliances and institutions of the whole Cold War period provide a dense political reality which cannot be opposed by moderate policies, but requires an absolute and exposed decision: for or against. That is why we cannot confine our critique of current foreign policy to local amendments and qualifications. We have to reject the whole world-view, and the consequent alliances, on which it continues to be based. Our problems are not the last stage of Britain's withdrawal from an imperial position. They are a continuing stage, in what if unchecked will be a very long conflict, of Britain's participation in an international military alliance against the colonial revolution and its allies.

Thus our indictment of the Cold War cannot be separated from our indictment of the new imperialism. It is not only that some of the giant companies have annexed this political conflict as a base from which they can really plan, in the now enormously profitable military contracts. It is not only that our political and intellectual life has been penetrated, in a hundred discrete areas, by Cold War agencies like the CIA, which evades even rudimentary democratic controls, and recruits and operates the mercenaries of anticommunism. It is also that in the financial difficulties over sterling, and in the increasing penetration of the British economy by United States capital, pressure to support particular policies can be put on us directly, in ways not unlike those of the new colonialism and imperialism in the most backward parts of the world. This is why, again, we see Britain's crisis as single and integrated. The fight against imperialism on an issue like Vietnam is substantially linked with the fight against direction of our own economic and political policies not only by the Americans, but specifically by the international institutions of monopoly capital which include elements of our own society. In fighting anywhere, we are fighting everywhere.

THE LABOR LEFT

The major division in contemporary British politics is between acceptance and rejection of the new capitalism: its priorities, its methods, its versions of man and of the future. Yet this major division cannot be made clear in any general way, because its line runs somewhere down the middle of the Labour Party, and is continually blurred by the orientation of the party toward preparation for and recovery from elections.

The most urgent political need in Britain is to make this basic line evident, and to begin the long process of unambiguous struggle and argument at this decisive point.

With Labour out of office, it could always be supposed, by a majority even of socialists, that the line ran between the Labour and Conservative parties, so that the electoral struggle was also the political struggle. To win a general election was to win power for the Left. All socialist policies could, by inclusion, be carried forward by the Labour Party in Parliament. This cannot any longer be reasonably supposed, yet for many years it has determined the basic strategy of the Left. This or that resolution would be got through the party Conference. This or that man would be backed in the contest for the leadership. Whenever the line became blurred and the political struggle confused, things could be set right by this kind of action: getting Labour in and keeping Labour left.

We do not now say these efforts were wrong, though when they come to contradict each other, still giving political priority to Labour in Parliament when Conference decisions have been ignored and the nominees of the Left are part of this corrupt power, some change of the strategy is obviously necessary. Even while the efforts at internal change are being made, the limitations must be clearly seen. Thus we can welcome some of the stands and speeches made by Left Labour M.P.'s, but for all the courage and sanity of many individual members, what is being shown, as a whole process, is their subordination. It is not only that, within the terms of the new politics, such efforts can only—at the very best—attain to marginal successes, which it is then the role of the managers to direct and contain. It is also that a strategy which is wholly enclosed within the forms of Labourism is directing energies into the very machines which socialists should fight. By endorsing the illusion that it is in this place—and in this place alone—that politics occur, energies are diverted from more public arenas and more uncompromising confrontations. And a Labour Left strategy of this kind becomes, of necessity, involved in the same kind of machine politics, the same manipulation of committee votes in the names of thousands, the same confusion of the emptying institutions of the movement with the people in whose name they are conducted, as that of the managers whom they seek to displace.

The principal distinction between what can be called the "old" and the "new" Left—cutting across what is often an agreement on policies—is in just this question of the nature of political power, and so of relevant political action in this kind of society. For, just as the Labour Party has been a compromise between working-class objectives and the existing power structures at the national level, so the traditional Labour left has been a compromise between socialist objectives and the existing power structure at the party level.

The purpose of any New Left must be to end this compromise. We therefore declare our intention to end the system of consensus politics, by drawing the political line where it actually is, rather than where it might be thought convenient for election or traditional descriptions.

THE POLITICS OF THE FUTURE

The shape of contemporary socialism, and of a New Left, must then be apparent. There are always local opportunities for effective action and particular campaigns, within the quarrels of the machines and the System, and sometimes these arise from the very fact that adjustments are incomplete, so that margins for movement remain. All such opportunities, we believe, must be taken. But what we must build beyond this is a new kind of movement, which is defined by the fact that it is opposing a new political system, and that it cannot defeat it by electoral action alone. Thus we stop subordinating every issue, and every strategy, to electoral calculations and organizations.

Instead we say:

(1) The System cannot solve the major problems of the society. It is keeping people going by pretending the difficulties are temporary. They are in fact permanent. The System is not designed to give, and cannot give, to the majority of our people: rising production and full employment; real social security; a humane education; peace and disarmament. These are not its objectives, but they are the conditions of its survival.

(2) The System cannot identify or solve the new problems of the society. It has opted against social change, and substituted its rising curve on existing lines and inequalities. But it must then absorb or deflect new kinds of demands in a changing world. It cannot provide for the growing demands for meaning in work and leisure, for participation in actual communities, for an urban environment shaped by human priorities, for the entry of women into fuller equality, for personal liberation from the routines of living inside the machine. All it can offer are its fashionable gimmicks and substitutes, and these feed on themselves. In the face of dissent, apathy, and violence, it can offer only new manipulation, new forms of control and force, for it cannot conceive what indeed would end it—a responsible, cooperative, and equal society.

(3) The System cannot operate with genuinely conflicting political parties and movements, and so it must try to drain these of meaning, which in practice involves taking significance and values and participation away from many thousands of actual people. To take away from the Labour Party its tenacious idea of a new and better society; to take away from the trade unions their daily commitments to the improvement of the lives of their members: these are things it must try to do, to

fit the machine, but that it will fail to do, because people will not hand themselves over, bound hand and foot, ballot-slip, party and union card, to that kind of convenience.
(4) The System cannot, finally, stand the pressure of the contemporary world. It is the last dream of a local group: a way of preserving its structures of minority power against a world revolution, with which the needs of its own people, for peace and democracy, must be eventually ranged. Centered in its dying concepts of what the world should be like, it is being driven to war and massive rearmament even while it proclaims its own version of life as an endless, mild, hand-to-mouth paradise. This contradiction is already breaking it, and will continue to break it. It is the weak link in its otherwise plausible policies. It is the point where change will begin, and where we must be ready to push the change right through, until the System as a whole is dismantled.

We can therefore begin a campaign of a new kind: a campaign of needs and issues, against what we have shown to be a system. In the coming years, the adjustments and the failures of the System itself will provoke repeated struggles, on particular issues, representing the urgent needs and expectations of millions of people. We intend to take part, as allies, in all the social conflicts, of every kind, which then follow. We will see each conflict as an opportunity for explaining the character of the System which is cheating us, and so as a way of helping to change consciousness: to follow the needs and the feelings through until they reach the point of demands which the System can neither satisfy nor contain. What has been our weakness, that we have run separate campaigns in so many different social and political fields, can become our strength: that we are present in the society where the System and the political leadership are not. To be a socialist, now, is to be at the point where a firm is taken over by foreign capital; to be where profit and convenience are hurrying, threatening, discarding men; to be where a wage is fought for, or a reduction of hours; to be where a school or a hospital needs urgent improvement, or where a bus-service, a housing development, a local clinic needs to be fought through against the ordinary commercial and bureaucratic priorities; to be where Council rents are being raised during a standstill on wages; to be on a newspaper or magazine threatened with closure by the calculations of the advertisers and combine proprietors; to be a student expected to pass quietly through to a prescribed job with no share in the definition of his subject or in the government of his institution; to be a teacher struggling to maintain his ideals against a bureaucratic grading of children and a perpetual shortage of resources; to be a social worker, knowing that where people are in need there is always shortage—of skilled helpers, of building and equipment, of the necessary respect; to be out in the streets, in the rush of society, demanding attention for what is happening to the unregarded poor in our own and in other countries; to be breaking the system of human indifference and opposing the preparation, the complicity, the lies of war; to be in any or all of these places and conditions, and to connect, to explain what is actually happening, so that ordinary people can begin to take control of it.

Older definitions have failed, and with them the traditional agencies of socialist change. The political machines have sought to expropriate us of our political identity: we have no alternative but to withdraw our allegiance from the machines and resume our own initiatives. We are now in a period of transition, in which we will seek to unite socialists, whatever their present affiliations, in new common forms of organization: for education; for propaganda; for international discussions; for mutual consultation and support in all active campaigns and interventions. We say that we must improvise for ourselves the kinds of organizations appropriate to our own communities and our own work, while seeking at all times for ways of uniting them in a common strategy.

In this necessary process, we mean, like our opponents, to keep our options open. The existing party structure is under great strain, and the pressures can be expected to increase. We do not intend to make any premature move which would isolate the Left, or confuse its actual and potential supporters. At the same time, we mean what we say when we declare an end to tactics and to allegiances which are wholly enclosed within traditional organizational forms. If our analysis is right, then socialists must make their voices heard, again and again, not only in committee rooms and in conference halls, but among the growing majority of the people who feel no commitment to these forms. Already thousands of young men and women who share many of our objectives and whose internationalist conscience and immediate personal concern are more alert than those of their predecessors and elders, stand outside the Labour Party and refuse to give it the kind of allegiance it demands. Other existing organizations of the Left represent, in many cases, the same hardening shells of old situations, old bearings, and old strategies. What matters now, everywhere, is movement. To those who say that there is no future without changing the Labour Party, we reply that we shall only change it by refusing to accept its machine definitions and demands, and that the real change required is so large and so difficult that it can only come about as part of very much wider changes of consciousness, and as a result of manifold struggles in many areas of life.

We shall generate our own pressures on the System as it now stands. But there will be other kinds of pressure that we are taking into account. The attempt to absorb the Labour Party and the unions into new capitalism in any permanent way will bring the movements to breaking point, sooner or later. Already, relations between the official Labour Party and the unions are under great strain. And behind these developments, a remodeled Conservative Party, of an aggressively new capitalist kind, is getting ready to take over when the present Labour government has done the necessary preparatory work.

Meanwhile, the important development of nationalist parties in Wales and Scotland is itself a response to the centralized politics of the System, and adds a new variation. If Britain joined the Common Market, there would be a radical crossing of political traditions and affiliations, out of which change would certainly come. As things stand now and can reasonably be foreseen, the formal party-political structure is not stable. Further, though the major parties will do all they can to prevent it, there is a strong and increasingly unanswerable case for electoral reform, to make representation more faithful to actual voting. Looking ahead, we see many possible opportunities for the recovery of active democracy, and it will be our duty as socialists both to respond to these opportunities and to make new ones.

The period will be confusing and testing, but we believe that by making a position clear now, we can take an effective part in a realignment of British politics. What we are defining is a socialism of the immediately coming generation, an emerging political process, rather than the formalities of a process that is already, as democratic practice, beginning to break up and disappear. We are looking to the political structure of the rest of the century, rather than to the forms which now embody the past and confuse recognition of the present.

This manifesto is intended to begin a sustained campaign. It is of course a challenge, and it asks for a response. There are thousands who share our general analysis and who stand in our situation. We invite their active support.

The Concept of the Left

LESZEK KOLAKOWSKI

In 1966, Gomulka expelled Kolakowski from the Polish Communist Party for having defended the 1956 rising which returned Gomulka to power. He has since been dismissed from the philosophy department at the University of Warsaw.

The story is by this time too familiar for comment. We need only observe that what the United States does to Iran, Guatemala, and Vietnam, the U.S.S.R approximates in Poland, Hungary, and Czechoslovakia, and that what the bloc countries do to their leading intellectuals, the United States approximates with dozens of its young professors. The signature of our period lies in part in the honor which surrounds a certain kind of defeat.

Throughout the collection from which this essay is taken, Toward a Marxist Humanism, *Kolakowski's constant meditation—cool, poised, never declining to bitterness—is upon precisely this impasse. In his gentleness which is never sentimental, his detachment which is never disengaged, his solitude which is never aloof, we may recognize the* real *Camus.*

EVERY WORK OF MAN is a compromise between the material and the tool. Tools are never quite equal to their tasks, and none is beyond improvement. Aside from differences in human skill, the tool's imperfection and the material's resistance together set the limits that determine the end product. But the tool must fit the material, no matter how remotely, if it isn't to produce a monstrosity. You cannot properly clean teeth with an oil drill or perform brain operations with a pencil. Whenever such attempts have been made the results have always been less than satisfactory.

THE LEFT AS NEGATION

Social revolutions are a compromise between utopia and historical reality. The tool of the revolution is utopia, and the material is the social reality on which one wants to impose a new form. And the tool must to some degree fit the substance if the results are not to become ludicrous.

There is, however, an essential difference between work on physical objects and work on history; for the latter, which is the substance, also creates the tools used to give this substance shape. Utopias which try to give history a new form are themselves a product of history, while history itself remains anonymous. That is why even when the tools turn out to be grossly unsuited to the material, no one is to blame, and it would be senseless to hold anyone responsible.

On the other hand, history is a human product. Although no individual is responsible for the results of the historical process, still each is responsible for his personal involvement in it. Therefore each is also responsible for his role in fashioning the intellectual tools used upon reality in order to change it—for accepting or rejecting a given utopia and the means employed to realize it.

To construct a utopia is always an act of negation toward an existing reality, a desire to transform it. But *negation is not the opposite of construction—it is only the opposite of affirming existing conditions*. That is why it makes little sense to reproach someone for committing a destructive rather than a constructive act, because every act of construction is necessarily a negation of the existing order. At most, you may reproach him for not supporting the reality that exists and for wanting to change it; or, on the other hand, for accepting it without qualification, without seeking change; or, finally, for seeking harmful changes. But a negative position is only the opposite of a conservative attitude toward the world, negation in itself being merely a desire for change. The difference between destructive and constructive work lies in a verbal mystification stemming from the adjectives used to describe the changes, which are considered either good or bad. Every change is, in fact, an act both negative and positive at one and the same time, and the opposite only of an affirmation of things as they are. To blow up a house is just as constructive as to build one—and at the same time just as negative. Of course, this does not mean that it is all the same whether one destroys or builds a house. The difference between the two acts is that the first, in most instances, works to the detriment of the people involved, and the second is almost always to their benefit. The opposite of blowing up a house is not to build a new house but to retain the existing one.

This observation will serve to lead to conclusions whose aim is to define more closely the meaning we give to the concept of the social Left.

The Left—and this is its unchangeable and indispensable quality, though by no means its only one—is a movement of negation toward the existing world. For this very reason it is, as we have seen, a constructive force. It is, simply, a quest for change.

That is why *the Left rejects the objection that its program is only a negative and not a constructive one.*

The Left can cope with reproaches directed at the potential harm or utility that may arise from its negations. It can also contend with the conservative attitude that wants to perpetuate things as they are. It will not defend itself, however, against the accusation of being purely negative, because every constructive program is negative, and vice versa. A Left without a constructive program cannot, by that token, have a negative one, since these two terms are synonymous. If there is no program, there is at the same time no negation, that is, no opposite of the Left—in other words, conservatism.

UTOPIA AND THE LEFT

But the act of negation does not in itself define the Left, for there are movements with retrogressive goals. Hitlerism was the negation of the Weimar Republic, but this does not make it leftist. In countries not controlled by the Right, an extreme counterrevolutionary movement is always a negation of the existing order. Thus the Left is defined by its negation, *but not only by this;* it is also defined by the direction of this negation, in fact, by the nature of its utopia.

I use the word "utopia" deliberately and not in the derogatory sense that expresses the absurd notion that all social changes are pipe dreams. By utopia I mean a state of social consciousness, a mental counterpart to the social movement striving for radical change in the world—a counterpart itself inadequate to these changes and merely reflecting them in an idealized and obscure form. It endows the real movement with the sense of realizing an ideal born in the realm of pure spirit and not in *current* historical experience. Utopia is, therefore, a mysterious consciousness of an actual historical tendency. As long as this tendency lives only a clandestine existence, without finding expression in mass social movements, it gives birth to utopias in the narrower sense, that is, to individually constructed models of the world, as it *should* be. But in time utopia becomes actual social consciousness; it invades the consciousness of a mass movement and becomes one of its essential driving forces. Utopia, then, crosses over from the domain of theoretical and moral thought into the field of practical thinking, and itself begins to govern human action.

Still, this does not make it realizable. Utopia always remains a phenomenon of the world of thought; even when backed by the power of a social movement and, more importantly, even when it enters its consciousness, it is inadequate, going far beyond the movement's potentials. It is, in a way, "pathological" (in a loose sense of the word, for utopian consciousness is in fact a natural social phenomenon). It is a warped attempt to impose upon a historically realistic movement goals that are beyond history.

However—and this is fundamental to an understanding of the internal contradictions of left-wing movements—the Left cannot do without a utopia. The Left gives forth utopias just as the pancreas discharges insulin—by virtue of an innate law. Utopia is the striving for changes which "realistically" cannot be brought about by immediate action, which lie beyond the forseeable future and defy planning. Still, utopia is a tool of action upon reality and of planning social activity.

A utopia, if it proves so remote from reality that the wish to enforce it would be grotesque, would lead to a monstrous deformation, to socially harmful changes threatening the freedom of man. The Left, if it succeeds, would then turn into its opposite —the Right. But then, too, the utopia would cease to be a utopia and become a slogan justifying every current practice.

On the other hand, the Left cannot renounce utopia; it cannot give up goals that are, for the time being, unattainable, but that impart meaning to social changes. I am speaking of the social Left as a whole, for though the concept of the Left is relative—one is a leftist only in comparison with something, and not in absolute terms—still the extreme element of every Left is a revolutionary movement. The revolutionary movement is a catch-all for all the ultimate demands made upon existing society. It is a total negation of the existing system and, therefore, also a total program. A total program is, in fact, a utopia. A utopia is a necessary component of the revolutionary Left, and the latter is a necessary product of the social Left as a whole.

Yet why is a utopia a condition of all revolutionary movements? Because much historical experience, more or less buried in the social consciousness, tells us that goals unattainable now will never be reached unless they are articulated when they are still unattainable. It may well be that the impossible at a given moment can become possible only by being stated at a time when it is impossible. To cite an example, a series of reforms will never attain the goals of revolution, a consistent reform party will never imperceptibly be transformed into the fulfillment of a revolution. *The existence of a utopia as a utopia is the necessary prerequisite for its eventually ceasing to be a utopia.*

A revolutionary movement cannot be born simultaneously with the act of revolution, for without a revolutionary movement to precede it the revolution could never come about. As long as the revolutionary act has not been accomplished, or is not indisputably and clearly evident, it is a utopia. For today's Spanish proletariat a social revolution is a utopia; but the Spanish proletariat will never achieve a revolution if it does not proclaim it when it is impossible. This is why tradition plays such an important role in the revolutionary movement: the movement would never know any victories if it had not in previous phases suffered inevitable defeats—if it had not initiated revolutionary activity when the historical situation precluded success.

The desire for revolution cannot be born only when the situation is ripe, because among the conditions for this ripeness are the revolutionary demands made of an unripe reality. The continuous influence of social consciousness is one of the necessary conditions for the maturation of history to the point of radical change; utopia is a prerequisite of social upheavals, just as unrealistic efforts are the precondition of realistic ones. That is the reason why revolutionary consciousness cannot be satisfied with mere participation in changes already taking place; it cannot merely follow events, but must precede them at a time when they are neither planned nor anticipated.

Therefore—and this is an elementary practical conclusion—*the Left doesn't mind being reproached for striving for a utopia.* It may have to defend itself against the accusation that the content of its utopia is damaging to society, but it need not defend itself against the charge of being utopian.

The Right, as a conservative force, needs no utopia; its essence is the affirmation of existing conditions—a fact and not a utopia—or else the desire to revert to a state which was once an accomplished fact. The Right strives to idealize actual conditions, not to change them. What it needs is fraud, not utopia.

The Left cannot give up utopia because it is a real force even when it is merely a utopia. The sixteenth-century revolt of the German peasants, the Babouvist movement, and the Paris Commune were all utopian. As it turned out, without such utopian activities no nonutopian, progressive social changes would have taken place. Obviously, it does not follow that the task of the Left is to undertake extreme actions in every historical situation. All we are saying is that to condemn utopia for the mere fact that it is a utopia is rightist, conservative, and hampers the prospects of ever creating a utopia. In any event, we are not at the moment formulating social tasks. We are considering the concept of the Left completely in the abstract, trying to ascertain and not to postulate. Since the Left is as "normal" a social phenomenon as the Right, and progressive social movements are as normal as reactionary ones, it is equally normal for the Left, which is a minority, to be persecuted by the Right.

THE LEFT AND SOCIAL CLASSES

The concept of the Left remains unclear to this day. Although only about a hundred and fifty years old, it has acquired universal historical dimensions and is applied to ancient history by virtue of a diffusion of meaning common to all languages. Broadly used, the term has a practical function, but its meaning becomes very obscure, more sensed than understood. One thing is certain: it is easier to say which movements, programs, and attitudes are Left in relation to others than to determine where the Left ends and the Right begins in the political power relationship within society's total structure. We speak of a Left within Hitler's party, but that does not, of course, mean that the German Right was restricted to the party Right and that everything else, including the left wing of that party, was the Left in an absolute sense. Society cannot be divided into a Right and a Left. A leftist attitude toward one movement can be linked with a rightist attitude toward another. It is only in their relative meanings that these words make sense.

But what do we mean when we say a movement or an attitude is Left in relation to another? More specifically, which aspect of the concept of the Left is valid in all social situations? For example, what do we mean when we speak of the Left in the Radical Party of France, or of the social-democratic, Catholic, or communist Left? Is there some common element in the word used in such varied contexts? Or are we simply stating that every political situation reveals some human activity we either approve or find to be the less repugnant, and which we therefore call "the Left"? (I say "we call" because the Left draws the dividing line between the Left and the Right, while the Right fights this division systematically—and in vain, for the Left's self-definition is strong enough to define the Right and, in any event, to establish the existence of the demarcation line.)

No doubt because it has taken on a positive aura, the term "Left" is often appropriated by reactionary groups. For example, there is the "European Left," a political annex of the European Coal and Steel Community. So the mere use of the word does not define the Left. We must look for other signposts to help us fix our position in this murky area. Slogans like "freedom" and "equality" belong, of course, to the tradition of the Left; but they lost their meaning once they became universal catchwords to which everyone attaches his own arbitrary interpretation. As time passes, the Left must define itself ever more precisely. For the more it influences social consciousness, the more its slogans take on a positive aura, the more they are appropriated by the Right and lose their defined meaning. Nobody today opposes such concepts as "freedom" and "equality"; that is why they can become implements of fraud, suspect unless they are explained. What is worse, the word "socialism" has also acquired many meanings.

Naturally, it is quite easy to define the Left in general terms, as we can define "progress." But general definitions are necessarily misleading and difficult to apply in concrete discussions. For example, we can say that "Leftness" is the degree of participation in the process of social development that strives to eliminate all conditions in which the possibility of satisfying human needs is obstructed by social relations. From such a definition we derive a certain number of equally general slogans that are too universally acceptable to be useful in fixing political demarcations. The concepts of the Left, of progress, and of freedom are full of internal contradictions; political disputes do not arise from the mere acceptance or rejection of the concepts.

Therefore, rather than construct an easy though ineffective general concept of the Left applicable to all eras, let us accept existing social reality as a fact and look for the basic conflicts that define current history. These are, first of all, class conflicts and, secondarily, political ones. However, the political battle is not completely identical with the pattern of class relations; it is not a carbon copy of them transposed to relations between political parties. This is so because class divisions are not the only kind, and classes themselves are becoming more, rather than less, complicated because they are split from within by nationality or ideology. Finally, there are political divisions, insofar as they assume diverse forms of autonomy. Under these conditions political life cannot reflect class conflicts purely and directly but, on the contrary, ever more indirectly and confusedly. As a matter of fact, it was never otherwise—if it had been, all historical conflicts would have been resolved centuries ago. That is why the statement that it must be in the interest of the working class to belong to the Left does not always hold true. On the one hand, it is characteristic of the Left to try not to realize men's wishes against their will, nor to force them to accept benefits they do not desire. On the other hand, the working class of a given country may be greatly influenced by nationalism, yet the Left will not support nationalistic demands; elsewhere, the working class may have deep roots in a religious tradition, yet the Left is a secular movement. Even real immediate interests of the working class can be in opposition to the demands of the Left. For example, for a long time the English workers benefited from colonial exploitation—and yet the Left is an enemy of colonialism.

That is why the Left cannot be defined by saying it will always, in every case, support every demand of the working class, or that it is always on the side of the majority. The Left must define itself on the level of ideas, conceding that in many instances it will find itself in the minority. Even though in today's world there is no leftist attitude independent of the struggle for the rights of the working class, though no leftist position can be realized outside the class structure, and though only the struggle of the oppressed can make the Left a material force, nevertheless the Left must be defined in intellectual, and not class, terms. This presupposes that concrete intellectual life is not and cannot be an exact replica of class interests.

On this basis, we can set forth certain characteristics of the position of the Left in various social orders:

In capitalist countries the fight of the Left is to abolish all social privilege. In noncapitalist countries, it is to remove privileges that have grown out of noncapitalist conditions.

In capitalist countries the Left fights all forms of colonial oppression. In noncapitalist ones, it demands the abolition of inequalities, discrimination, and the exploitation of certain countries by others.

In capitalist countries the Left struggles against limitations on freedom of speech and expression. It does so also in noncapitalist lands. In one and the other the Left fights all the contradictions of freedom that arise in *both kinds* of social conditions: how far can one push the demand for tolerance without turning against the idea of tolerance itself? How can one guarantee that tolerance will not lead to the victory of forces that will strangle the principle of tolerance? This is the great problem of all leftist movements. It is also true, obviously, that the Left can make mistakes and act ineffectively, and thus engender a situation that is inimical to itself. However, it is not faulty tactics that are the distinguishing feature of the Left, for, as we have said, its criteria are established on an ideological plane.

In capitalist countries the Left strives to secularize social life. This is also true in noncapitalist countries.

In capitalist countries the destruction of all racism is an essential part of the Left's position. This is so in noncapitalist lands as well.

Everywhere the Left fights against the encroachment of any type of obscurantism in social life; it fights for the victory of rational thought, which is by no means a luxury reserved for the intellectuals, but an integral component of social progress in this century. Without it any form of progress becomes a parody of its own premises.

Finally, under both systems, the Left does not exclude the use of force when necessary, though the use of force is not an invention of the Left, but rather an unavoidable form of social existence. The Left accepts the antinomy of force, but only as an antinomy and not as a gift of fate. Everywhere the Left is ready to compromise with historical facts, but it rejects ideological compromises; that is, it does not abdicate the right to proclaim the basic tenets of its existence regardless of its political tactics.

The Left is free of sacred feelings; it has no sense of sanctity toward any existing historical situation. It takes a position of permanent revisionism toward reality, just as the Right assumes an attitude of opportunism in respect to the world as it is. The Right is the embodiment of the inertia of historical reality—that is why it is as eternal as the Left.

In both systems the Left strives to base its prospects on the experience and evolutionary tendencies of history; whereas the Right is the expression of capitulation to the situation of the moment. For this reason the Left can have a political ideology, while the Right has nothing but tactics.

Within the context of both systems, the Left knows that every human freedom satisfies a specific need, but that there is also a need for freedom as such.

The Left does not fear history. It believes in the flexibility of social relations and of human nature—in the possibility of changing them. Within both camps it rejects all humility vis-à-vis existing situations, authorities, doctrines, the majority, prejudgments, or material pressures.

In both, the Left—not excluding the use of force, not ashamed of it, and not calling it "upbringing" or "benevolence" or "care for children," etc.—nevertheless rejects any means of political warfare that lead to moral consequences which contradict its premises.

All this time I have been describing the Left as a certain ideological and moral attitude. For the Left is not a single, defined political movement, or party, or group of parties. The Left is a characteristic which to a greater or lesser degree can serve particular movements or parties, as well as given individuals or human activities, attitudes, and ideologies. One can be leftist from one point of view and not from another. There rarely occur political movements that are totally leftist in every aspect throughout the entire course of their existence. A man of the Left can participate in the political struggle and be a politician in a leftist party, but refuse to approve actions and opinions that are clearly inimical to a leftist attitude. Which does not mean, obviously, that the leftist position does not lead to internal conflicts and contradictions.

For these reasons the Left, as such and as a whole, cannot be an organized political movement. The Left is always to the left in certain respects with relation to some political movements. Every party has its left wing, a current which is farther to the left than the rest of the party in regard to some trait that can be cited as an example. Still, this does not mean that all the leftist elements of all parties taken together form a single movement, or that they are more closely allied to each other than they are to the party that gave birth to them. This would be so if they fulfilled all the requirements of being Left in every aspect; but in that case they would not have been segments of so many diverse parties with such varied programs to begin with. The left wing of the Christian Democratic parties has, as a rule, infinitely more in common with them than with the socialist Left, yet it is the Christian Democratic Left on this very basis. Its "Leftness" may be shown by a stand on one or another actual political problem that, in the particular instance, brings it nearer the left of other parties—for example, a condemnation of colonialism or racism. On the other hand, the demands of the Left are met to varying degrees by different parties, which for this reason are called more or less leftist.

THE LEFT AND COMMUNISM IN POLAND

Can one speak of a pure party of the Left, and if so, when? Is the Communist Party one? Since we cannot at this time define all the Communist parties, let us apply this question to the Polish Party.

For a long time the division into a Party Left and Right did not exist, although some members were more or less to the left. It did not exist because the Party was deprived of any real political life, because its ideology did not grow out of its own historical experience but was to a large degree imposed upon it regardless of experience. The division into a Left and a Right was drawn only when the political life of the Party came into being.

The split took place according to positions on the problems that always divide a movement into a Left and a Right. The Party Left was made up of those who fought to abolish all forms of privilege in social life, to recognize the principle of equality in dealings among nations, and to oppose local and foreign nationalism, reserving the right to call it by its real name of nationalism. The Left stands for the abolition, without chicanery, of all kinds of anti-Semitism in Poland, for freedom of speech and discussion, for *victory over dogma* and over dull, doctrinaire, or else magical thinking in political life, for legality in public relations, for the maximum increase in the role of the working class within the system of government, for the liquidation of the lawlessness of the police. It fights against calling crimes "communism" and gangsters "communists"—and against a thousand other things.

I am listing these items summarily, without going into specifics, only to show that the direction of the changes intended to lead to the triumph of socialist democracy was inspired in the Party by its Left, whose demands on all vital points are included in what we call a leftist position. The Party Right consists of the forces of Stalinist inertia, defending a system based on principles that renounce Polish sovereignty in favor of a foreign nationalism. It supports the dictatorship of doctrinaire schemas in intellectual life, the dictatorship of the police in public life, and military dictatorship in economic life. It suppresses freedom of speech and uses the terminology of government by the people to conceal government by a political apparatus that disregards both the opinion of the public and its needs. The forces of Stalinism within the Party were and are a concentration of all the basic characteristics that define the Right, conservatism, and reaction.

However, the Left in the Polish Communist Party finds itself in a peculiar position, in which political tendencies do not cover a single unbroken gamut "from left to right," but abound in complications. The forces of the Left stand between two rightist tendencies: the reaction within the Party, and traditional reaction. This is a new historical development, awareness of which has arisen only in the past few years. It is as yet a very restricted phenomenon, but its implications are international. We will refrain from describing the historical causes of this situation, which in a certain phase of its development created a crisis in the communist movement, and simply state that the New Left appeared within the movement when it became apparent that a New Right existed. We will not at this time take up the question of just how the Old Left degenerated and survived in the form of a Right—a process of which the history of Stalinism furnishes an instructive example—but it does not seem that this process was caused by the mere fact of the Left's coming to power. That is, it does not seem that the Left can exist only in a position of opposition, or that the possession of power is incompatible with the nature of the Left and leads inevitably to its downfall.

For although the negation of reality is part of the nature of the Left, it does not follow necessarily that reality must always be contrary to the demands of the Left. History, it is true, provides countless experiences that seem to speak for such a view and tempt us to see the Left as condemned to be an "eternal opposition." Yet over the years history has witnessed many setbacks to demands (for example, equality before the law) that subsequently, after centuries of suffering and defeat, became reality. Love of martyrdom and heroics is as alien to the

Left as opportunism in a current situation or renunciation of utopian goals. The Left protests against the existing world, but it does not long for a void. It is an explosive charge that disrupts the stability of social life, but it is not a movement toward nothingness.

THE WEAKNESSES OF THE LEFT

The main weakness of the Left was not that it grew out of negation, but that its negation attained only the level of *moral protest* and not of practical thought. A leftist attitude that stops at the stage of moral experience has little practical effect. "Bleeding-heartism" is not a political position.

Another trait, one that was unavoidable in our circumstances, was that the Left could not be an organized movement but only an unclear, fragmented, negative consciousness opposed to the Right, which was bound by no scruples of loyalty regarding the formation of splinter factions within the Party. Thus the Left did not become a political movement in the true sense, but merely the sum total of spontaneous moral positions.

One weakness of the Left arose from the regressive circumstances of the international situation, the details of which I won't go into but which distinctly favored rightist activities.

Other weaknesses of the Left were those elements of the immediate situation from which the efforts of the Right could draw strength. The Right has no scruples about using every kind of demagogy, every political and ideological slogan that will enable it to dominate the situation of the moment. When necessary, it makes use of anti-Semitism to gain a certain number of allies from the bigots within or outside the party. The Right is primarily after power. In the fight for power (which, for example, it does not possess in Poland today) it is prepared to advance any leftist slogans that can count on popular appeal. Let us speak openly: contempt for ideology is the strength of the Right because it allows for greater flexibility in practice and for the arbitrary use of any verbal façade that will facilitate the seizure of power. The Right is backed not only by the inertia of old customs and institutions, but also by the power of the lie; true, only a little way, but far enough to enable it to master the situation. At a given moment these ideological slogans are exposed as tactical imposture; but the trick is to make sure this moment comes only after the situation is in hand and the police are at one's disposal. That is why it is important for the Left to have available at all times criteria of recognition in the form of attitudes toward those actual political matters which, for one reason or another, force the Right to reveal itself for what it is. Today such criteria exist chiefly in the domain of international affairs.

The Left was also weakened by the fact that the general social protest against the compromised methods of the government was too often linked with reactionary demands unacceptable to the Left. But at that stage of its development, the Left was not strong enough to assume leadership of this protest.

As a result of these circumstances, the Left (on an international scale) could not help but be defeated. Nevertheless, if it is to exist, the Left must above all be aware of the danger of its *ideological* position.

The danger lies in its double exposure to two forms of rightist pressure. The Left must be particularly alert to its need to define its special position as *constantly and simultaneously* opposed to both those forces. It must clearly and continuously proclaim its negative stand against both rightist currents, of which one is the expression of Stalinist inertia and the other of the inertia of capitalism in its most backward and obscurantist cast. The Left is in grave danger if it directs its criticism toward only one pressure, for it thus blurs its political demarcations. Its position must be expressed in simultaneous negation. The Left must oppose Polish nationalism as adamantly as it does foreign nationalisms that threaten Poland. It must take the same clear rational attitude toward both the sclerotic religiosity of the Stalinist version of Marxism and the obscurantism of the clergy. It must simultaneously reject socialist phraseology as a façade for police states and democratic phraseology as a disguise for bourgeois rule. Only thus can the Left retain its separate, distinct position, which is that of a minority. Nevertheless, the Left does not desire to become a majority at any price.

In the current situation, the Left's greatest claim is ideological. To be more precise, it is to differentiate exactly between ideology and *current political tactics*. The Left does not refuse to compromise with reality as long as compromises are so labeled. It will always counteract any attempt to bend ideology to the demands of the moment, to temporarily necessary concessions, to tactics. While the Left realizes that on occasion it is powerless in the face of crime, it refuses to call crime a "blessing."

This is definitely not a trivial or secondary matter. A political party that does not rely on an authentic ideological base can exist for a long time in a state of vegetation, but it will collapse like a house of cards if confronted by difficulties. A case in point is the Hungarian Party. A communist movement that subordinates its ideology to immediate tactics is destined for degeneration and defeat. It can exist only with the support of the power and the repressive capacity of the State. The intellectual and moral values of communism are not luxurious ornaments of its activity, but the conditions of its existence. That is why it is difficult to create leftist socialism in a reactionary country. A communist movement whose sole form of existence is sheer tactics and which permits the loss of its original intellectual and moral premises ceases to be a leftist movement. Hence the word "socialism" has come to have more than one meaning, and is no longer synonymous with the word "Left." And this is why a regeneration of the concept of the Left is necessary—also so that we can delimit the meaning of socialist slogans. We therefore propose the term "leftist socialism."

Without surrendering any of the premises of its existence, the Left is obviously ready to make alliances with any groups, no matter how small, and with all "leftist foci" wherever they may be. But it must refuse to support rightist situations and activities; or if compelled to do so under duress, it must call this "duress" and refrain from seeking ideological justification for its actions.

The Left knows that these demands merely seem modest, and realizes they may lead to new defeats—but such defeats are more fruitful than capitulation. For this reason the Left is not afraid of being a minority, which is what it is on an international scale. It knows that history itself calls forth in every situation a leftist side which is as necessary a component of social life as its aspect of conservatism and inertia.

The contradictions of social life cannot be liquidated; this means that the history of man will exist as long as man itself. And the Left is the fermenting factor in even the most hardened mass of the historical present. Even though it is at times weak and invisible, it is nonetheless the dynamite of hope that blasts the dead load of ossified systems, institutions, customs, intellectual habits, and closed doctrines. The Left unites those dispersed and often hidden atoms whose movement is, in the last analysis, what we call progress.

PART TWO:

The Revolutionary Frontier

Algeria Unveiled

FRANTZ FANON

Fanon, says Adolfo Gilly, "was not a Marxist." If so, so much the worse for Marxism.

Marxism is only incidentally a technical method; it is not a technique at all, or pliers with which to pull history's teeth. And as much as it is a way of seeing history, it is equally a way of feeling about it. The compassionate grasp of social process and of the divided collectivity of mankind: Marx.

Fanon: Beginning with the Algerian woman's veil, he ends with a description of the modern confrontation which, even if only implicitly, is still all but total, encompassing not only the native's mind and the revolutionary's means, but the sickness of the master culture, too. All by itself, this chapter from A Dying Colonialism[1] *would have made Fanon a permanent Marxist requirement. Its relevance for the current women's liberation movement does not need comment.*

THE WAY PEOPLE clothe themselves, together with the traditions of dress and finery that custom implies, constitutes the most distinctive form of a society's uniqueness, that is to say the one that is the most immediately perceptible. Within the general pattern of a given costume, there are of course always modifications of detail, innovations which in highly developed societies are the mark of fashion. But the effect as a whole remains homogeneous, and great areas of civilization, immense cultural regions, can be grouped together on the basis of original, specific techniques of men's and women's dress.

It is by their apparel that types of society first become known,

[1] New York: Monthly Review Press, 1965.

whether through written accounts and photographic records or motion pictures. Thus, there are civilizations without neckties, civilizations with loin-cloths, and others without hats. The fact of belonging to a given cultural group is usually revealed by clothing traditions. In the Arab world, for example, the veil worn by women is at once noticed by the tourist. One may remain for a long time unaware of the fact that a Moslem does not eat pork or that he denies himself daily sexual relations during the month of Ramadan, but the veil worn by the women appears with such constancy that it generally suffices to characterize Arab society.

In the Arab Maghreb, the veil belongs to the clothing traditions of the Tunisian, Algerian, Moroccan, and Libyan national societies. For the tourist and the foreigner, the veil demarcates both Algerian society and its feminine components.[2] In the case of the Algerian man, on the other hand, regional modifications can be noted: the *fez* in urban centers, turbans and *djellabas*[3] in the countryside. The masculine garb allows a certain margin of choice, a modicum of heterogeneity. The woman seen in her white veil unifies the perception that one has of Algerian feminine society. Obviously what we have here is a uniform which tolerates no modification, no variant.[4]

[2] We do not here consider rural areas where the woman is often unveiled. Nor do we take into account the Kabyle woman, who, except in the large cities, never uses a veil. For the tourist who rarely ventures into the mountains, the Arab woman is first of all one who wears a veil. This originality of the Kabyle woman constitutes, among others, one of the themes of colonialist propaganda bringing out the opposition between Arabs and Berbers. Such studies, devoted to the analysis of psychological modifications, neglect considerations that are properly historical. We shall presently take up this other aspect of Algerian reality in action. Here we shall content ourselves with pointing out that the Kabyle women, in the course of 130 years of domination, have developed other defense mechanisms with respect to the occupier. During the war of liberation their forms of action have likewise assumed absolutely original aspects.

[3] *Djellaba*—a long, hooded cloak. (Translator's note)

[4] One phenomenon deserves to be recalled. In the course of the Moroccan people's struggle for liberation, and chiefly in the cities, the white veil was replaced by the black veil. This important modification is explained by the Moroccan women's desire to express their attachment to His Majesty Mohammed V. It will be remembered that it was immediately after the exiling of the King of Morocco that the black veil, a sign of mourning, made its appearance. It is worth noting that black, in Moroccan or Arab society, has never expressed mourning or affliction. As a combat measure, the adoption of black is a response to the desire to exert a symbolic pressure on the occupier, and hence to make a logical choice of one's own symbols.

The *haïk*[5] very clearly demarcates the Algerian colonized society. It is of course possible to remain hesitant before a little girl, but all uncertainty vanishes at the time of puberty. With the veil, things become well-defined and ordered. The Algerian woman, in the eyes of the observer, is unmistakably "she who hides behind a veil."

We shall see that this veil, one of the elements of the traditional Algerian garb, was to become the bone of contention in a grandiose battle, on account of which the occupation forces were to mobilize their most powerful and most varied resources, and in the course of which the colonized were to display a surprising force of inertia. Taken as a whole, colonial society, with its values, its areas of strength, and its philosophy, reacts to the veil in a rather homogeneous way. The decisive battle was launched before 1954, more precisely during the early 1930's. The officials of the French administration in Algeria, committed to destroying the people's originality, and under instructions to bring about the disintegration, at whatever cost, of forms of existence likely to evoke a national reality directly or indirectly, were to concentrate their efforts on the wearing of the veil, which was looked upon at this juncture as a symbol of the status of the Algerian woman. Such a position is not the consequence of a chance intuition. It is on the basis of the analyses of sociologists and ethnologists that the specialists in so-called native affairs and the heads of the Arab Bureaus coordinated their work. At an initial stage, there was a pure and simple adoption of the well-known formula, "Let's win over the women and the rest will follow." This definition of policy merely gave a scientific coloration to the "discoveries" of the sociologists.

Beneath the patrilineal pattern of Algerian society, the specialists described a structure of matrilineal essence. Arab society has often been presented by Westerners as a formal society in which outside appearances are paramount. The Algerian woman, an intermediary between obscure forces and the group, appeared in this perspective to assume a primordial importance. Behind the visible, manifest patriarchy, the more significant existence of a basic matriarchy was affirmed. The role of the Algerian mother, that of the grandmother, the aunt, and the "old woman," were inventoried and defined.

This enabled the colonial administration to define a precise political doctrine: "If we want to destroy the structure of Algerian society, its capacity for resistance, we must first of all

[5] The *haik*—the Arab name for the big square veil worn by Arab women, covering the face and the whole body. (Translator's note.)

conquer the women; we must go and find them behind the veil where they hide themselves and in the houses where the men keep them out of sight." It is the situation of woman that was accordingly taken as the theme of action. The dominant administration solemnly undertook to defend this woman, pictured as humiliated, sequestered, cloistered . . . It described the immense possibilities of woman, unfortunately transformed by the Algerian man into an inert, demonetized, indeed dehumanized object. The behavior of the Algerian was very firmly denounced and described as medieval and barbaric. With infinite science, a blanket indictment against the "sadistic and vampirish" Algerian attitude toward women was prepared and drawn up. Around the family life of the Algerian, the occupier piled up a whole mass of judgments, appraisals, reasons, accumulated anecdotes and edifying examples, thus attempting to confine the Algerian within a circle of guilt.

Mutual aid societies and societies to promote solidarity with Algerian women sprang up in great number. Lamentations were organized. "We want to make the Algerian ashamed of the fate that he metes out to women." This was a period of effervescence, of putting into application a whole technique of infiltration, in the course of which droves of social workers and women directing charitable works descended on the Arab quarters.

The indigent and famished women were the first to be besieged. Every kilo of semolina distributed was accompanied by a dose of indignation against the veil and the cloister. The indignation was followed up by practical advice. Algerian women were invited to play "a functional, capital role" in the transformation of their lot. They were pressed to say no to a centuries-old subjection. The immense role they were called upon to play was described to them. The colonial administration invested great sums in this combat. After it had been posited that the woman constituted the pivot of Algerian society, all efforts were made to obtain control over her. The Algerian, it was assured, would not stir, would resist the task of cultural destruction undertaken by the occupier, would oppose assimilation, so long as his woman had not reversed the stream. In the colonialist program, it was the woman who was given the historic mission of shaking up the Algerian man. Converting the woman, winning her over to the foreign values, wrenching her free from her status, was at the same time achieving a real power over the man and attaining a practical, effective means of destructuring Algerian culture.

Still today, in 1959, the dream of a total domestication of Algerian society by means of "unveiled women aiding and sheltering the occupier" continues to haunt the colonial authorities.[6]

The Algerian men, for their part, are a target of criticism for their European comrades, or more officially for their bosses. There is not a European worker who does not sooner or later, in the give and take of relations on the job site, the shop, or the office, ask the Algerian the ritual questions: "Does your wife wear the veil? Why don't you take your wife to the movies, to the fights, to the café?"

European bosses do not limit themselves to the disingenuous query or the glancing invitation. They use "Indian cunning" to corner the Algerian and push him to painful decisions. In connection with a holiday—Christmas or New Year, or simply a social occasion with the firm—the boss will invite *the Algerian employee and his wife*. The invitation is not a collective one. Every Algerian is called in to the director's office and invited by name to come with "your little family." "The firm being one big family, it would be unseemly for some to come without their wives, you understand? . . ." Before this formal summons, the Algerian sometimes experiences moments of difficulty. If he comes with his wife, it means admitting defeat, it means "prostituting his wife," exhibiting her, abandoning a mode of resistance. On the other hand, going alone means refusing to give satisfaction to the boss; it means running the risk of being

[6] The ground is prepared in the school establishments as well. The teachers to whom the parents have entrusted their children soon acquire the habit of passing severe judgment on the fate of woman in Algerian society. "We firmly hope that you at least will be strong enough to impose your point of view . . ." Schools for "young Moslem girls" are multiplying. At their pupils' approach to puberty, the teachers or the nuns exercise a truly exceptional activity. The mothers are first felt out, besieged, and given the mission of shaking up and convincing the father. Much is made of the young student's prodigious intelligence, her maturity; a picture is painted of the brilliant future that awaits those eager young creatures, and it is none too subtly hinted that it would be criminal if the child's schooling were interrupted. The shortcomings of colonized society are conceded, and it is proposed that the young student be sent to boarding school in order to spare the parents the criticism of "narrow-minded neighbors." For the specialist in the colonial affairs, veterans and the "developed" natives are the commandos who are entrusted with destroying the cultural resistance of a colonized country. The regions are accordingly classified in terms of the number of developed "active units," in other words, agents of erosion of the national culture that they contain.

out of a job. The study of a case chosen at random—a description of the traps set by the European in order to bring the Algerian to expose himself, to declare: "My wife wears a veil, she shall not go out," or else to betray: "Since you want to see her, here she is,"—would bring out the sadistic and perverse character of these contacts and relationships and would show in microcosm the tragedy of the colonial situation on the psychological level, the way the two systems directly confront each other, the epic of the colonized society, with its specific ways of existing in the face of the colonialist hydra.

With the Algerian intellectual, the aggressiveness appears in its full intensity. The *fellah*, "the passive slave of a rigidly structured group," is looked upon with a certain indulgence by the conqueror.[7] The lawyer and the doctor, on the other hand, are severely frowned upon. These intellectuals, who keep their wives in a state of semi-slavery, are literally pointed to with an accusing finger. Colonial society blazes up vehemently against this inferior status of the Algerian woman. Its members worry and show concern for those unfortunate women, doomed "to produce brats," kept behind walls, banned.

Before the Algerian intellectual, racialist arguments spring forth with special readiness. For all that he is a doctor, people will say, he still remains an Arab. "You can't get away from nature." Illustrations of this kind of race prejudice can be multiplied indefinitely. Clearly, the intellectual is reproached for limiting the extension of learned Western habits, for not playing his role as an active agent of upheaval of the colonized society, for not giving his wife the benefit of the privileges of a more worthy and meaningful life . . . In the large population centers it is altogether commonplace to hear a European confess acidly that he has never seen the wife of an Algerian he has known for twenty years. At a more diffuse, but highly revealing, level of apprehension, we find the bitter observation that "we work in vain" . . . that "Islam holds its prey."

The method of presenting the Algerian as a prey fought over with equal ferocity by Islam and France with its Western culture reveals the whole approach of the occupier, his philosophy and his policy. This expression indicates that the occupier, smarting from his failures, presents in a simplified and pejorative way the system of values by means of which the colonized person resists his innumerable offensives. What is in fact the assertion of a distinct identity, concern with keeping intact a

[7] *fellah*—a peasant. (Translator's note)

few shreds of national existence, is attributed to religious, magical, fanatical behavior.

This rejection of the conqueror assumes original forms, according to circumstances or to the type of colonial situation. On the whole, these forms of behavior have been fairly well studied in the course of the past twenty years; it cannot be said, however, that the conclusions that have been reached are wholly valid. Specialists in basic education for underdeveloped countries or technicians for the advancement of retarded societies would do well to understand the sterile and harmful character of any endeavor which illuminates preferentially a given element of the colonized society. Even within the framework of a newly independent nation, one cannot attack this or that segment of the cultural whole without endangering the work undertaken (leaving aside the question of the native's psychological balance). More precisely, the phenomena of counter-acculturation must be understood as the organic impossibility of a culture to modify any one of its customs without at the same time re-evaluating its deepest values, its most stable models. To speak of counteracculturation in a colonial situation is an absurdity. The phenomena of resistance observed in the colonized must be related to an attitude of counterassimilation, of maintenance of a cultural, hence national, originality.

The occupying forces, in applying their maximum psychological attention to the veil worn by Algerian women, were obviously bound to achieve some results. Here and there it thus happened that a woman was "saved," and symbolically unveiled.

These test-women, with bare faces and free bodies, henceforth circulated like sound currency in the European society of Algeria. These women were surrounded by an atmosphere of newness. The Europeans, overexcited and wholly given over to their victory, carried away in a kind of trance, would speak of the psychological phenomena of conversion. And in fact, in the European society, the agents of this conversion were held in esteem. They were envied. The benevolent attention of the administration was drawn to them.

After each success, the authorities were strengthened in their conviction that the Algerian woman would support Western penetration into the native society. Every rejected veil disclosed to the eyes of the colonialists horizons until then forbidden, and revealed to them, piece by piece, the flesh of Algeria laid bare. The occupier's aggressiveness, and hence his hopes, multiplied tenfold each time a new face was uncovered. Every new Algerian woman unveiled announced to the occupier an Algerian society whose systems of defense were in the process of dislocation, open and breached. Every veil that fell, every body that became liberated from the traditional embrace of the *haïk,* every face that offered itself to the bold and impatient glance of the occupier, was a negative expression of the fact that Algeria was beginning to deny herself and was accepting the rape of the colonizer. Algerian society with every abandoned veil seemed to express its willingness to attend the master's school and to decide to change its habits under the occupier's direction and patronage.

We have seen how colonial society, the colonial administration, perceives the veil, and we have sketched the dynamics of the efforts undertaken to fight it as an institution and the resistances developed by the colonized society. At the level of the individual, of the private European, it may be interesting to follow the multiple reactions provoked by the existence of the veil, which reveal the original way in which the Algerian woman manages to be present or absent.

For a European not directly involved in this work of conversion, what reactions are there to be recorded?

The dominant attitude appears to us to be a romantic exoticism, strongly tinged with sensuality.

And, to begin with, the veil hides a beauty.

A revealing reflection—among others—of this state of mind was communicated to us by a European visiting Algeria who, in the exercise of his profession (he was a lawyer), had had the opportunity of seeing a few Algerian women without the veil. These men, he said, speaking of the Algerians, are guilty of concealing so many strange beauties. It was his conclusion that a people with a cache of such prizes, of such perfections of nature, owes it to itself to show them, to exhibit them. If worst came to worst, he added, it ought to be possible to force them to do so.

A strand of hair, a bit of forehead, a segment of an "overwhelmingly beautiful" face glimpsed in a streetcar or on a train, may suffice to keep alive and strengthen the European's persistence in his irrational conviction that the Algerian woman is the queen of all women.

But there is also in the European the crystallization of an aggressiveness, the strain of a kind of violence before the Algerian woman. Unveiling this woman is revealing her beauty; it is baring her secret, breaking her resistance, making her available for adventure. Hiding the face is also disguising a secret; it is also creating a world of mystery, of the hidden. In a confused way, the European experiences his relation with the Algerian woman at a highly complex level. There is in it the will to bring this woman within his reach, to make her a possible object of possession.

This woman who sees without being seen frustrates the colonizer. There is no reciprocity. She does not yield herself, does not give herself, does not offer herself. The Algerian has an attitude toward the Algerian woman which is on the whole clear. He does not see her. There is even a permanent intention not to perceive the feminine profile, not to pay attention to women. In the case of the Algerian, therefore, there is not, in the street or on a road, that behavior characterizing a sexual encounter that is described in terms of the glance, of the physical bearing, the muscular tension, the signs of disturbance to which the phenomenology of encounters has accustomed us.

The European faced with an Algerian woman wants to see. He reacts in an aggressive way before this limitation of his perception. Frustration and aggressiveness, here too, evolve apace. Aggressiveness comes to light, in the first place, in structurally ambivalent attitudes and in the dream material that can be revealed in the European, whether he is normal or suffers from neuropathological disturbances.[8]

In a medical consultation, for example, at the end of the morning, it is common to hear European doctors express their disappointment. The women who remove their veils before them are commonplace, vulgar; there is really nothing to make such a mystery of. One wonders what they are hiding.

European women settle the conflict in a much less round-

[8] Attention must be called to a frequent attitude, on the part of European women in particular, with regard to a special category of evolved natives. Certain unveiled Algerian women turn themselves into perfect Westerners with amazing rapidity and unsuspected ease. European women feel a certain uneasiness in the presence of these women. Frustrated in the presence of the veil, they experience a similar impression before the bared face, before that unabashed body which has lost all awkwardness, all timidity, and become downright offensive. Not only is the satisfaction of supervising the evolution and correcting the mistakes of the unveiled woman withdrawn from the European woman, but she feels herself challenged on the level of feminine charm, of elegance, and even sees a competitor in this novice metamorphosed into a professional, a neophyte transformed into a propagandist. The European woman has no choice but to make common cause with the Algerian man who had fiercely flung the unveiled woman into the camp of evil and of depravation. "Really!" the European women will exclaim, "these unveiled women are quite amoral and shameless." Integration, in order to be successful, seems indeed to have to be simply a continued, accepted paternalism.

about way. They bluntly affirm that no one hides what is beautiful and discern in this strange custom an "altogether feminine" intention of disguising imperfections. And they proceed to compare the strategy of the European woman, which is intended to correct, to embellish, to bring out (beauty treatments, hairdos, fashion), with that of the Algerian woman who prefers to veil, to conceal, to cultivate the man's doubt and desire. On another level, it is claimed that the intention is to mislead the customer, and that the wrapping in which the "merchandise" is presented does not really alter its nature, nor its value.

The content of the dreams of Europeans brings out other special themes. Jean-Paul Sartre, in his *Réflections Sur la Question Juive,* has shown that on the level of the unconscious, the Jewish woman almost always has an aura of rape about her.

The history of the French conquest in Algeria, including the overrunning of villages by the troops, the confiscation of property and the raping of women, the pillaging of a country, has contributed to the birth and the crystallization of the same dynamic image. At the level of the psychological strata of the occupier, the evocation of this freedom given to the sadism of the conqueror, to his eroticism, creates faults, fertile gaps through which both dreamlike forms of behavior and, on certain occasions, criminal acts can emerge.

Thus the rape of the Algerian woman in the dream of a European is always preceded by a rending of the veil. We here witness a double deflowering. Likewise, the woman's conduct is never one of consent or acceptance, but of abject humility.

Whenever, in dreams having an erotic content, a European meets an Algerian woman, the specific features of his relations with the colonized society manifest themselves. These dreams evolve neither on the same erotic plane, nor at the same tempo, as those that involve a European woman.

With an Algerian woman, there is no progressive conquest, no mutual revelation. Straight off, with the maximum of violence, there is possession, rape, near-murder. The act assumes a para-neurotic brutality and sadism, even in a normal European. This brutality and this sadism are in fact emphasized by the frightened attitude of the Algerian woman. In the dream, the woman-victim screams, struggles like a doe, and as she weakens and faints, is penetrated, martyrized, ripped apart.

Attention must likewise be drawn to a characteristic of this dream content that appears important to us. The European never dreams of an Algerian woman taken in isolation. On the rare occasions when the encounter has become a binding relationship that can be regarded as a couple, it has quickly been transformed by the desperate flight of the woman, who, inevitably, leads the male "among women." The European always dreams of a group of women, of a field of women, suggestive of the gynaeceum, the harem—exotic themes deeply rooted in the unconscious.

The European's aggressiveness will express itself likewise in contemplation of the Algerian woman's morality. Her timidity and her reserve are transformed in accordance with the commonplace laws of conflictual psychology into their opposite, and the Algerian woman becomes hypocritical, perverse, and even a vertitable nymphomaniac.

We have seen that on the level of individuals the colonial strategy of destructuring Algerian society very quickly came to assign a prominent place to the Algerian woman. The colonialist's relentlessness, his methods of struggle were bound to give rise to reactionary forms of behavior on the part of the colonized. In the face of the violence of the occupier, the colonized found himself defining a principled position with respect to a formerly inert element of the native cultural configuration. It was the colonialist's frenzy to unveil the Algerian woman, it was his gamble on winning the battle of the veil at whatever cost, that were to provoke the native's bristling resistance. The deliberately aggressive intentions of the colonialist with respect to the *haïk* gave a new life to this dead element of the Algerian cultural stock—dead because stabilized, without any progressive change in form or color. We here recognize one of the laws of the psychology of colonization. In an initial phase, it is the action, the plans of the occupier that determine the centers of resistance around which a people's will to survive becomes organized.

It is the white man who creates the Negro. But it is the Negro who creates negritude. To the colonialist offensive against the veil, the colonized opposes the cult of the veil. What was an undifferentiated element in a homogeneous whole acquires a taboo character, and the attitude of a given Algerian woman with respect to the veil will be constantly related to her over-all attitude with respect to the foreign occupation. The colonized, in the face of the emphasis given by the colonialist to this or that aspect of his traditions, reacts very violently. The attention devoted to modifying this aspect, the emotion the conqueror puts into his pedagogical work, his prayers, his threats, weave a whole universe of resistances around this particular element of the culture. Holding out against the occupier on this precise element means inflicting upon him a spectacular setback; it means more particularly maintaining "coexistence" as a form of conflict and latent warfare. It means keeping up the atmosphere of an armed truce.

Upon the outbreak of the struggle for liberation, the attitude of the Algerian woman, or of native society in general, with regard to the veil was to undergo important modifications. These innovations are of particular interest in view of the fact that they were at no time included in the program of the struggle. The doctrine of the Revolution, the strategy of combat, never postulated the necessity for a revision of forms of behavior with respect to the veil. We are able to affirm even now that when Algeria has gained her independence such questions will not be raised, for in the practice of the Revolution the people have understood that problems are resolved in the very movement that raises them.

Until 1955, the combat was waged exclusively by the men. The revolutionary characteristics of this combat, the necessity for absolute secrecy, obliged the militant to keep his woman in absolute ignorance. As the enemy gradually adapted himself to the forms of combat, new difficulties appeared which required original solutions. The decision to involve women as active elements of the Algerian Revolution was not reached lightly. In a sense, it was the very conception of the combat that had to be modified. The violence of the occupier, his ferocity, his delirious attachment to the national territory, induced the leaders no longer to exclude certain forms of combat. Progressively, the urgency of a total war made itself felt. But involving the women was not solely a response to the desire to mobilize the entire nation. The women's entry into the war had to be harmonized with respect for the revolutionary nature of the war. In other words, the women had to show as much spirit of sacrifice as the men. It was therefore necessary to have the same confidence in them as was required from seasoned militants who had served several prison sentences. A moral elevation and a strength of character that were altogether exceptional would therefore be required of the women. There was no lack of hesitations. The revolutionary wheels had assumed such proportions; the mechanism was running at a given rate. The machine would have to be complicated; in other words its network would have to be extended without affecting its efficiency. The women could not be conceived of as a replacement product, but as an element capable of adequately meeting the new tasks.

In the mountains, women helped the *guerrilla* during halts or when convalescing after a wound or a case of typhoid contracted in the *djebel.*[9] But deciding to incorporate women as essential elements, to have the Revolution depend on their presence and their action in this or that sector, was obviously a wholly revolutionary step. To have the Revolution rest at any point on their activity was an important choice.

Such a decision was made difficult for several reasons. During the whole period of unchallenged domination, we have seen that Algerian society, and particularly the women, had a tendency to flee from the occupier. The tenacity of the occupier in his endeavor to unveil the women, to make of them an ally in the work of cultural destruction, had the effect of strengthening the traditional patterns of behavior. These patterns, which were essentially positive in the strategy of resistance to the corrosive action of the colonizer, naturally had negative effects. The woman, especially the city woman, suffered a loss of ease and of assurance. Having been accustomed to confinement, her body did not have the normal mobility before a limitless horizon of avenues, of unfolded sidewalks, of houses, of people dodged or bumped into. This relatively cloistered life, with its known, categorized, regulated comings and goings, made any immediate revolution seem a dubious proposition. The political leaders were perfectly familiar with these problems, and their hesitations expressed their consciousness of their responsibilities. They were entitled to doubt the success of this measure. Would not such a decision have catastrophic consequences for the progress of the Revolution?

To this doubt there was added an equally important element. The leaders hesitated to involve the women, being perfectly aware of the ferocity of the colonizer. The leaders of the Revolution had no illusions as to the enemy's criminal capacities. Nearly all of them had passed through their jails or had had sessions with survivors from the camps or the cells of the French judicial police. Not one of them failed to realize that any Algerian woman arrested would be tortured to death. It is relatively easy to commit oneself to this path and to accept among different eventualities that of dying under torture. The matter is a little more difficult when it involves designating someone who manifestly runs the risk of certain death. But the decision as to whether or not the women were to participate in the Revo-

[9] *djebel*—mountain. (Translator's note)

lution had to be made; the inner oppositions became massive, and each decision gave rise to the same hesitations, produced the same despair.

In the face of the extraordinary success of this new form of popular combat, observers have compared the action of the Algerian women to that of certain women resistance fighters or even secret agents of the specialized services. It must be constantly borne in mind that the committed Algerian woman learns both her role as "a woman alone in the street" and her revolutionary mission instinctively. The Algerian woman is not a secret agent. It is without apprenticeship, without briefing, without fuss, that she goes out into the street with three grenades in her handbag or the activity report of an area in her bodice. She does not have the sensation of playing a role she has heard about ever so many times in novels, or seen in motion pictures. There is not that coefficient of play, of imitation, almost always present in this form of action when we are dealing with a Western woman.

What we have here is not the bringing to light of a character known and frequented a thousand times in imagination or in stories. It is an authentic birth in a pure state, without preliminary instruction. There is no character to imitate. On the contrary, there is an intense dramatization, a continuity between the woman and the revolutionary. The Algerian woman rises directly to the level of tragedy.[10]

The growth in the number of the FLN cells, the range of new tasks—finance, intelligence, counterintelligence, political training—the necessity to provide for one active cell three or four replacement cells to be held in reserve, ready to become active at the slightest alert concerning the front cell, obliged the leaders to seek other avenues for the carrying out of strictly individual assignments. After a final series of meetings among leaders, and especially in view of the urgency of the daily problems that the Revolution faced, the decision to concretely involve women in the national struggle was reached.

The revolutionary character of this decision must once again be emphasized. At the beginning, it was the married women who were contacted. But rather soon these restrictions were

[10] We are mentioning here only realities known to the enemy. We therefore say nothing about the new forms of action adopted by women in the Revolution. Since 1958, in fact, the tortures inflicted on women militants have enabled the occupier to have an idea of the strategy used by women. Today new adaptations have developed. It will therefore be understood if we are silent as to these.

abandoned. The married women whose husbands were militants were the first to be chosen. Later, widows or divorced women were designated. In any case, there were never any unmarried girls—first of all, because a girl of even twenty or twenty-three hardly ever has occasion to leave the family domicile unaccompanied. But the woman's duties as mother or spouse, the desire to limit to the minimum the possible consequences of her arrest and her death, and also the more and more numerous volunteering of unmarried girls, led the political leaders to make another leap, to remove all restrictions, to accept indiscriminately the support of all Algerian women.

Meanwhile the woman who might be acting as a liaison agent, as a bearer of tracts, as she walked some hundred or two hundred meters ahead of the man under whose orders she was working, still wore a veil; but after a certain period the pattern of activity that the struggle involved shifted in the direction of the European city. The protective mantle of the Kasbah, the almost organic curtain of safety that the Arab town weaves round the native, withdrew, and the Algerian woman, exposed, was sent forth into the conqueror's city. Very quickly she adopted an absolutely unbelievable offensive tactic. When colonized people undertake an action against the oppressor, and when this oppression is exercised in the form of exacerbated and continuous violence in Algeria, they must overcome a considerable number of taboos. The European city is not the prolongation of the native city. The colonizers have not settled in the midst of the natives. They have surrounded the native city; they have laid siege to it. Every exit from the Kasbah of Algiers opens on enemy territory. And so it is in Constantine, in Oran, in Blida, in Bone.

The native cities are deliberately caught in the conqueror's vise. To get an idea of the rigor with which the immobilizing of the native city, of the autochthonous population, is organized, one must have in one's hands the plans according to which a colonial city has been laid out, and compare them with the comments of the general staff of the occupation forces.

Apart from the charwomen employed in the conquerors' homes, those whom the colonizer indiscriminately calls the "Fatmas," the Algerian women, especially the young Algerian women, rarely venture into the European city. Their movements are almost entirely limited to the Arab city. And even in the Arab city their movements are reduced to the minimum. The rare occasions on which the Algerian woman abandons the city are almost always in connection with some event, either of an exceptional nature (the death of a relative residing in a nearby locality), or more often, traditional family visits for religious feasts, or a pilgrimage. In such cases, the European city is crossed in a car, usually early in the morning. The Algerian woman, the young Algerian woman—except for a very few students (who, besides, never have the same ease as their European counterparts)—must overcome a multiplicity of inner resistances, of subjectively organized fears, of emotions. She must at the same time confront the essentially hostile world of the occupier and the mobilized, vigilant, and efficient police forces. Each time she ventures into the European city, the Algerian woman must achieve a victory over herself, over her childish fears. She must consider the image of the occupier lodged somewhere in her mind and in her body, remodel it, initiate the essential work of eroding it, make it inessential, remove something of the shame that is attached to it, devalidate it.

Initially subjective, the breaches made in colonialism are the result of a victory of the colonized over their old fear and over the atmosphere of despair distilled day after day by a colonialism that has incrusted itself with the *prospect of enduring forever*.

The young Algerian woman, whenever she is called upon, establishes a link. Algiers is no longer the Arab city, but the autonomous area of Algiers, the nervous system of the enemy apparatus. Oran, Constantine develop their dimensions. In launching the struggle, the Algerian is loosening the vise that was tightening around the native cities. From one area of Algiers to another, from the Ruisseau to Hussein-Dey, from El-Biar to the rue Michelet, the Revolution creates new links. More and more, it is the Algerian woman, the Algerian girl, who will be assuming these tasks.

Among the tasks entrusted to the Algerian woman is the bearing of messages, of complicated verbal orders learned by heart, sometimes despite complete absence of schooling. But she is also called upon to stand watch, for an hour and often more, before a house where district leaders are conferring.

During those interminable minutes when she must avoid standing still, so as not to attract attention, and avoid venturing too far since she is responsible for the safety of the brothers within, incidents that are at once funny and pathetic are not infrequent. An unveiled Algerian girl who "walks the street" is very often noticed by young men who behave like young men all over the world, but who use a special approach as the result of the idea people habitually have of one who has discarded the veil. She is treated to unpleasant, obscene, humiliating remarks. When such things happen, she must grit her teeth, walk away a few steps, elude the passers-by who draw attention to her, who give other passers-by the desire either to follow their example, or to come to her defense. Or it may be that the Algerian woman is carrying in her bag or in a small suitcase twenty, thirty, forty million francs, money belonging to the Revolution, money which is to be used to take care of the needs of the families of prisoners, or to buy medicine and supplies for the guerrillas.

This revolutionary activity has been carried on by the Algerian woman with exemplary constancy, self-mastery, and success. Despite the inherent, subjective difficulties and notwithstanding the sometimes violent incomprehension of a part of the family, the Algerian woman assumes all the tasks entrusted to her.

But things were gradually to become more complicated. Thus the unit leaders who go into the town and who avail themselves of the women-scouts, of the girls whose function it is to lead the way, are no longer new to political activity, are no longer unknown to the police. Authentic military chiefs have now begun to pass through the cities. These are known, and are being looked for. There is not a police superintendent who does not have their pictures on his desk.

These soldiers on the move, these fighters, always carry their weapons—automatic pistols, revolvers, grenades, sometimes all three. The political leader must overcome much resistance in order to induce these men, who under no circumstance would allow themselves to be taken prisoner, to entrust their weapons to the girl who is to walk ahead of them, it being up to them, if things go badly, to recover the arms immediately. The group accordingly makes its way into the European city. A hundred meters ahead, a girl may be carrying a suitcase and behind her are two or three ordinary-looking men. This girl who is the group's lighthouse and barometer gives warning in case of danger. The file makes it way by fits and starts; police cars and patrols cruise back and forth.

There are times, as these soldiers have admitted after completing such a mission, when the urge to recover their weapons is almost irresistible because of the fear of being caught short and not having time to defend themselves. With this phase, the Algerian woman penetrates a little further into the flesh of the Revolution.

But it was from 1956 on that her activity assumed really gigantic dimensions. Having to react in rapid succession to the massacre of Algerian civilians in the mountains and in the cities, the revolutionary leadership found that if it wanted to prevent the people from being gripped by terror it had no choice but to adopt forms of terror which until then it had rejected. This phenomenon has not been sufficiently analyzed; not enough attention has been given to the reasons that lead a revolutionary movement to choose the weapon that is called terrorism.

During the French Resistance, terrorism was aimed at soldiers, at Germans of the Occupation, or at strategic enemy installations. The technique of terrorism is the same. It consists of individual or collective attempts by means of bombs or by the derailing of trains. In Algeria, where European settlers are numerous and where the territorial militias lost no time in enrolling the postman, the nurse, and the grocer in the repressive system, the men who directed the struggle faced an absolutely new situation.

The decision to kill a civilian in the street is not an easy one, and no one comes to it lightly. No one takes the step of placing a bomb in a public place without a battle of conscience.

The Algerian leaders who, in view of the intensity of the repression and the frenzied character of the oppression, thought they could answer the blows received without any serious problems of conscience, discovered that the most horrible crimes do not constitute a sufficient excuse for certain decisions.

The leaders in a number of cases canceled plans or even in the last moment called off the *fidaï*[11] assigned to place a given bomb. To explain these hesitations there was, to be sure, the memory of civilians killed or frightfully wounded. There was the political consideration not to do certain things that could compromise the cause of freedom. There was also the fear that the Europeans working with the Front might be hit in these attempts. There was thus a threefold concern: not to pile up possibly innocent victims, not to give a false picture of the Revolution, and finally the anxiety to have the French democrats on their side, as well as the democrats of all the countries of the world and the Europeans of Algeria who were attracted by the Algerian national ideal.

Now the massacres of Algerians, the raids in the countryside,

[11] *fidaï*—a death volunteer, in the Islamic tradition. (Translator's note.)

strengthened the assurance of the European civilians, seemed to consolidate the colonial status, and injected hope into the colonialists. The Europeans who, as a result of certain military actions on the part of the Algerian National Army in favor of the struggle of the Algerian people, had soft-pedaled their race prejudice and their insolence, recovered their old arrogance, their traditional contempt.

I remember a woman clerk in Birtouta who, on the day of the interception of the plane transporting the five members of the National Liberation Front, waved their photographs in front of her shop, shrieking: "They've been caught! They're going to get their what-you-call-'ems cut off!"

Every blow dealt the Revolution, every massacre perpetrated by the adversary, intensified the ferocity of the colonialists and hemmed in the Algerian civilian on all sides.

Trains loaded with French soldiers, the French Navy on maneuvers and bombarding Algiers and Philippeville, the jet planes, the militiamen who descended on the *douars*[12] and decimated uncounted Algerians, all this contributed to giving the people the impression that they were not defended, that they were not protected, that nothing had changed, and that the Europeans could do what they wanted. This was the period when one heard Europeans announcing in the streets: "Let's each one of us take ten of them and bump them off and you'll see the problem solved in no time." And the Algerian people, especially in the cities, witnessed this boastfulness which added insult to injury and noted the impunity of these criminals who did not even take the trouble to hide. Any Algerian man or woman in a given city could in fact name the torturers and murderers of the region.

A time came when some of the people allowed doubt to enter their minds, and they began to wonder whether it was really possible, quantitatively and qualitatively, to resist the occupant's offensives. Was freedom worth the consequences of penetrating into that enormous circuit of terrorism and counterterrorism? Did this disproportion not express the impossibility of escaping oppression?

Another part of the people, however, grew impatient and conceived the idea of putting an end to the advantage the enemy derived by pursuing the path of terror. The decision to strike the adversary individually and by name could no longer be eluded. All the prisoners "shot and killed while trying to

[12] *douar*—a village. (Translator's note.)

escape," and the cries of the tortured, demanded that new forms of combat be adopted.

Members of the police and the meeting places of the colonialists (cafés in Algiers, Oran, Constantine) were the first to be singled out. From this point on the Algerian woman became wholly and deliberately immersed in the revolutionary action. It was she who would carry in her bag the grenades and the revolvers that a *fidaï* would take from her at the last moment, before the bar, or as a designated criminal passed. During this period Algerians caught in the European city were pitilessly challenged, arrested, searched.

This is why we must watch the parallel progress of this man and this woman, of this couple that brings death to the enemy, life to the Revolution. The one supporting the other, but apparently strangers to each other. The one radically transformed into a European woman, poised and unconstrained, whom no one would suspect, completely at home in the environment, and the other, a stranger, tense, moving toward his destiny.

The Algerian *fidaï*, unlike the unbalanced anarchists made famous in literature, does not take dope. The *fidaï* does not need to be unaware of danger, to befog his consciousness, or to forget. The "terrorist," from the moment he undertakes an assignment, allows death to enter into his soul. He has a rendezvous with death. The *fidaï*, on the other hand, has a rendezvous with the life of the Revolution, and with his own life. The *fidaï* is not one of the sacrificed. To be sure, he does not shrink before the possibility of losing his life or the independence of his country, but at no moment does he choose death.

If it has been decided to kill a given police superintendent responsible for tortures or a given colonialist leader, it is because these men constitute an obstacle to the progress of the Revolution. Froger, for example, symbolized a colonialist tradition and a method inaugurated at Sétif and at Guelma in 1954.[13] Moreover, Froger's apparent power crystallized the colonization and gave new life to the hopes of those who were beginning to have doubts as to the real solidity of the System. It was around people like Froger that the robbers and murderers of the Algerian people would meet and encourage one another. This was something the *fidaï* knew, and that the woman who accompanied him, his woman-arsenal, likewise knew.

Carrying revolvers, grenades, hundreds of false identity cards

[13] Froger, one of the colonialist leaders. Executed by a *fidaï* in late 1956.

or bombs, the unveiled Algerian woman moves like a fish in the Western waters. The soldiers, the French patrols, smile to her as she passes, compliments on her looks are heard here and there, but no one suspects that her suitcases contain the automatic pistol which will presently mow down four or five members of one of the patrols.

We must come back to that young girl, unveiled only yesterday, who walks with sure steps down the streets of the European city teeming with policemen, parachutists, militiamen. She no longer slinks along the walls as she tended to do before the Revolution. Constantly called upon to efface herself before a member of the dominant society, the Algerian woman avoided the middle of the sidewalk which in all countries in the world belongs rightfully to those who command.

The shoulders of the unveiled Algerian woman are thrust back with easy freedom. She walks with a graceful, measured stride, neither too fast nor too slow. Her legs are bare, not confined by the veil, given back to themselves, and her hips are free.

The body of the young Algerian woman, in traditional society, is revealed to her by its coming to maturity and by the veil. The veil covers the body and disciplines it, tempers it, at the very time when it experiences its phase of greatest effervescence. The veil protects, reassures, isolates. One must have heard the confessions of Algerian women or have analyzed the dream content of certain recently unveiled women to appreciate the importance of the veil for the body of the woman. Without the veil she has an impression of her body being cut up into bits, put adrift; the limbs seem to lengthen indefinitely. When the Algerian woman has to cross a street, for a long time she commits errors of judgment as to the exact distance to be negotiated. The unveiled body seems to escape, to dissolve. She has an impression of being improperly dressed, even of being naked. She experiences a sense of incompleteness with great intensity. She has the anxious feeling that something is unfinished, and along with this a frightful sensation of disintegrating. The absence of the veil distorts the Algerian woman's corporal pattern. She quickly has to invent new dimensions for her body, new means of muscular control. She has to create for herself an attitude of unveiled-woman-outside. She must overcome all timidity, all awkwardness (for she must pass for a European), and at the same time be careful not to overdo it, not to attract notice to herself. The Algerian woman who walks stark naked into the European city relearns her body, re-establishes it in a totally revolutionary fashion. This new dialectic of the body and of the world is primary in the case of one revolutionary woman.[14]

But the Algerian woman is not only in conflict with her body. She is a link, sometimes an essential one, in the revolutionary machine. She carries weapons, knows important points of refuge. And it is in terms of the concrete dangers that she faces that we must gauge the insurmountable victories that she has had to win in order to be able to say to her chief, on her return: "Mission accomplished . . . R.A.S."[15]

Another difficulty to which attention deserves to be called appeared during the first months of feminine activity. In the course of her comings and goings, it would happen that the unveiled Algerian woman was seen by a relative or a friend of the family. The father was sooner or later informed. He would naturally hesitate to believe such allegations. Then more reports would reach him. Different persons would claim to have seen "Zohra or Fatima unveiled, walking like a . . . My Lord,

[14] The woman, who before the Revolution never left the house without being accompanied by her mother or her husband, is now entrusted with special missions such as going from Oran to Constantine or Algiers. For several days, all by herself, carrying directives of capital importance for the Revolution, she takes the train, spends the night with an unknown family, among militants. Here too she must harmonize her movements, for the enemy is on the lookout for any false step. But the important thing here is that the husband makes no difficulty about letting his wife leave on an assignment. He will make it, in fact, a point of pride to say to the liaison agent when the latter returns, "You see, everything has gone well in your absence." The Algerian's age-old jealousy, his "congenital" suspiciousness, have melted on contact with the Revolution. It must be pointed out also that militants who are being sought by the police take refuge with other militants not yet identified by the occupier. In such cases the woman, left alone all day with the fugitive, is the one who gets him his food, the newspapers, the mail, showing no trace of suspicion or fear. Involved in the struggle, the husband or the father learns to look upon the relations between the sexes in a new light. The militant man discovers the militant woman, and jointly they create new dimensions for Algerian society.

[15] R.A.S.—*Rien à signaler*—a military abbreviation for "Nothing to report."

We here go on to a description of attitudes. There is, however, an important piece of work to be done on the woman's role in the Revolution: the woman in the city, in the *djebel*, in the enemy administrations; the prostitute and the information she obtains; the women in prison, under torture, facing death, before the courts. All these chapter headings, after the material has been sifted, will reveal an incalculable number of facts essential for the history of the national struggle.

protect us! . . ." The father would then decide to demand explanations. He would hardly have begun to speak when he would stop. From the young girl's look of firmness the father would have understood that her commitment was of long standing. The old fear of dishonor was swept away by a new fear, fresh and cold—that of death in battle or of torture of the girl. Behind the girl, the whole family—even the Algerian father, the authority for all things, the founder of every value—following in her footsteps, becomes committed to the new Algeria.

Removed and reassumed again and again, the veil has been manipulated, transformed into a technique of camouflage, into a means of struggle. The virtually taboo character assumed by the veil in the colonial situation disappeared almost entirely in the course of the liberating struggle. Even Algerian women not actively integrated into the struggle formed the habit of abandoning the veil. It is true that under certain conditions, especially from 1957 on, the veil reappeared. The missions in fact became increasingly difficult. The adversary now knew, since certain militant women had spoken under torture, that a number of women very Europeanized in appearance were playing a fundamental role in the battle. Moreover, certain European women of Algeria were arrested, to the consternation of the adversary, who discovered that his own System was breaking down. The discovery by the French authorities of the participation of Europeans in the liberation struggle marks a turning point in the Algerian Revolution. From that day, the French patrols challenged every person. Europeans and Algerians were equally suspect. All historic limits crumbled and disappeared. Any person carrying a package could be required to open it and show its contents. Anyone was entitled to question anyone as to the nature of a parcel carried in Algiers, Philippeville, or Batna. Under those conditions it became urgent to conceal the package from the eyes of the occupier and again to cover oneself with the protective *haïk*.

Here again, a new technique had to be learned: how to carry a rather heavy object dangerous to handle under the veil and still give the impression of having one's hands free, that there was nothing under this *haïk*, except a poor woman or an insignificant young girl. It was not enough to be veiled. One had to look so much like a "Fatma" that the soldier would be convinced that this woman was quite harmless.

Very difficult. Three meters ahead of you the police challenge a veiled woman who does not look particularly suspect. From the anguished expression of the unit leader you have guessed that she is carrying a bomb, or a sack of grenades, bound to her body by a whole system of strings and straps. For the hands must be free, exhibited bare, humbly and abjectly presented to the soldiers so that they will look no further. Showing empty and apparently mobile and free hands is the sign that disarms the enemy soldier.

The Algerian woman's body, which in an initial phase was pared down, now swelled. Whereas in the previous period the body had to be made slim and disciplined to make it attractive and seductive, it now had to be squashed, made shapeless and even ridiculous. This, as we have seen, is the phase during which she undertook to carry bombs, grenades, machine-gun clips.

The enemy, however, was alerted, and in the streets one witnessed what became a commonplace spectacle of Algerian women glued to the wall, on whose bodies the famous magnetic detectors, the "frying pans," would be passed. Every veiled woman, every Algerian woman became suspect. There was no discrimination. This was the period during which men, women, children, the whole Algerian people, experienced at one and the same time their national vocation and the recasting of the new Algerian society.

Ignorant or feigning to be ignorant of these new norms of conduct, French colonialism, on the occasion of May 13th, re-enacted its old campaign of Westernizing the Algerian woman. Servants under the threat of being fired, poor women dragged from their homes, prostitutes, were brought to the public square and *symbolically* unveiled to the cries of "*Vive l'Algérie française!*" Before this new offensive old reactions reappeared. Spontaneously and without being told, the Algerian women who had long since dropped the veil once again donned the *haïk,* thus affirming that it was not true that woman liberated herself at the invitation of France and of General de Gaulle.

Behind these psychological reactions, beneath this immediate and almost unanimous response, we again see the over-all attitude of rejection of the values of the occupier, even if these values objectively be worth choosing. It is because they fail to grasp this intellectual reality, this characteristic feature (the famous sensitivity of the colonized), that the colonizers rage at always "doing them good in spite of themselves." Colonialism wants everything to come from it. But the dominant psychological feature of the colonized is to withdraw before any invitation of the conqueror's. In organizing the famous cavalcade of May 13th, colonialism has obliged Algerian society to go back to methods of struggle already outmoded. In a certain sense, the different ceremonies have caused a turning back, a regression.

Colonialism must accept the fact that things happen without its control, without its direction. We are reminded of the words spoken in an international assembly by an African political figure. Responding to the standard excuse of the immaturity of colonial peoples and their incapacity to administer themselves, this man demanded for the underdeveloped peoples "the right to govern themselves badly." The doctrinal assertions of colonialism in its attempt to justify the maintenance of its domination almost always push the colonized to the position of making uncompromising, rigid, static counterproposals.

After the 13th of May, the veil was resumed, but stripped once and for all of its exclusively traditional dimension.

There is thus a historic dynamism of the veil that is very concretely perceptible in the development of colonization in Algeria. In the beginning, the veil was a mechanism of resistance, but its value for the social group remained very strong. The veil was worn because tradition demanded a rigid separation of the sexes, but also because the occupier *was bent on unveiling Algeria.* In a second phase, the mutation occurred in connection with the Revolution and under special circumstances. The veil was abandoned in the course of revolutionary action. What had been used to block the psychological or political offensives of the occupier became a means, an instrument. The veil helped the Algerian woman to meet the new problems created by the struggle.

The colonialists are incapable of grasping the motivations of the colonized. It is the necessities of combat that give rise in Algerian society to new attitudes, to new modes of action, to new ways.

"The Universal Conscience" Speech to the Cultural Congress of Havana

FIDEL CASTRO

The following text of Castro's closing speech to the Havana Cultural Congress of January, 1968, is the official Cuban translation as published in the January 21 Granma. *The stenographer's notes—applause, laughter, ovation—are retained here. Unobtrusive reminders of the situation, they suggest the auditorium and imply the mood.*

As Castro points out early in his speech, the Congress's participants formed an unusual group: they had not come as "militants in any political organizations." In other words, they were not the official representatives of so many communist parties, and the Havana meeting was no mere Cuban replica of the CP congresses of the U.S.S.R. Rather, it constituted another episode of the new revolutionary's attempt to overcome the reluctant-dragon apparatus of the communist parties of Europe and Latin America: the spirit of revolution discarding its no longer serviceable forms. This is the unifying theme of a speech which touches on all the major problems that confront men of all three worlds in their distinctively modern collectivity.

DELEGATES TO THE Cultural Congress of Havana,
Comrades:

I feel I must express the opinion of many participants in the Congress to the effect that this, the first international event of its kind, has been a complete success.

Some predicted that it would be difficult, if not impossible, to hold a congress of this kind—an international assemblage of numerous workers in the intellectual field, coming from no less than seventy countries, speaking a great number of different languages, whose ideas may differ on many points and who, therefore, might have turned the Cultural Congress into a sort of arena for all kinds of polemics and misunderstandings. Some predicted that it would be very difficult for the workers in the intellectual field to reach practically unanimous conclusions.

Perhaps this is the result of several factors, among them the general tendency of intellectual workers to be excessively individualistic at times and the fact—analyzed in the Congress itself—that men of any society, independently of their positions, are greatly influenced by the ideas, habits, and way of life that permeate the world in which they are developing. And possibly this supposition is based on an underestimation of intellectual workers.

So we ought to give some thought to what factors have made this Congress possible, what factors have inspired the discussions in this Congress, what factors have contributed to giving it a profoundly revolutionary quality, a revolutionary quality that may truly be said to surpass the most optimistic expectations. The factor that made this Congress possible and guaranteed its results is the universal conscience that is developing today, the universal awareness of the grave threats hanging over all the peoples of the world, the universal awareness of the need for struggle, the universal awareness of the need for justice, which is spreading throughout the world.

The strange thing is that the men and women gathered here did not come as militants in any political organizations. Many times and in many places congresses of similar militant organizations, of similar parties, have been held; but this Congress has been characterized by its broad representation, by its participants having come from vastly different places, by their having carried out a variety of activities and, in spite of this, by the fact that a series of questions, a series of fundamental principles, was approached with unusual unanimity.

Intellectual workers from the most diverse sectors, intellectual workers having the most diverse philosophical ideas, the most diverse scientific and artistic concepts, the most diverse political opinions gathered here, and yet a common ground could be found. We believe that this constitutes a genuine cause for concern for the enemies of humanity.

What determines this universal conscience? Is it perhaps an idealistic sentiment nurtured by those who participated in this Congress? Is it perhaps simply the expression of noble, generous, humanitarian sentiments? Even though these sentiments clearly abounded in this Congress, the factor that created this universal conscience was, unquestionably, the danger, the threats of aggression, and the actual acts of aggression hanging over and victimizing many peoples of the world—practically the whole world. This universal conscience has grown on a par with the spirit of aggression, the acts of oppression and subjugation, and the threats that hang over humanity. What must be said is that the men and women meeting here undoubtedly constitute the vanguard, a nucleus that is able to get to the bottom of things, to grasp quickly the nature, the character, and the seriousness of the contemporary problems from which humanity is suffering or that are threatening humanity.

We have read all the resolutions on the different topics, and it is clear that the fundamental questions, the most serious dangers that face humanity today, were dealt with, and they were dealt with, we feel, very correctly.

There are some things before which no one with a modicum of conscience, no one with human sentiments or feelings of justice can remain unmoved.

That is why, for example, the aggression against Vietnam, this act unparalleled in modern times, this mass murder which Yankee imperialism is brutally perpetrating against that people, this action which is unjustifiable from any point of view, which relies on vastly destructive weapons and acts of barbarism, unquestionably reminds all those who have lived through Nazism in Europe or are familiar with it through reading . . . of the crimes of the Fascists. It reminds them, for example, of all those actions which later were qualified as war crimes and for which the Nazis were punished and in some cases executed—although not so many as should have been, only those principally responsible for those acts.

The imperialist Yankee policy today reminds us of the policy of Hitler. It reminds us of the Nazis' acts of barbarism, but with a difference: imperialism has succeeded in amassing technical and therefore also military resources; it has succeeded in amassing forces of death and destruction incomparably greater than anything the Nazi-Fascists ever dreamed of.

It is logical that humanity should be concerned when it sees such tremendous forces advancing along the same road.

Not only does the nature of the crimes committed contribute to developing conscience, but so does the admiration we feel for the heroic people who are facing those powerful forces so bravely, so successfully, and so incredibly, who are combating them and, moreover, defeating them.

The indignation and hatred against one side and the admiration for the other, regarding events in Vietnam, have contributed to a considerable extent—perhaps more than any other single thing in today's world—to the creation of this awareness of justice and universal ethics which has been in such great evidence during this Congress.

But humanity, at the same time, sees more and more clearly that these deeds are not mere isolated incidents—far from it! They are the fruits of a concept, of a whole system which the imperialists are trying to impose on the whole world.

The unusual unanimity with which the actions of Yankee imperialism are today condemned is the logical result of a whole chain of similar events which have taken place throughout the world in recent times. Because those imperialists who brutally murder in Vietnam are the same imperialists who invaded and occupied the Dominican Republic. They are the same imperialists who participated in the repression of revolutionary movements all over the world. They are the same imperialists who triggered the events that culminated in the murder of Lumumba. They are the same imperialists who carry out acts of provocation and aggression against Korea, who intervene in Laos, who threaten Cambodia, who keep a notorious puppet in power in Formosa, and who, with their weapons and resources, prop up the oligarchic governments of Latin America, the tyrannies, the archaic systems that prevail on this continent. They are the same ones who not only support coups d'état in Latin America—which have become daily occurrences—and coups d'état in Africa—which have become so fashionable nowadays—but even support the reactionary military coups d'état in Greece, in Europe itself, and abet acts of aggression against the Arab peoples. *(Applause)*

Actually, there is no need to mention Cuba, as our case ceases to be an isolated one, to become just one more. Our experience has taught us only too well about the activities and behavior of imperialism. But today our people's stand, their indignation and hatred of imperialism, is motivated not precisely by imperialist aggression against us but by the comprehension of the role imperialism plays in the entire world.

There is not a single people, there is not a single contemporary problem where the activities of imperialism are not clearly seen and felt; there is not a single infamous cause in today's world that is not supported by imperialism, as there is not a single just cause in the world that is not opposed by imperialism.

It is no longer just the case of imperialism aiming at and attacking what is called the Third World or the underdeveloped world—or developing world, as others call it. This term, "developing world," is a misnomer, an incorrectly applied concept, because, if we go by the reality of that world, we could call it, rather than a "developing" world—from an economic and technical standpoint, and as a result of the conditions imposed by imperialism on that part of the world—a "world in retrogression."

The voracious actions of imperialism are not limited to this part of the world; the actions of that imperialism are directed, ever more seriously, against the interests of the so-called developed countries as well. There are discrepancies of terminology in this concept of "developed" and "underdeveloped" countries, since it is said that at times a country which is highly developed industrially and economically is at the same time politically and socially underdeveloped, and that a country that is economically underdeveloped is politically and socially more developed.

We do not feel in the least offended if we are included among the underdeveloped countries. Because development of awareness, our social as well as our general cultural development, is steadily becoming a prerequisite to our economic and industrial development. In this country—as must occur in any other country where conditions are similar to ours—the development of a political as well as social awareness among the people becomes a prerequisite for winning the battle against economic underdevelopment.

Imperialism as a world phenomenon, as a world evil, as a wolf at large in the world, can exist only if it acts in this wolflike manner all over the world, if it acts against the interest of the entire world. And that imperialism behaves identically toward the rest of the so-called developed world, the industrialized world.

Nowadays it is common, in political terminology, to speak of imperialism headed by the United States. The fact is that in today's world there is only one truly powerful imperialism; in today's world the mainstay of imperialism, imperialism in essence, is U.S. imperialism. The powerful imperialisms of yesteryear are today extraordinarily weak in comparison with Yankee imperialism. That is the reason why—and this is becoming understood more and more clearly by the whole world

—the effort, the struggle, is being concentrated against Yankee imperialism, the mainstay of every reactionary government, of every evil cause in the world.

That imperialism even threatens to devour—and is actually, to a certain extent, devouring—the other imperialist powers. It is needless to dwell on this point. It was discussed in the Congress; brilliant ideas were expressed and proposals made in this sense. A paper presented to the Congress examined, and substantiated with statistics, the phenomenon of Yankee imperialist penetration in Europe, the drain of capital—it is no longer a question of the exportation of capital but of the drain of capital—which Yankee imperialism is carrying out in the underdeveloped world. An insight was given into the mechanism of the brain drain which Yankee imperialism perpetrates all over the world. And facts showing the phenomenon today of a monopoly over science and technology, showing how the imperialists utilize the great advances in science and modern technology. All of this was brilliantly set forth at the Congress, as was the explanation of how, at present, when the Yankee imperialists make investments in Europe they only have to bring in ten per cent of the total amount invested, mobilizing the rest of the resources within Europe itself.

We know the degree of Yankee penetration in Europe. And we must say, seriously, that, perhaps to an extent unimagined by Europeans themselves, Yankee imperialism governs Europe. (*Applause*)

We know this; we have constant proof of it. Because, for example, the imperialists carry on incessant economic sabotage, economic blockade against us, doing everything possible to keep us from acquiring anything useful in any part of the world. The worst of this is that on many, many occasions the imperialists sabotage and frustrate our efforts in countries that consider themselves quite independent, quite sovereign, and quite developed.

The imperialists hold controlling interests in countless European enterprises; the imperialists control numerous patents used in Europe. And if we seek to purchase a machine that is manufactured under a patent held by a U.S. company, or if part of the machine has been manufactured under such a patent, we cannot buy the machine or the technological process involved. At times we may buy a part of a factory, but we cannot purchase the complete process because the patent is held by a U.S. company. In many other cases, in which neither patents nor the participation of U.S. capital in a factory is involved, we are also unable to purchase what we want because U.S. citizens are important clients of that industry and will be offended if the industry sells something to us. And in this way they sabotage and frustrate our efforts in the economic field.

Thus they govern Europe, as owners of enterprises, as owners of patents, as important clients, and as allies of some European governments, using their influence to sabotage Cuba's economic activities.

And the lengths to which they go and their thoroughness in this activity seem incredible. Therefore, we, without being Europeans, know to what extent the economy of Europe is ruled by the United States. And the problem confronting Europe—including capitalist Europe—is to see if any way exists to control, to check that economic penetration; to see if a way exists to resist that penetration, and if such a way exists within the capitalist conception, within a capitalist legal structure. No matter how much they try to protect themselves with tariffs and import duties, the financial and technological power of the United States is so great that on many occasions it is able to sell cheaper and even "dump" certain products, overcoming every kind of trade barrier. And often the U.S. capitalists do not have to overcome any barrier whatever because they simply buy up the European enterprises.

We have even had the following type of experience: after we have purchased trucks from a European firm and received them, U.S. businessmen have bought the factory. From that point on, we have been unable to purchase a single spare part for those trucks.

Sometimes we have the impression that they are voraciously taking over everything, and sometimes we even have the impression that whenever a European plant supplies us with products which are important to our development the imperialists won't rest until they have bought that plant. Fortunately, they have not been able to do this in all industries; fortunately, contradictions arise; fortunately, in spite of everything and as a result of those contradictions, and as a result of that penetration and of the competition of Yankee imperialism with Europe, in spite of all difficulties, trade between Cuba and Europe is on the increase.

We have a ready index to the steadily increasing resistance of European industrialists and governments, to their increasing concern or increasing anguish over the economic penetration and domination of the European economy by the United States, in the fact that at present it is not so hard to purchase certain things which a few years ago were very difficult for Cuba to acquire. Our country's credit—and please forgive me for this disquisition—and the number of commercial offers made to us are increasing.

These facts show us the contradictions; these facts show us the tremendous influence the Yankee imperialists have in Europe. And at the same time we see a growing concern in the capitalist circles of Europe over this phenomenon that is affecting that continent.

Therefore, there is an enemy that can indeed be called a universal enemy. If, in the history of mankind, there ever was a truly universal enemy, an enemy whose attitude and deeds alarmed the whole world, threatened the whole world, assaulted the whole world in one way or another, that real enemy, that truly universal enemy, is precisely Yankee imperialism. And, as mankind becomes aware of this problem, mankind begins, in one way or another, to act.

At times we have heard self-criticism by intellectuals, scientists, and artists to the effect that they are not in close contact with problems. I am not referring, in this case, to the intellectual workers of the Third World—if we may use this name —I am referring, in particular, to the intellectual workers of Europe. They criticize themselves for having a distant—at times they call it paternalistic—relationship with the problems of the world. What do we think of this? It seems to me that we would be deceiving ourselves, we would fall into idealism, if we were to expect this awareness we were speaking of to appear overnight, in a glorious awakening.

We are not going to spend time analyzing the degree to which intellectual workers all over the world are mobilizing in favor of just causes; rather, we shall stress that whatever the degree of that development, whatever the effectiveness of that solidarity, the fact is that such a movement is on the increase, the fact is that it is developing, the fact is that it is growing.

And, in all sincerity, we could say that we have often seen how certain causes which most affect today's world, how certain aggressions, certain crimes have aroused greater defense movements, greater response, greater protest, and greater militancy in groups of intellectual workers than in organizations of a political kind which might have been expected to react with the most militancy! (*Applause*) At times we have seen alleged vanguards far back in the rearguard in the struggle against imperialism! (*Applause*)

In truth, it is not our intention to offend or hurt anyone from this rostrum. Besides, we do not like to offend or attack anyone indirectly. I say this because we must refer to a truth that we know from firsthand experience. After all, this is the point of view of the victims of aggression, the point of view of the revolutionary combatants of a country struggling against imperialism, of a country which, if it does not occupy the front-line trench—for the front-line trench is, unquestionably, Vietnam —(*Applause*) is a country occupying a modest battle post and defending it firmly and resolutely. When we see someone who is supposed to be a member of the vanguard actually in the vanguard it seems the most natural thing in the world to us. But when we see those who were not thought of as being members of the vanguard actually in the vanguard of protest and struggle this arouses our admiration. Therefore, we do not stop to gauge the degree of their fight, but rather we see tangible proof of the fact that when the banners of just causes are not raised in certain countries there are honest men who will raise those banners! (*Applause*) We have seen many an example of such phenomena.

In the course of these years of revolution we have learned a lot, and one of the things we have learned is to distinguish between what is false and what is true, between a revolutionary slogan and a revolutionary attitude, between words and deeds, between dogmas and realities.

Could anyone feel that our experience during the October Crisis was not an unforgettable one for us? We do not want to speak about that episode, but our people unquestionably lived through moments of extreme danger. And no one should take it as bragging when we state here that our people acted with dignity, with integrity, and with bravery. (*Applause*)

But let us say at the same time that for years, almost since we were teenagers, we have been hearing about a great campaign for peace. And I do not say this to criticize the men who have fought for peace, the men who honestly, in one way or another, have taken up the banner of the struggle for peace and have raised it as high as they could.

What really caught our attention was the fact that, when peace was truly endangered, when the world was on the brink of a nuclear war, we did not see mass mobilizations in Europe —and we take it for granted that there would be war in Europe, too, if there were a nuclear war; we take it for granted that, in an encounter between the great nuclear powers, Europe, tied by military pacts to one of these powers, Yankee imperialism, would suffer from the consequences of this war, would be involved in the war—yet we did not see great mass mobilizations. And truly, if there were any, we didn't hear of them; great or small, we didn't hear of them. And we had the strong feeling, the impression—and if this strong impression is incorrect we would be grateful if someone would set us straight—that that slogan was nothing but a slogan, something to be taken lightly, and that that slogan was not able to mobilize any masses, that that slogan was not even able to awaken the masses' instinct of self-preservation.

Where was the vanguard? Where were the revolutionary vanguards?

We have a recent example, very recent, which was very close to us: the death of our heroic Comrade Ernesto Guevara. (*Ovation*)

It will be difficult to find a man who is his equal; it will be difficult to find a revolutionary purer than he, more consistent than he, more complete than he, more exemplary than he. And when we are asked to give an example of what a revolutionary is or should be, could we find a better example than his?

Nevertheless, who were the ones who raised his banner on high? Who were the ones who created a stir in the world? And, above all, who were the ones who raised high his name in Europe, who raised high and extolled his example? Who were the ones who mobilized people, painted signs, and organized meetings in Europe? In which sector was the impact of Che Guevara's death most profound? Precisely among the intellectual workers! (*Applause*) It was not organizations, it was not parties! It was honest, sensitive men and women, who were able to assimilate, understand, and do justice, as compared with those who are unable to understand and who will never understand why he died, who will never be capable of dying as he did, of being the kind of revolutionary he was. (*Applause*)

We know the heartfelt sorrow of true revolutionaries throughout the world. Above all, we know how this event grieved the most exemplary revolutionaries of this epoch, the Vietnamese combatants. (*Applause*)

We have received many condolences, true condolences and formal condolences. We speak of condolences because there is no other word, even though the death of a combatant is not an occasion for mourning, if we believe, as we have always believed, as our people have believed, as revolutionaries in all epochs have always believed, that no true man, no true revolutionary dies in vain.

We have been given irrefutable proof of that by our own enemies, who, with no respect for his condition as a wounded combatant unable to continue fighting because even his weapon had been destroyed, cravenly assassinated him. And not only did they, as cowards, assassinate him, but, even more cowardly, they did away with his body.

In recent days the wire services have been publishing news items, have been speaking of an exchange of counterrevolutionary prisoners in Cuba for Régis Debray. Of course, we are sure—for we have seen Debray's attitude, we have seen his powerful defense, we have seen the serenity, courage, and integrity with which he unmasked his accusers—we are sure that Régis Debray would never accept such an exchange. But we are not running away from the "gorilla" Barrientos's challenge. If he wants counterrevolutionaries freed, if he wants petty counterrevolutionary leaders freed, we say, we propose: return the remains of Major Guevara and we will release one hundred imprisoned counterrevolutionaries! (*Ovation*) We will release, at once, not one counterrevolutionary, but one hundred, chosen by the CIA and by the Pentagon, if they have the courage to return the remains of Major Guevara! (*Applause*) For they are the ones who will show whether or not it is true that they fear Che even more dead than alive. (*Applause*)

This is a mighty example of what an example is! This is a mighty example of the fact that ideas cannot be destroyed! This is a mighty example of the fact that revolutionary causes, just causes, cannot be crushed, no matter what blows or losses they are dealt! Because we are human beings, we are men, for a reason; and a man's ideas are values that are above and beyond anything else, and, of course, above and beyond his own life.

We have gone through these experiences, and it is for that reason that—with no intentions of flattery, but with absolute sincerity—we want to express the sentiments aroused in us at seeing how the intellectual workers, in ever increasing numbers, have united and become mighty standard-bearers and defenders of just causes.

I mentioned Che's example; but we have also seen the strength that the movement for support of and solidarity with Vietnam is gaining throughout the world; we have seen how more and more intellectual workers in the United States are raising the banners of struggle against the savage aggression in Vietnam; we have seen the increasing support that the intellectual workers of the world are giving the black Movement in the United States; we have seen how intellectual workers throughout the world have raised the banner of struggle against the imprisonment of Régis Debray; and we have seen in recent events, in definitive actions, how the movement of solidarity has increased among intellectual workers throughout the world. And we know how to give this phenomenon its due and deeply deserved estimation!

By this I don't mean that we should be satisfied. I don't mean that the maximum has been done; far from it. I don't mean that this movement has the strength it should have; I simply mean that we feel optimistic because this movement—a movement of conscience, of justice—is growing and developing. And there is no doubt that it will continue growing and developing, because as our common enemy becomes increasingly aggressive, as its crimes become increasingly repulsive, as it becomes increasingly rapacious, this movement, this strength will grow.

And, saying Yankee imperialism is powerful, that Yankee imperialism has amassed great financial and technical resources, great means of causing death and destruction, we do not consider, and never will, that this threat to humanity, that all the forces accumulated by imperialism, can be more powerful than humanity. Vietnam, a very small part of humanity, has shown us once again how to face, how to fight, and how to defeat this superpowerful imperialism! An imperialism that is trying to intimidate the world, that is trying to blackmail the world, and that has only succeeded in increasing political awareness in the world, in increasing the indignation and fighting spirit in the world, as its actions become more repulsive, as its actions become more criminal and abhorrent—an enemy that wants to solve everything by force, that wants to solve everything with its gold, that is just as ready to assassinate as to bribe, that is just as ready to oppress by force as by corruption, an enemy that penetrates all fields, penetrates all activities.

It is logical that intellectual workers must feel revolted when they see the best creations of man, the most marvelous products of human intelligence, the creations of scientists and technicians, the advances that man has developed for the welfare of mankind, being used today to kill, to destroy, to oppress, and to corrupt. The advances in physics, as well as in chemistry, in electronics, and in biology, are applied to making everything from bombs that explode into thousands of pieces to poisons, chemical means of destruction, weapons of germ warfare—in short, everything that men of science have created is used.

It is logical for the intellectual workers of the world to feel that in one way or another they are victims of this plunder, to feel they are under attack in one way or another, just as they feel they are under attack from the brain drain policy of stealing technicians, from this whole policy aimed at monopolizing science through the recruiting of scientists from all over the world, from so-called developed countries and from underdeveloped countries. This situation is no secret; it is very widely recognized, since the statistics have been published in the United States itself. Thus, the country with a more developed technology is following—as I pointed out on January 2—this policy of brain draining, this stealing of specialists.

In the face of this situation, what can be strange about men and women, intellectuals who hold the most varied philosophical views, who take very different political positions, who are apolitical, or who sustain differing beliefs, having met here?

We also want to point out that certain aspects of this Congress have been truly impressive. One of them is the general awareness of what constitutes imperialism, what it represents, the general awareness that the problems raised in the modern world cannot be solved by outdated social systems rendered obsolete by the development of science and technology as well as human conscience. And there was unanimous agreement among intellectuals of the Third World as well as those of the developed countries that it was impossible (through these obsolete social systems) to overcome the deep-seated problems of any modern country, be it developed or underdeveloped: for the developed countries to meet or overcome the serious contradictions that exist under capitalism in order to pass beyond a society that is practically rendered obsolete by history, or the underdeveloped countries to take their only possible road, because how can a country which is falling further behind the rest of the world achieve an accelerated rate of development going through the *via crucis* of capitalist development under the conditions of imperialist domination?

But these were elementary questions for those who took part in this Congress.

However, there were other matters, and one thing in particular which quite frankly impressed us very much, because it indicated just how vast the scope of the world revolutionary movement actually is. This was a paper presented by a group of Catholic priests who took part in the Congress. I am not going to mention their names, because I have not consulted them about it, but I am going to read their paper to our people—I suppose you delegates have all read it.

> We, Catholic priests, delegates to the Cultural Congress of Havana, are convinced of the following:
>
> That imperialism today, and especially in the Third World, constitutes a dehumanizing factor which destroys the very basis of individual dignity, violates the freedom of cultural development, impedes true forms of human development, and propitiates a state of underdevelopment that grows more acute and oppressive by the day.
>
> That in spite of the differences existing between Christianity and Marxism concerning interpretations of mankind and the world, it is Marxism which provides the most exact scientific analysis of the real nature of imperialism and provides the most effective impetus to revolutionary action by the masses.
>
> That the Christian faith involves the concept of love expressed through effective help to each and every man.
>
> That the priest Camilo Torres Restrepo, by dying for the revolutionary cause, provided us with the greatest example of a Christian intellectual dedicated to the people. [*Applause*]
>
> We pledge ourselves to the anti-imperialist revolutionary cause, come what may, in order to achieve the liberation of every man and of all mankind.
>
> Therefore, we condemn the economic and cultural blockade which imperialism has placed on the Republic of Cuba, first free territory of America. We condemn the United States' war against Vietnam as a most monstrous imperialist aggression against the freedom of a people living in the Third World.
>
> We reject any form of colonialism and neocolonialism as the product of imperialism, an alienating and dehumanizing force.

This statement is an indication of how revolutionary ideas, in one form or another, are spreading, how they are broadening in scope, how these ideas are even penetrating religious sectors, and how more and more revolutionary combatants are emerging from these sectors.

A few days ago we read one of the numerous news dispatches received here from the Yankee news services, dealing precisely with this movement, expressing concern over the movement developing within the Catholic clergy in Latin America. And, of course, it stated that this was a movement linked to Cuba, to the Cuban Revolution, to Castro, and so on. It even made accusations against the Papal Nuncio. (*Laughter*) Accusations were made against the Papal Nuncio in Cuba as well as the Canadian Papal Nuncio who had come to Cuba to invest the Cuban Papal Nuncio with the office of bishop.

There was a reception, and we attended that reception. And of course, for the imperialists, for the counterrevolutionary clique, for the reactionaries, and undoubtedly for the CIA, that was a conspiratorial council. (*Laughter*) Unquestionably, the reactionaries are more and more alarmed; they live in fear, seeing conspiracy everywhere, seeing specters everywhere, seeing subversion everywhere. And it's true, it is true! They are the specters that they have created, the rebellions that they have aroused, and the universal conspiracy by men worthy of mankind that they have incited.

Unquestionably, we are observing new events, new phenomena. It is certain that revolutionaries, we who consider ourselves revolutionaries, and, among those who consider themselves revolutionaries, we who consider ourselves Marxist-Leninists, all have the obligation of analyzing these new phenomena. Because nothing could be more anti-Marxist than dogma, (*Applause*) nothing could be more anti-Marxist than the petrification of ideas. And there are even ideas propounded in the name of Marxism which seem to be truly fossils. (*Applause*) Marxism has had thinkers of genius: Karl Marx, Friedrich Engels, Lenin, to mention the outstanding founders. But Marxism needs to develop, break away from a certain rigidity, interpret today's reality from an objective, scientific viewpoint, conduct itself as a revolutionary force and not as a pseudo-revolutionary church. (*Applause*)

These are the paradoxes of history. How, seeing sectors of the clergy becoming revolutionary forces, can we resign ourselves to seeing revolutionary forces becoming ecclesiastical forces? (*Applause*)

We trust that because of our affirmation of such ideas we shall not be subjected to excommunication (*Laughter*) nor to a Holy Inquisition either. But we must meditate on this, we must act with a more dialectical sense—that is, with a more revolutionary sense.

We must analyze contemporary phenomena, study them profoundly. Naturally such analysis, such concepts, must be more and more the work of groups rather than individuals. Just as in scientific fields the isolated researcher scarcely any longer exists, nor can he exist, so in politics, in economics, in sociology, isolated researchers—the appearance of men of genius under modern conditions—become more and more improbable. And in reality there is a certain underdevelopment in the field of political ideas, in the field of revolutionary ideas. And this is the basis of the enormous confusion that exists in today's world, the enormous crisis that exists in the field of ideas—that is, in the field of doctrines—at the very moment in which revolutionary sentiments and attitudes are spreading. No one can state that he is the possessor of all truth. Today no one can state, amidst the great complexity of the world, that he is completely right. We have our truths here, which arose from our experience, applicable to our conditions, and we have our deductions and our conclusions. But we have never attempted to be mentors; we have never pretended to have a monopoly on revolutionary truth. Nonetheless, we have seen how revolutionary truths have appeared, how revolutionary ideas emerge from analysis, from the efforts of many minds.

And what will the imperialists say, what will they think? Perhaps they will say that this is a Vietnam in the field of culture; they will say that guerrillas have begun to appear among intellectual workers—that is, the intellectual workers are adopting an increasingly militant position. And we have not the slightest doubt that the imperialists will be deeply concerned at this event and the resolutions adopted at this event, the revolutionary tone of this event.

And the thinking of the imperialists is increasingly evident, their intentions ever more unmistakable. Today, for example, two dispatches, quoting two great oligarchs of imperialism, arrived in Cuba: one concerning a general, the U.S. Chief of Staff, and the other reporting on statements made by Mr. Rusk. Are they any different from the usual declarations? They are no different. Are they any different from numerous statements mentioned in this Congress? No! But they do reveal the precision and clarity of the intellectual workers and their resolutions.

Let's see what they say—whichever of the two, the one you prefer. Mr. Rusk spoke and, among other things, referred to the October Crisis. The cable reads: " 'The October Crisis, in which the United States showed considerable moderation, has surely served as a warning to various powers, both large and small,' stressed U.S. Secretary of State Dean Rusk at a press conference yesterday, adding that many countries had learned their lesson."

This is the vulgar language of vulgar blackmail! (*Applause*)

All right. But, even more important, it says: "Another continuing problem is that constituted by aggressions such as the one in Vietnam"—Vietnamese aggression!—"adding that once the so-called wars of liberation are curbed"—once the so-called wars of liberation are curbed!—"the world will be able to enjoy a long era of peace." A pax romana! (*Laughter*)

The dispatch continues: "Speaking of the population explosion, Dean Rusk stressed the pressing need to find a solution to it before this danger reaches the point of causing the outbreak of a nuclear war.

" 'Science and technology will have to overcome these problems, which, in the '80s, will acquire a character at least as explosive as the question of nuclear weapons,' he concluded."

And the general? What did the general have to say?

"General Harold K. Johnson, U.S. Army Chief of Staff, stated today that the experience of this country (the United States) in the Dominican Republic and Cuba shows that war in Vietnam is necessary to end the spread of communism.

"In an address given in this city General Johnson stated, 'The spread of communism ended when our country began directly assisting resistance to the establishment of the system.'

"He added, 'Even in our hemisphere, when we stand up to the communists swiftly and vigorously, as was the case in the Dominican Republic, they are halted.'

" 'But,' continued Johnson, 'when the United States did not recognize a communist coup, as was the case in Cuba, the tumor put down roots and tried to spread.'

"General Johnson, who returned a week ago from his ninth inspection tour of Vietnam, denied that the communists had taken the initiative in the war, or that the war had become stalemated."

Two statements issued on the same day: one from a general with numerous defeats to his credit, the other from an eminent and dismal spokesman of imperialism. And what do all these declarations so brazenly issued by the spokesmen of imperialism—generals and civilians—mean? Do they perhaps hide the strategy of imperialism? Do they somehow disguise its intentions and ambitions?

They say that "Communism ceases to spread when we combat it vigorously." They cite the case of Cuba—"that tumor"—a tumor that is still not rooted out, is perhaps what they mean to say—how can its spread be stopped? "And that's why we intervened in Santo Domingo, at the cost of blood and fire . . . to assist the resistance." They assisted the gorillas! Resistance? They couldn't have held out for half an hour against the people! (*Applause*)

And what does the other one say? Just the same: that "When liberation struggles cease there will be peace." But they don't stop there. It is not enough for liberation struggles to cease. No. The birth rate must be controlled; population growth must be controlled. For it's not enough for liberation struggles to cease; if humanity continues growing there will be explosions more powerful and dangerous than nuclear weapons. Imperialism wants science and technology to come to its aid! It wants education on birth control; it wants birth control to come to its aid!

The solutions put forth by imperialism are the quintessence of simplicity. Two thirds of humanity is hungry; in order to rid themselves of hunger and misery, these people must make revolutions. Ah! But there must not be revolutions! Revolutions will be put down with blood and fire! There will be peace only if there are no revolutions. But, moreover, even if there are no revolutions, what will happen to that two thirds of mankind that multiplies like rabbits? When they speak of the problems of population and birth, they are in no way moved by concepts related to the interests of the family or of society. No! Their premise is that humanity will die of hunger if it continues multiplying; and they advance this concept in these days, which are not the days of Malthus or of Methuselah! Just when science and technology are making incredible advances in all fields, they resort to technology to suppress revolutions and ask the help of science to prevent population growth. In short, the peoples are not to make revolutions, and women are not to give birth. This sums up the philosophy of imperialism.

But at the same time we see the insoluble contradictions of that imperialism, its insecurity, its fear of the future. Here is evidence that this oligarchy, established on guns and on piles of gold, lives in worry, lives in distrust, lives in fear of the future.

And that, in essence, is what the political thinking of imperialism today is reduced to, the political thinking of the oligarchy that governs the United States and that, despite its savage repression, its technological and military resources, feels insecure. For it knows that, without revolution, none of these countries will emerge from underdevelopment.

The imperialists admit, they understand—they know—that there is no formula for passing from feudalism to progress. They know that without revolution there is no development, and they feel powerless in view of the reality that there is growth and development in the world, that the population is growing and that—as a natural and inevitable phenomenon—revolutionary awareness is growing.

The imperialists know that the gap between the developed and the underdeveloped world is growing; the United Nations constantly publishes the statistics. It is known, for example, that the gross national product in the United States will increase from approximately 400 thousand million dollars in 1960 to approximately 800 thousand million in 1975—a fifteen-year period; that in the European Common Market the gross product will increase in the same period from approximately 200 thousand million dollars to 400 thousand million dollars, this by 1975. All economists and all those who work in problems of commercial exchange know that industrial products are sold at increasingly higher prices to the underdeveloped world and that the latter's products bring lower and lower prices.

A Latin American oligarch recently said that his country could buy only one jeep now with the same amount of a product which ten years ago could pay for three jeeps.

And while the living standards go up in one part of the world, poverty grows in the rest of the world; the inequality grows, exploitation grows.

According to the same data, the imbalance in trade between the underdeveloped and the developed world amounted to 4 thousand million dollars in 1960 and will amount to approximately 20 thousand million dollars by 1970.

While the gross national product grows, while the per capita income grows in one part of the world, in the most populated part of the world the per capita income diminishes, the imbalance grows; prices for the products of those who have the best living conditions increase, while the prices paid those who live in the worst conditions drop; resources, moreover, are often squandered by feudal barons and by oligarchies; the extraction of monetary resources increases.

And that is simply an insoluble problem, a problem that has no solution; it is a simple fact. Therefore, it seems that those who use cybernetics and calculate, add, subtract, multiply, and divide have consulted their computers and learned that this situation has no solution, that it is a situation without solution.

So what is the imperialists' remedy? Repressive wars against revolutions, and there will be peace when there are no more revolutions; let populations cease to grow, because if the population does not stop increasing there will be uprisings and there will be nuclear wars.

In no previous period of history has man heard such barbarous, genocidal, brutal manifestations against mankind!

That is the fact, that is the undeniable truth, that is what contributes to the creation of a universal revolutionary awareness; that is what has brought you here; these unquestionable facts are what has given a revolutionary tone to this Congress.

And it is true that in the field of culture there are many problems to be solved, there are many questions to be answered, and we by no means wish to disguise the fact that there are still many things for which solutions must be found; there are many new problems still unsolved. And those are problems that face us as revolutionaries, above all when, as revolutionaries, in special conditions, we find ourselves obliged to use an immense part of our efforts to merely survive, to defend ourselves, and to advance.

However, we are determined to find the adequate answers, the best solutions, to the countless problems that emerge in the process of development of a society. Problems to be solved and solutions to be found exist; we do not deny it. And we will find the solutions. And we sincerely believe that this Congress is a contribution to us and to the revolutionary movements.

But the way that the intellectual workers of the Congress took hold of fundamental problems, of the most essential questions, of the things that most concern man in today's world, and worked on these questions and, united around these questions, carried this Congress forward, has been instructive.

Numerous questions could be debated within the revolutionary camp on the problems of culture, because they are real problems.

Perhaps that was what the imperialists expected. But attention and efforts were centered on fundamental contradictions, on decisive contradictions, that are not contradictions within the heart of the revolutionary movement, not problems of culture within the heart of the revolutionary movement, but contradictions and problems of culture created by imperialism.

We do not, certainly, believe that this Congress has solved all problems or clarified all questions, but we do believe that it has been an extraordinary step forward; we do believe that it has been very, very positive; and we do believe that the topics that have been discussed here are essential and that the preoccupations concerning revolutionary society were important and essential—above all, those relating to the new man.

Fortunately, in this question of the future we have the magnificent exposition left to us by Che, in which he so clearly and brilliantly analyzed some of these problems with the sincerity, honesty, and frankness that invariably characterized him, and in which he expressed his idea of what the new man should be like, what the man of tomorrow, the man of the twenty-first century, should be like. We have seen how these concerns were taken up in this Congress. We have also seen how the example of Che, his attitude, his conduct, his honesty, his integrity, presided over and inspired many of the resolutions of this Congress.

For us, this successful event, whose results are greater than the most optimistic predictions, will be unforgettable. It is true that our people live hours, days, and months intensely immersed in work, overcoming obstacles, battling for the development of our economy under difficult conditions, against an aggressive imperialism and with a socialism which is very limited in all fields; and in this battle, in this titanic struggle, in this effort that grows by the day, immersed in work, our people may have appeared to be indifferent to the Congress, but really that is not the case. In reality, our people have acquired an extraordinary sensitivity, an extraordinary perceptiveness, and you had an opportunity to observe in several mass rallies the rapidity, the agility, of our masses to understand any problem, the degree of political understanding of our people, their revolutionary spirit, the internationalist spirit which they have developed; their feeling of solidarity acquired in the struggle itself that has inspired and received the encouragement of everyone. In every event, be it the Tricontinental Conference, a conference of Latin American revolutionary organizations, or events such as this one, they have increasingly broadened their knowledge, their information, their revolutionary horizons.

For our part, we take pleasure in saying that your presence here has been a very great honor. We hope that our people have expressed in a thousand different ways their warmth, their recognition, and their sympathy. It is a high honor for us to have shared these days with men and women of value, of prestige, whose works and labor are known to a much greater extent than you perhaps imagine. We shall remember this high honor, always. This sentiment expresses the sentiment of the Revolutionary Government, the sentiment of our Party, the sentiment of our people. And so, in a spirit of friendship, of fraternity, and of affection, we declare this Congress closed. Many thanks to all of you. Be assured that this effort for advancement in all fields, in economy, in culture, in revolutionary struggle, in the construction of a better society, in the development of a better man, will not cease, and that our Revolution will not defraud the confidence and hope that you may place in it!

Patria o Muerte!
Venceremos!
(*Ovation*)

"I Don't Mean Bananas"

MALCOLM X

By the fall of 1968, the disarray of the Black Power movement had become critical. In part: sharp police repression. In part: the difficulty of achieving the concrete practice of a forward strategy, of avoiding the pitfalls of self-defensiveness. But these reasons may themselves largely be explained by still a third: nationalism and radicalism, caste politics and class politics, had somehow been forced apart by black militants and defined as competing *points of departure, the former becoming ascendant in key black groups.*

Malcolm's political method had presupposed rather the unity *of nationalism and radicalism, a unity which therefore connected Mississippi with the Congo and Africa with Asia, and which understood a viable politics for black Americans to require both a demand for Africanhood* and a conception of pro-Africanhood as an explicitly anti-imperialist stance. *The decision of many black militants to leave the anti-war protest to whites—"their war, not ours"—drained that protest of its needed volatility and led at the same time to the further psychological and political confinement of the Black Power movement in the weakest of all definitions of blackness. "Black is beautiful." Very well, but only provisionally: only when it asserts itself against the full plenitude of whiteness's oppressive meanings. One understands the need to develop black consciousness. But there is just no such thing as a black consciousness which is not also a consciousness of the structural sources of* global *subjugation: caste* is *class and cannot otherwise be understood.*

That is, black is beautiful only under the same conditions in which white is also beautiful. It is only men and women that can be beautiful, and it is only their fully understood stipulation of freedom that can make them so. Either negritude is antiracist, anti-imperialist, and therefore anticapitalist—in other words, radical, revolutionary, and socialist—or it is nothing but a demand for privileged servitude, gilded chains. "First things first," someone says; "the program is black capitalism." But how can such a thing be, since capitalism has so clearly said that black is ugly? In our context, blackness and capitalism are each other's negations, and they cannot be joined.

Malcolm's enshrinement has been his banalization. He is not a "surpassed" figure, someone whose insights, fresh once upon a time, have since become immobile commonplaces. His message—as in the following passages from a 1964 Audubon Ballroom speech—must be taken out of the political museum where inattention has very prematurely deposited it.

SEVERAL PERSONS have asked me recently, since I've been back, "What is your program?" I purposely, to this day, have not in any way mentioned what our program is, because there will come a time when we will unveil it so that everybody will understand it. Policies change, and programs change, according to time. But the objective never changes. You might change your method of achieving the objective, but the objective never changes. Our objective is complete freedom, complete justice, complete equality, by any means necessary. That never changes. Complete and immediate recognition and respect as human beings, that doesn't change, that's what all of us want. I don't care what you belong to—you still want that, recognition and respect as a human being. But you have changed your methods from time to time on how you go about getting it. The reason you change your method is that you have to change your method according to time and conditions that prevail. And one of the conditions that prevails on this earth right now, that we know too little about, is our relationship with the freedom struggle of people all over the world.

Here in America, we have always thought that we were struggling by ourselves, and most Afro-Americans will tell you just that—that we're a minority. By thinking we're a minority, we struggle like a minority. We struggle like we're an underdog. We struggle like all of the odds are against us. This type of struggle takes place only because we don't yet know where we fit in the scheme of things. We've been maneuvered out of a position where we could rightly know and understand where we fit into the scheme of things. It's impossible for you and me to know where we stand until we look around on this entire earth. Not just look around in Harlem or New York, or Mississippi, or America—we have got to look all around this earth. We don't know where we stand until we know where America stands. You don't know where you stand in America until you know where America stands in the world. We don't know where you and I stand in this context, known to us as America, until we know where America stands in the world context.

When you and I are inside of America and look at America, she looks big and bad and invincible. Oh, yes, and when we approach her in that context, we approach her as beggars, with our hat in our hands. As Toms, actually, only in the twentieth-century sense, but still as Toms. While if we understand what's going on on this earth and what's going on in the world today, and fit America into that context, we find out she's not so bad, after all; she's not very invincible. And when you find out she's not invincible, you don't approach her like you're dealing with someone who's invincible.

As a rule, up to now, the strategy of America has been to tuck all of our leaders up into her dress, and besiege them with money, with prestige, with praise, and make them jump, and tell them what to tell us. And they always tell us we're the underdog, and that we don't have a chance, and that we should do it nonviolently and carefully; otherwise, we'll get hurt or we'll get wasted. We don't buy that.

Number one, we want to know: What are we? How did we get to be what we are? Where did we come from? How did we come from there? Who did we leave behind? Where was it that we left them behind, and what are they doing over there where we used to be? This is something that we have not been told. We have been brought over here and isolated—you know the funniest thing about that: they accuse *us* of introducing "separation" and "isolation." No one is more isolated than you and I. There's no system on earth more capable of thoroughly separating and isolating a people than this system that they call the democratic system; and you and I are the best proof of it, the best example of it. We were separated from our people, and have been isolated here for a long time.

So thoroughly has this been done to us that now we don't even know that there is somebody else that looks like we do. When we see them, we look at them like they're strangers. And when we see somebody that doesn't look anything like us, we call them our friends. That's a shame. It shows you what has been done to us. Yes, I mean our own people—we see our people come here who look exactly like we do, our twins, can't tell them apart, and we say, "Those are foreigners." Yet we're getting our heads busted trying to snuggle up to somebody who not only doesn't look like us, but doesn't even smell like us.

So you can see the importance of these meetings on Sunday nights during the past two or three weeks, and for a couple more weeks. It is not so much to spell out any program; you can't give a people a program until they realize they need one, and until they realize that all existing programs aren't programs that are going to produce productive results. So what we would like to do on Sunday nights is to go into our problem, and just analyze and analyze and analyze; and question things that you don't understand, so we can at least try and get a better picture of what faces us.

I, for one, believe that if you give people a thorough understanding of what it is that confronts them, and the basic causes that produce it, they'll create their own program; and when the people create a program, you get action. When these "leaders" create programs, you get no action. The only time you see them is when the people are exploding. Then the leaders are shot into the situation and told to control things. You can't show me a leader that has set off an explosion. No, they come and contain the explosion. They say, "Don't get rough, you know, do the smart thing." This is their role—they're there just to restrain you and me, to restrain the struggle, to keep it in a certain groove, and not let it get out of control. Whereas you and I don't want anybody to keep us from getting out of control. We want to get out of control. We want to smash anything that gets in our way that doesn't belong there.

Listen to the last part of what I said: I didn't just say we want to smash anything that gets in our way. I said we want to smash anything that gets in our way that doesn't belong there. You see, I had to give you the whole thing, because when you read it, you'll hear we're going to smash up everybody. No, I didn't say that. I said we'll smash up anything that gets in the way that doesn't belong there. I mean that. If it doesn't belong there, it's worthy to be smashed. This country practices that—power. This country smashes anything that gets in its way. It crushes anything that gets in its way. And since we're Americans, they tell us, well, we'll do it the American way. We'll smash anything that gets in our way.

This is the type of philosophy that we want to express among our people. We don't need to give them a program, not yet. First, give them something to think about. If we give them something to think about, and start them thinking in a way that they should think, they'll see through all this camouflage that's going on right now. It's just a show—the result of a script written by somebody else. The people will take that script and tear it up and write one for themselves. And you can bet that when you write the script for yourself, you're always doing something different than you'd be doing if you followed somebody else's script.

So, brothers and sisters, the thing that you and I must have an understanding of is the role that's being played in world affairs today, number one, by the continent of Africa; number two, by the people on that continent; number three, by those of us who are related to the people on that continent, but who, by some quirk in our own history, find ourselves today here in the Western hemisphere. Always bear that in mind that our being in the Western hemisphere differs from anyone else, because everyone else here came voluntarily. Everyone that you see in this part of the world got on a boat and came here voluntarily; whether they were immigrants or what have you, they came here voluntarily. So they don't have any real squawk, because they got what they were looking for. But you and I can squawk because we didn't come here voluntarily. We didn't ask to be brought here. We were brought here forcibly, against our will, and in chains. And at no time since we have been here, have they even acted like they wanted us here. At no time. At no time have they even tried to pretend that we were brought here to be citizens. Why, they don't even *pretend.* So why should we pretend?

Look at the continent of Africa today and see what position it occupies on this earth, and you realize that there's a tussle going on between East and West. It used to be between America and the West and Russia, but they're not tussling with each other any more. Kennedy made a satellite out of Russia. He put Khrushchev in his pocket; yes, he did—lost him his job. The tussle now is between America and China. In the camp of the West, America is foremost. Most other Western nations are satellites to America. England is an American satellite. All of them are satellites, perhaps with the exception of France. France wants America to be her satellite. You never can tell what the future might bring. Better nations than this have fallen, if you read history. Most of the European communist nations are still satelliting around Russia. But in Asia, China is the center of power.

Among Asian countries, whether they are communist, socialist—you don't find any capitalist countries over there too much nowadays. Almost every one of the countries that has gotten independence has devised some kind of socialistic system, and this is no accident. This is another reason why I say that you and I here in America—who are looking for a job, who are looking for better housing, looking for a better education—before you start trying to be incorporated, or integrated, or disintegrated, into this capitalistic system, should look over there and find out what are the people who have gotten their freedom adopting to provide themselves with better housing and better education and better food and better clothing.

None of them are adopting the capitalistic system because they realize they can't. You can't operate a capitalistic system unless you are vulturistic; you have to have someone else's blood to suck to be a capitalist. You show me a capitalist, I'll show you a bloodsucker. He cannot be anything but a bloodsucker if he's going to be a capitalist. He's got to get it from somewhere other than himself, and that's where he gets it—from somewhere or someone other than himself. So, when we look at the African continent, when we look at the trouble that's going on between East and West, we find that the nations in Africa are developing socialistic systems to solve their problems.

There's one thing that Martin Luther King mentioned at the Armory the other night, which I thought was most significant. I hope he really understood what he was saying. He mentioned that while he was in some of those Scandinavian countries he saw no poverty. There was no unemployment, no poverty. Everyone was getting education, everyone had decent housing, decent whatever-they-needed to exist. But why did he mention those countries in his list as different?

This is the richest country on earth and there's poverty, there's bad housing, there's slums, there's inferior education. And this is the richest country on earth. Now, you know, if those countries that are poor can come up with a solution to their problems so that there's no unemployment, then instead of you running downtown picketing city hall, you should stop and find out what they do over there to solve their problems. This is why the Man doesn't want you and me to look beyond Harlem or beyond the shores of America. As long as you don't know what's happening on the outside, you'll be all messed up dealing with this Man on the inside. I mean what they use to solve the problem is not capitalism. What they are using to solve their problem in Africa and Asia is not capitalism. So what you and I should do is find out what they are using to get rid of poverty and all the other negative characteristics of a rundown society.

Africa is strategically located geographically between East and West; it's the most valuable piece of property involved in the struggle between East and West. You can't get to the East without going past it, and can't get from the East to West without going past it. It sits right there between all of them. It sits snuggled into a nest between Asia and Europe; it can reach either one. None of the natural resources that are needed in Europe that they get from Asia can get to Europe without coming either around Africa, over Africa, or in between the Suez Canal which is sitting at the tip of Africa. She can cut off Europe's bread. She can put Europe to sleep overnight, just like that. Because she's in a position to; the African continent is in a position to do this. But they want you and me to think Africa is a jungle, of no value, of no consequence. Because they also know that if you knew how valuable it was, you'd realize why they're over there killing our people. And you'd realize that it's not for some kind of humanitarian purpose or reason.

Also, Africa as a continent is important because of its tropical climate. It's so heavily vegetated you can take any section of Africa and use modern agricultural methods and turn that section alone into the breadbasket for the world. Almost any country over there can feed the whole continent, if it only had access to people who had the technical know-how to bring into that area modern methods of agriculture. It's rich. A jungle is only a place that's heavily vegetated—the soil is so rich and the climate is so good that everything grows, and it doesn't grow in season—it grows all the time. All the time is the season. That means it can grow anything, produce anything.

Added to its richness and its strategic position geographically is the fact of the existence of the Suez Canal and the Strait of Gibraltar. Those two narrow straits can cut off from Europe anything and everything Europe needs. All of the oil that runs Europe goes through the Suez Canal, up the Mediterranean Sea to places like Greece and Italy and Southern Spain and France and along through there; or through the Strait of Gibraltar and around on into England. And they need it. They need access through the Suez. When Nasser took over the Suez, they almost died in Europe. It scared them to death—why? Because Egypt is in Africa, in fact, Egypt is in both Africa and Asia . . .

Before the Suez Canal was built, it was all one, you couldn't really make a distinction between Africa and Asia. It was all one. When President Nasser took the Suez Canal, that meant that for the first time the Suez Canal was under the complete jurisdiction of an African nation, and it meant that other nations had to cater to this African nation if they wanted to survive, if they didn't want their oil and other sources of supply cut off. Immediately this had an effect on European attitudes and European economic measures. They began to try and devise new means, new routes, to get the things that they needed.

Another reason the continent is so important is because of its gold. It has some of the largest deposits of gold on earth, and diamonds. Not only the diamonds you put on your finger and in your ear, but industrial diamonds, diamonds that are needed to make machines—machines that can't function or can't run unless they have these diamonds. These industrial diamonds play a major role in the entire industrialization of the European nations, and without these diamonds their industry would fall . . .

Not only diamonds, but also cobalt. Cobalt is one of the most valuable minerals on this earth today, and I think Africa is one of the only places where it is found. They use it in cancer treatment, plus they use it in this nuclear field that you've heard so much about. Cobalt and uranium—the largest deposits are right there on the African continent. And this is what the Man is after. The Man is after keeping you over here worrying about a cup of coffee, while he's over there in your motherland taking control over minerals that have so much value they make the world go around. While you and I are still walking around over here, yes, trying to drink some coffee—with a cracker.

It's one of the largest sources of iron and bauxite and lumber and even oil, and Western industry needs all of these minerals in order to survive. All of these natural minerals are needed by the Western industrialists in order for their industry to keep running at the clip that it's been used to. Can we prove it? Yes. You know that France lost her French West African possessions, Belgium lost the Congo, England lost Nigeria and Ghana and some of the other English-speaking areas; France also lost Algeria, or the Algerians took Algeria.

As soon as these European powers lost their African possessions, Belgium had an economic crisis—the same year she turned the Congo loose. She had to rearrange her entire economy and her economic methods had to be revised, because she had lost possession of the source of most of her raw materials—raw materials that she got almost free, almost with no price or output whatsoever. When she got into a position where she didn't have access to these free raw materials anymore, it affected her economy. It affected the French economy. It affected the British economy. It drove all of these European countries to the point where they had to come together and form what's known as the European Common Market. Prior to that, you wouldn't hear anything about a European Common Market.

Being the gateway to Southwest Africa, Southern Rhodesia, Basutoland, Swaziland, and South Africa, the Congo is a country on the African continent which is so strategically located geographically that if it were to fall into the hands of a real dyed-in-the-wool African nationalist, he could then make it possible for African soldiers to train in the Congo for the purpose of invading Angola. When they invade Angola, that means Angola must fall, because there are more Africans than there are Portuguese, and they just couldn't control Angola any longer. And if the Congo fell into good hands, other than Tshombe, then it would mean that Angola would fall, Southern Rhodesia would fall, Southwest Africa would fall, and South Africa would fall. And that's the only way they would fall.

When these countries fall, it would mean that the source of raw materials, natural resources, some of the richest mineral deposits on earth, would then be taken away from the European economy. And without free access to this, the economy of Europe wouldn't be worth two cents. All of your European countries would be of no more importance than a country like Norway, which is all right for Norwegians, but has no influence beyond that. It's just another country stuck up some place in the northern part, like Sweden and some of those places. Every European country would be just as insignificant as the smallest insignificant country in Europe right now—if they lost the rest of Africa. Because the rest of Africa that's still colonized is the part of the African continent that's still backing up the European economy. And if the economy of Europe was to sink any farther, it would really wash away the American economy. American economy can never be any stronger than the European economy because both of them are one. It's one and the same economy. They are brothers.

I say this because it is necessary for you and me to understand what is at stake. You can't understand what is going on in Mississippi if you don't understand what is going on in the Congo. And you can't really be interested in what's going on in Mississippi if you're not also interested in what's going on in the Congo. They're both the same. The same interests are at stake. The same sides are drawn up, the same schemes are at work in the Congo that are at work in Mississippi. The same stakes—no difference whatsoever.

Another frightening thing for this continent and the European continent is the fact that the Africans are trying to industrialize. One of the most highly industrialized African nations is Egypt. They have had a limited source of power up to now, but they are building a dam in upper Egypt, where the black Egyptians live . . . The Aswan Dam is something that everybody should see. The Aswan is being built on the Nile in the heart of the desert, surrounded by mountains. One of the most outstanding things about this dam isn't so much its miraculous technical aspects, but the human aspects . . .

So the Aswan Dam creates enough additional power to make it possible to step up or speed up the industrialization of that particular African nation. And as their industrialization is stepped up, it means that they can produce their own cars, their own tractors, their own tools, their own machinery, plus a lot of other things. Not only Egypt, but Ghana too. Ghana is building a dam, they're damming the Volta River. There's the Volta High Dam, and it's being built for the purpose of increasing the power potential of Ghana, so that Ghana also can increase its industrial output.

As these African nations get in a position to increase their own power and to industrialize, what does it mean? It means that where they now are a market for American goods and America's finished products, and a market for European finished products, when they're able to finish their own products, they will be able to get their products cheaper because they're putting their own raw materials into the finished products. Now the raw materials are taken from Africa, shipped all the way to Europe, used to feed the machines of the Europeans, and make jobs for them, and then turned around and sold back to the Africans as finished products. But when the African nations become industrialized, they can take their own products and stick them in the machines and finish them into whatever they want. Then they can live cheaper. The whole system will be a system with a high standard of living but a cheaper standard of living.

This standard of living automatically will threaten the standard of living in Europe because it will cut off the European market. European factories can't produce unless they have some place to market the products. American factories can't produce unless they have some place to market their products. It is for this reason that the European nations in the past have kept the nations in Latin America and in Africa and in Asia from becoming industrial powers. They keep the machinery and the ability to produce and manufacture limited to Europe and limited to America. Then this puts America and the Europeans in a position to control the economy of all other nations and keep them living at a low standard.

These people are beginning to see that. The Africans see it, the Latin Americans see it, the Asians see it. So when you hear them talking about freedom, they're not talking about a cup of coffee with a cracker. No, they're talking about getting in a position to feed themselves and clothe themselves and make these other things that, when you have them, make life worth living. So this is the way you and I have to understand the world revolution that's taking place right now.

When you understand the motive behind the world revolution, the drive behind the African and the drive behind the Asian, then you get some of that drive yourself. You'll be driving for real. The Man downtown knows the difference between when you're driving for real and when you're driving not for real. As long as you keep asking about coffee, he doesn't have to worry about you; he can send you to Brazil. So these dams being set up over there in different parts of the continent are putting African nations in a position to have more power, to become more industrial and also to be self-sustained and self-sufficient.

In line with that: in the past it was the World Bank, controlled again by Europeans and from Europe, that subsidized most of the effort that was being made by African nations and Asian nations to develop underdeveloped areas. But the African nations are now getting together and forming their own bank, the African bank. The details of it aren't as much in my mind as I would like them to be, but when I was in Lagos, Nigeria, they were having a meeting there. It was among African bankers and African nations, and the Organization of African Unity, which is the best thing that has ever happened on the African continent, had taken up as part of its program the task of getting all of the African nations to pool their efforts in creating an African bank, so that there would be an internal bank in the internal African structure to which underdeveloped African nations can turn for financial assistance in projects that they're trying to undertake that would be beneficial to the whole continent . . .

Politically, Africa as a continent, and the African people as a people, have the largest representation of any continent in the United Nations. Politically, the Africans are in a more strategic position and in a stronger position whenever a conference is taking place at the international level. Today, power is international, real power is international; today, real power is not local. The only kind of power that can help you and me is international power, not local power. Any power that's local, if it's real power, is only a reflection or a part of that international power. If you think you've got some power, and it isn't in some way tied into that international thing, brother, don't get too far out on a limb.

If your power base is only here, you can forget it. You can't build a power base here. You have to have a power base among brothers and sisters. You have to have your power base among people who have something in common with you. They have to have some kind of cultural identity, or there has to be some relationship between you and your power base. When you build a power base in this country, you're building it where you aren't in any way related to what you build it on. No, you have to have that base somewhere else. You can work here, but you'd better put your base somewhere else. Don't put it in this Man's hand. Any kind of organization that is based here can't be an effective organization. Anything you've got going for you, if the base is here, is not going to be effective. Your and my base must be at home, and this is not at home.

When you see that the African nations at the international level comprise the largest representative body and the largest force of any continent, why, you and I would be out of our minds not to identify with that power bloc. We would be out of our minds, we would actually be traitors to ourselves, to be reluctant or fearful to identify with people with whom we have so much in common. If it was a people who had nothing to offer, nothing to contribute to our well-being, you might be justified, even though they looked like we do; if there was no contribution to be made, you might be justified. But when you have people who look exactly like you, and you are catching hell to boot, and you still are reluctant or hesitant or slow to identify with them, then you need to catch hell, yes. You deserve all the hell you get.

The African representatives, coupled with the Asians and Arabs, form a bloc that's almost impossible for anybody to contend with. The African-Asian-Arab bloc was the bloc that started the real independence movement among the oppressed peoples of the world. The first coming together of that bloc was at the Bandung conference . . .

To show you the power of that bloc and the results that they've gotten and how well the Europeans know it: on the African continent, when I was there, one thing I noticed was the twenty-four-hour-a-day effort being made in East Africa to turn the African against the Asian; and in West Africa to turn the African against the Arab; and in parts of Africa where there are no Asians or Arabs, to turn the Muslim African against the Christian African. When you go over there and study this thing, you can see that it is not something that's indigenous, it's not a divisive situation that's indigenous to the African himself. But someone realizes that the power of the oppressed black, brown, red, and yellow people began at the Bandung conference, which was a coalition between the Arab and the Asian and the African, and how much pressure they've been able to put on the oppressor since then.

So, very shrewdly they have moved in. Now when you travel on the continent, you see the African in East Africa is being sicked on the Asian—there's a division taking place. And in West Africa he's being sicked on the Arab—there's a division taking place. And where the oppressor, this ingenious oppressor, diabolically ingenious—where he hasn't found an Asian to sic the African on, or an Arab to sic the African on, he uses the Muslim African against the Christian African. Or the one that believes in religion against the one that doesn't believe in religion. But the main thing he's doing is causing this division, division, division to in some way keep the African, the Arab, and the Asian from beating up on him.

He's doing the same thing in British Guiana. He's got the black Guianians down there fighting against the so-called Indians. He's got them fighting each other. They didn't fight each other when the British were there in full control. If you notice, as long as the place was an old-style colony, no fight. But as soon as the British are supposed to be moving away, the black one starts fighting the red one. Why? This is no accident. If they didn't fight before, they don't need to fight now. There's no reason for it. But their fighting each other keeps the Man on top. The fact that he can turn one against the other keeps the Man on top.

He does the same thing with you and me right here in Harlem. All day long. I turned on the radio last night. I heard them say, every hour on the hour, that James Farmer, the head of

CORE, was going to Africa, Egypt, and Israel. And they said the reason he was going was because he wanted to correct false statements made by black nationalist leader Malcolm X when he was over there. If I hadn't had this experience before, immediately I would have started blasting Farmer. But I called him up today. He said he didn't know what they were talking about. But why do they do it? They do it to make us fight each other. As long as we're fighting each other, we can't get at the Man who should be fought against from the start. Do you understand? Once we see the strategy that they use at the international level, then we can better understand the strategy that they use at the national and at the local level.

Lastly, I would like to point out my understanding of what I think is the position taken in African policy. Their policy, in a nutshell, is positive neutrality, nonalignment. They don't line up either way. Africa is for the Africans. And the Africans are for the Africans. The policy of the independent African states, by and large, is positive neutrality, nonalignment. Egypt is a good example. They take from East and West and don't take sides with either one. Nasser took everything Russia could give him, and then put all the communists in jail. Not that I mean the communists should necessarily have been put in jail. For the communist is a man, a capitalist is a man, and a socialist is a man. Well, if all of them are men, why should they be put in jail, unless one of them is committing a crime? And if being a communist or being a capitalist or being a socialist is a crime, first you have to study which of those systems is the most criminal. And then you'll be slow to say which one should be in jail.

I cite that as an example just to show what this positive neutrality means: if you want to help us, help us; we're still not with you. If you have a contribution to make to our development, do it. But that doesn't mean we're with you or against you. We're neutral. We're for ourselves. Whatever is good for us, that's what we're interested in. That doesn't mean we're against you. But it does mean we're for ourselves.

This is what you and I need to learn. You and I need to learn how to be positively neutral. You and I need to learn how to be nonaligned. And if you and I ever study the science of nonalignment, then you'll find out that there's more power in nonalignment than there is in alignment. In this country, it's impossible for you to be aligned—with either party. Either party that you align yourself with is suicide. Because both parties are criminal. Both parties are responsible for the criminal condition that exists. So you can't align yourself with a party.

What you can do is get registered so that you have power—political potential. When you register your political potential, that means your gun is loaded. But just because it's loaded, you don't have to shoot until you see a target that will be beneficial to you. If you want a duck, don't shoot when you see a bear; wait till you see a duck. And if you want a bear, don't shoot when you see a duck; wait till you see a bear. Wait till you see what you want—then take aim and shoot!

What they do with you and me is tell us, "Register and vote." Don't register and vote—register! That's intelligent. Don't register and vote—you can vote for a dummy, you can vote for a crook, you can vote for another who'd want to exploit you. "Register" means being in a position to take political action any time, any place, and in any manner that would be beneficial to you and me; being in a position to take advantage of our position. Then we'll be in a position to be respected and recognized. But as soon as you get registered, and you want to be a Democrat or a Republican, you are aligning. And once you are aligning, you have no bargaining power—none whatsoever. We've got a program we are going to launch, which will involve the absolute maximum registering of as many of our people as we can. But they will be registered as independents. And by being registered as independents, it means we can do whatever is necessary, wherever it's necessary, and whenever the time comes. Do you understand? . . .

As I mentioned today—and you'll probably read about it tomorrow; they'll blow it up, and out of context—what we need in this country (and I believe it with all my heart, and with all my mind, and with all my soul) is the same type of Mau Mau here that they had over there in Kenya. Don't you ever be ashamed of the Mau Mau. They're not to be ashamed of. They are to be proud of. Those brothers were freedom fighters. Not only brothers, there were sisters over there. I met a lot of them. They're brave. They hug you and kiss you—glad to see you. In fact, if they were over here, they'd get this problem straightened up just like that.

I read a little story once, and Mau Mau proved it. I read a story once where someone asked some group of people how many of them wanted freedom. They all put up their hand. Think there were about 300 of them. Then the person says, "Well, how many of you are ready to kill anybody who gets in your way for freedom?" About fifty put up their hands. And he told those fifty, "You stand over here." That left 250 sitting who wanted freedom, but weren't ready to kill for it. So he told this fifty, "Now you wanted freedom and you said you'd kill anybody who'd get in your way. You see those 250? You get them first. Some of them are your own brothers and sisters and mothers and fathers. But they're the ones who stand in the way of your freedom. They're afraid to do whatever is necessary to get it and they'll stop you from doing it. Get rid of them and freedom will come naturally."

I go for that. That's what the Mau Mau learned. The Mau Mau realized that the only thing that was standing in the way of the independence of the African in Kenya was another African. So they started getting them one by one, all those Toms. One after another, they'd find another Uncle Tom African by the roadside. Today they're free. The white man didn't even get involved—he got out of the way. That's the same thing that will happen here. We've got too many of our own people who stand in the way. They're too squeamish. They want to be looked upon as respectable Uncle Toms. They want to be looked upon by the white man as responsible. They don't want to be classified by him as extremist, or violent, or, you know, irresponsible. They want that good image. And nobody who's looking for a good image will ever be free. No, that kind of image doesn't get you free. You've got to take something in your hand and say, "Look, it's you or me." And I guarantee you he'll give you freedom then. He'll say, "This man is ready for it." I said something in your hand—I won't define what I mean by "something in your hand." I don't mean bananas.

A Prison Interview

HUEY NEWTON

Black Panther Minister of Defense Huey P. Newton, a luminous man, is in prison because he is black, compassionate, sensitive, courageous, and unprepared to cooperate with his would-be assassins, however shiny their badges.

He is not the first revolutionary who has found it both necessary and possible to keep working behind bars. His teaching, as the Panthers call it, like that of all prophets and organizers, is at its best when it is most direct, when there is a fluent rhythm set up between the word and the deed, the small circle of faces and the motion in the streets. Interrupting that rhythm, imprisonment obliged the refinement of another mode of speech—the interview, which better than any other printed form retains the quickness, the ease, and the scope of conversation.

The interview printed here, made in the summer of 1968 by Movement *editor Joe Blum, was immediately recognized as one of the richest statements to have been produced by the black revolutionary movement in America. Perhaps Newton is naïve about the state of Algerian socialism and the motives of white radicals. But his insight into the political psychology of master and slave, mother country and colony, is as sharp as Fanon's. And it may be that a white man can learn more about his civilization and its discontents from these few words than from a whole library of Freudian analysis.*

THE MOVEMENT: The question of nationalism is a vital one in the black movement today. Some have made a distinction between cultural nationalism and revolutionary nationa
Would you comment on the differences and give us your vi

HUEY P. NEWTON: There are two kinds of nationalism,

lutionary nationalism and reactionary nationalism. Revolutionary nationalism is first dependent upon a people's revolution with the end goal being the people in power. Therefore to be a revolutionary nationalist you would by necessity have to be a socialist. If you are a reactionary nationalist you are not a socialist and your end goal is the oppression of the people.

Cultural nationalism, or pork-chop nationalism, as I sometimes call it, is basically a problem of having the wrong political perspective. It seems to be a reaction instead of responding to political oppression. The cultural nationalists are concerned with returning to the old African culture and thereby regaining their identity and freedom. In other words, they feel that the African culture will automatically bring political freedom. Many times cultural nationalists fall into line as reactionary nationalists.

Papa Doc in Haiti is an excellent example of reactionary nationalism. He oppresses the people but he does promote the African culture. He's against anything other than black, which on the surface seems very good, but for him it is only to mislead the people. He merely kicked out the racists and replaced them with himself as the oppressor. Many of the nationalists in this country seem to desire the same ends.

The Black Panther Party, which is a revolutionary group of black people, realizes that we have to have an identity. We have to realize our black heritage in order to give us strength to move on and progress. But as far as returning to the old African culture, it's unnecessary and it's not advantageous in many respects. We believe that culture itself will not liberate us. We're going to need some stronger stuff.

REVOLUTIONARY NATIONALISM

A good example of revolutionary nationalism was the revolution in Algeria when Ben Bella took over. The French were kicked out but it was a people's revolution because the people ended up in power. The leaders that took over were not interested in the profit motive where they could exploit the people and keep them in a state of slavery. They nationalized the industry and plowed the would-be profits into the community That's what socialism is all about in a nutshell. The people's representatives are in office strictly on the leave of the people. The wealth of the country is controlled by the people and they are considered whenever modifications in the industries are made

The Black Panther Party is a revolutionary nationalist group and we see a major contradiction between capitalism in this country and our interests. We realize that this country became very rich upon slavery and that slavery is capitalism in the extreme. We have two evils to fight, capitalism and racism. We must destroy both racism and capitalism.

MOVEMENT: Directly related to the question of nationalism is the question of unity within the black community. There has been some question about this since the Black Panther Party has run candidates against other black candidates in recent California elections. What is your position on this matter?

HUEY: Well, a very peculiar thing has happened. Historically you got what Malcolm X calls the field nigger and the house nigger. The house nigger had some privileges, a little more. He got the worn-out clothes of the master and he didn't have to work as hard as the field black. He came to respect the master to such an extent that he identified with the master because he got a few of the leftovers that the field blacks did not get. And through this identity with him, he saw the slavemaster's interest as being his interest. Sometimes he would even protect the slavemaster more than the slavemaster would protect himself. Malcolm makes the point that if the master's house happened to catch on fire the house Negro will work harder than the master to put the fire out and save the master's house. While the field Negro, the field black, was praying that the house burned down. The house black identified with the master so much that when the master would get sick the house Negro would say, "Master, we's sick!"

BLACK BOURGEOISIE

The Black Panther Party are the field blacks; we're hoping the master dies if he gets sick. The black bourgeoisie seem to be acting in the role of the house Negro. They are pro-administration. They would like a few concessions made, but as far as the over-all setup goes, they have a few more material goods, a little more advantage, a few more privileges than the black have-nots, the lower class. And so they identify with the power structure and they see their interests as the power structure's interest . . .

The Black Panther Party was forced to draw a line of demarcation. We are for all of those who are for the promotion of the interests of the black have-nots, which represents about ninety-eight per cent of blacks here in America. We're not controlled by the white mother country radicals nor are we controlled by the black bourgeoisie. We have a mind of our own and if the black bourgeoisie cannot align itself with our complete program, then the black bourgeoisie sets itself up as our enemy. And they will be attacked and treated as such.

MOVEMENT: The Black Panther Party has had considerable contact with white radicals since its earliest days. What do you see as the role of these white radicals?

HUEY: The white mother country radical is the offspring of the beast that has plundered the world, exploiting all people, concentrating on the people of color. These are children of the beast that seek now to be redeemed because they realize that their former heroes, who were slavemasters and murderers, put forth ideas that were only façades to hide the treachery they inflicted upon the world. They are turning their backs on their fathers.

The white mother country radical, in resisting the System, becomes somewhat of an abstract thing because he's not oppressed as much as black people are. As a matter of fact, his oppression is somewhat abstract simply because he doesn't have to live in a reality of oppression.

Black people in America and colored people throughout the world suffer not only from exploitation, but they suffer from racism. Black people here in America, in the black colony, are oppressed because we're black and we're exploited. The whites are rebels, many of them from the middle class, and as far as any overt oppression goes, this is not the case with them. So therefore I call their rejection of the System somewhat of an abstract thing. They're looking for new heroes. They're looking to wash away the hypocrisy that their fathers have presented to the world. In doing this they see the people who are really fighting for freedom. They see the people who are really standing for justice and equality and peace throughout the world. They are the people of Vietnam, the people of Latin America, the people of Asia, the people of Africa, and the black people in the black colony here in America.

WHITE REVOLUTIONARIES

This presents somewhat of a problem in many ways to the black revolutionary, especially to the cultural nationalist. The cultural nationalist doesn't understand the white revolutionaries because he can't see why anyone white would turn on the System. So they think that maybe this is some more hypocrisy being planted by white people.

I personally think that there are many young white revolutionaries who are sincere in attempting to realign themselves with mankind, and to make a reality out of the high moral standards that their fathers and forefathers only expressed. In pressing for new heroes the young white revolutionaries found the heroes in the black colony at home and in the colonies throughout the world.

The young white revolutionaries raised the cry for the troops to withdraw from Vietnam, hands off Latin America, withdraw from the Dominican Republic, and also to withdraw from the black community or the black colony. So you have a situation in which the young white revolutionaries are attempting to identify with the oppressed people of the colonies and against the exploiter.

The problem arises then: What part they can play? How can they aid the colony? How can they aid the Black Panther Party or any other black revolutionary group? They can aid the black revolutionaries first by simply turning away from the Establishment, and secondly by choosing their friends. For instance, they have a choice between whether they will be a friend of Lyndon Baines Johnson or a friend of Fidel Castro. A friend of Robert Kennedy or a friend of Ho Chi Minh. And these are direct opposites. A friend of mine or a friend of Johnson's. After they make this choice then the white revolutionaries have a duty and a responsibility to act.

The imperialistic or capitalistic system occupies areas. It occupies Vietnam now. They occupy them by sending soldiers there, by sending policemen there. The policemen or soldiers are only a gun in the Establishment's hand. They make the racist secure in his racism. The gun in the Establishment's hand makes the Establishment secure in its exploitation. The first problem, it seems, is to remove the gun from the Establishment's hand. Until lately the white radical has seen no reason to come into conflict with the policemen in his own community. The reason I said until recently is because there is friction now in the mother country between the young white revolutionaries and the police. Because now the white revolutionaries are attempting to put some of their ideas into action, and there's the rub. We say that it should be a permanent thing.

Black people are being oppressed in the colony by white policemen, by white racists. We are saying they must withdraw. We realize that it is not only the Oakland police department but rather the security forces in general. On April 6 it wasn't just the Oakland police department who ambushed the Panthers. It was the Oakland police department, the Emeryville police department, and I wouldn't be surprised if there were others. When the white revolutionaries went down to close up the Army terminal in October 1965 it wasn't the Oakland police by themselves who tried to stop them. It was the Oakland police, the Berkeley police, the Highway Patrol, the Sheriff's Department, and the National Guard was standing by. So we see that they're all part of one organization. They're all a part of the security force to protect the status quo; to make sure that the institutions carry out their goals. They're here to protect the System.

As far as I'm concerned, the only reasonable conclusion would be to first realize the enemy, realize the plan, and then when something happens in the black colony—when we're attacked and ambushed in the black colony—then the white revolutionary students and intellectuals and all the other whites who support the colony should respond by defending us, by attacking the enemy in their community. Every time that we're attacked in our community there should be a reaction by the white revolutionaries, they should respond by defending us, by attacking part of the security force. Part of that security force that is determined to carry out the racist ends of the American institutions.

As far as our party is concerned, the Black Panther Party is an all-black party, because we feel as Malcolm X felt that there can be no black-white unity until there first is black unity. We have a problem in the black colony that is particular to the colony, but we're willing to accept aid from the mother country as long as the mother country radicals realize that we have, as Eldridge Cleaver says in *Soul On Ice*, a mind of our own. We've regained our mind that was taken away from us and we will decide the political as well as the practical stand that we'll take. We'll make the theory and we'll carry out the practice. It's the duty of the white revolutionary to aid us in this.

So the role of the mother country radical, and he does have a role, is to first choose his friend and his enemy and after doing this, which it seems he's already done, then to not only articulate his desires to regain his moral standard and align himself with humanity, but also to put this into practice by attacking the protectors of the institutions.

MOVEMENT: You have spoken a lot about dealing with the protectors of the System, the armed forces. Would you like to elaborate on why you place so much emphasis on this?

HUEY: The reason that I feel very strongly about dealing with the protectors of the System is simply because without this protection from the army and the police, the institutions could not go on in their racism and exploitation. For instance, as the Vietnamese are driving the American imperialist troops out of Vietnam, it automatically stops the racist imperialist institutions of America from oppressing that particular country. The country cannot implement its racist program without the guns. And the guns are the military and the police. If the military were disarmed in Vietnam, then the Vietnamese would be victorious.

We are in the same situation here in America. Whenever we attack the System, the first thing the administrators do is to send out their strong-arm men. If it's a rent strike, because of the indecent housing we have, they will send out the police to throw the furniture out the window. They don't come themselves. They send their protectors. So to deal with the corrupt exploiter you are going to have to deal with his protector, which is the police who take orders from him. This is a must.

MOVEMENT: Would you like to be more specific on the conditions which must exist before an alliance or coalition can be formed with predominantly white groups? Would you comment specifically on your alliance with the California Peace and Freedom Party?

HUEY: We have an alliance with the Peace and Freedom Party. The Peace and Freedom Party has supported our program in full and this is the criterion for a coalition with the black revolutionary group. If they had not supported our program in full, then we would not have seen any reason to make an alliance with them, because we are the reality of the oppression. They are not. They are only oppressed in an abstract way; we are oppressed in the real way. We are the real slaves! So it's a problem that we suffer from more than anyone else and it's our problem of liberation. Therefore we should decide what measures and what tools and what programs to use to become liberated. Many of the young white revolutionaries realize this and I see no reason not to have a coalition with them.

MOVEMENT: Other black groups seem to feel that from past experience it is impossible for them to work with whites and impossible for them to form alliances. What do you see as the reasons for this and do you think that the history of the Black Panther Party makes this less of a problem?

SNCC AND LIBERALS

HUEY: There was somewhat of an unhealthy relationship in the past with the white liberals supporting the black people who were trying to gain their freedom. I think that a good example of this would be the relationship that SNCC had with its white liberals. I call them white liberals because they differ strictly from the white radicals. The relationship was that the whites controlled SNCC for a very long time. From the very start of SNCC until here recently whites were the mind of SNCC. They controlled the program of SNCC with money and they controlled the ideology, or the stands SNCC would take. The blacks in SNCC were completely controlled program-wise; they couldn't do any more than these white liberals wanted them to do, which wasn't very much. So the white liberals were not working for self-determination for the black community. They were interested in a few concessions from the power structure. They undermined SNCC's program.

Stokely Carmichael came along and, realizing this, started to follow Malcolm X's program of Black Power. This frightened many of the white liberals who were supporting SNCC. Whites were afraid when Stokely came along with Black Power and said that black people have a mind of their own and that SNCC would be an all-black organization and that SNCC would seek self-determination for the black community. The white liberals withdrew their support, leaving the organization financially bankrupt. The blacks who were in the organization, Stokely and H. Rap Brown, were left very angry with the white liberals who had been aiding them under the disguise of being sincere. They weren't sincere.

The result was that the leadership of SNCC turned away from the white liberal, which was very good. I don't think they distinguished between the white liberal and the white revolutionary, because the white revolutionary is white also and they are very much afraid to have any contact whatsoever with white people. Even to the point of denying that the white revolutionaries could give support, by supporting the programs of SNCC in the mother country. Not by making any programs, not by being a member of the organization, but simply by resisting. Just as the Vietnamese people realize that they are supported whenever other oppressed people throughout the world resist. Because it helps divide the troops. It drains the country militarily and economically. If the mother country radicals are sincere then this will definitely add to the attack that we are making on the power structure. The Black Panther Party's program is a program where we recognize that the revolution in the mother country will definitely aid us in our freedom and has everything to do with our struggle!

HATE THE OPPRESSOR

I think that one of SNCC's great problems is that they were controlled by the traditional administrator: the omnipotent administrator, the white person. He was the mind of SNCC. And so SNCC regained its mind, but I believe that it lost its political perspective. I think that this was a reaction rather than a response. The Black Panther Party has *never* been controlled by white people. The Black Panther Party has always been a black group. We have always had an integration of mind and body. We have never been controlled by whites and therefore we don't fear the white mother country radicals. Our alliance is one of organized black groups with organized white groups. As soon as the organized white groups do not do the things that would benefit us in our struggle for liberation, that will be our departure point. So we don't suffer in the hangup of a skin color. We don't hate white people; we hate the oppressor. And if the oppressor happens to be white then we hate him. When he stops oppressing us then we no longer hate him. And right now in America you have the slavemaster being a white group. We are pushing him out of office through revolution in this country. I think the responsibility of the white revolutionary will be to aid us in this. And when we are attacked by the police or by the military then it will be up to the white mother country radicals to attack the murderers and to respond as we respond, to follow our program.

SLAVEMASTERS

MOVEMENT: You indicate that there is a psychological process that has historically existed in white-black relations in the United States that must change in the course of revolutionary struggle. Would you like to comment on this?

HUEY: Yes. The historical relationship between black and white here in America has been the relationship between the slave and the master; the master being the mind and the slave the body. The slave would carry out the orders that the mind demanded him to carry out. By doing this the master took the manhood from the slave because he stripped him of a mind. He stripped black people of their mind. In the process the slavemaster stripped himself of a body. As Eldridge puts it, the slavemaster became the omnipotent administrator and the slave became the supermasculine menial. This put the omnipotent administrator into the controlling position or the front office and the supermasculine menial into the field.

The whole relationship developed so that the omnipotent administrator and the supermasculine menial became opposites. The slave, being a very strong body doing all the practical things, all of the work, becomes very masculine. The omnipotent administrator in the process of removing himself from all body functions realizes later that he has emasculated himself. And this is very disturbing to him. So the slave lost his mind and the slavemaster his body.

PENIS ENVY

This caused the slavemaster to become very envious of the slave because he pictured the slave as being more of a man, being superior sexually, because the penis is part of the body. The omnipotent administrator laid down a decree when he realized that his plan to enslave the black man had a flaw, when he discovered that he had emasculated himself. He attempted to bind the penis of the slave. He attempted to show that his penis could reach further than the supermasculine menial's penis. He said "I, the omnipotent administrator, can have access to the black woman." The supermasculine menial then had a psychological attraction to the white woman (the ultra-feminine freak) for the simple reason that it was forbidden fruit. The omnipotent administrator decreed that this kind of contact would be punished by death. At the same time in order to reinforce his sexual desire, to confirm, to assert his manhood, he would go into the slave quarters and have sexual relations with the black women (the self-reliant Amazon). Not to be satisfied but simply to confirm his manhood. Because if he could only satisfy the self-reliant Amazon then he would be sure that he was a man. Because he doesn't have a body, he doesn't have a penis, he psychologically wants to castrate the black man. The slave was constantly seeking unity within himself: a mind and a body. He always wanted to be able to decide, to gain respect from his woman. Because women want one who can control. I give this outline to fit into a framework of what is happening now. The white power structure today in America defines itself as the mind. They want to control the world. They go off and plunder the world. They are the policemen of the world, exercising control especially over people of color.

RECAPTURE THE MIND

The white man cannot gain his manhood, cannot unite with the body because the body is black. The body is symbolic of slavery and strength. It's a biological thing as he views it. The slave is in a much better situation because his not being a full man has always been viewed psychologically. And it's always easier to make a psychological transition than a biological one. If he can only recapture his mind, recapture his balls, then he will lose all fear and will be free to determine his destiny. This is what is happening at this time with the rebellion of the world's oppressed people against the controller. They are regaining their mind and they're saying that we have a mind of our own. They're saying that we want freedom to determine the destiny of our people, thereby uniting the mind with their bodies. They are taking the mind back from the omnipotent administrator, the controller, the exploiter.

In America black people are also chanting that we have a mind of our own. We must have freedom to determine our destiny. It's almost a spiritual thing, this unity, this harmony. This unity of the mind and of the body, this unity of man within himself. Certain slogans of Chairman Mao, I think, demonstrate this theory of uniting the mind with the body within the man. An example is his call to the intellectuals to go to the countryside. The peasants in the countryside are all bodies; they're the workers. And he sent the intellectuals there because the dictatorship of the proletariat has no room for the omnipotent administrator; there's no room for the exploiter. So therefore he must go to the countryside to regain his body; he must work. He is really done a favor, because the people force him to unite his mind with his body by putting them both to work. At the same time the intellectual teaches the people political ideology, he educates them, thus uniting the mind and the body in the peasant. Their minds and bodies are united and they control their country. I think this is a very good example of this unity and it is my idea of the perfect man.

THE GUERRILLA

MOVEMENT: You mentioned at another point that the guerrilla was the perfect man and this kind of formulation seems to fit in directly with the guerrilla as a political man. Would you like to comment on this?

HUEY: Yes. The guerrilla is a very unique man. This is in contrast to Marxist-Leninist orthodox theories where the party controls the military. The guerrilla is not only the warrior, the military fighter; he is also the military commander as well as the political theoretician. Debray says "poor the pen without the gun, poor the gun without the pen." The pen being just an extension of the mind, a tool to write down concepts, ideas. The gun is only an extension of the body, the extension of our fanged teeth that we lost through evolution. It's the weapon, it's the claws that we lost, it's the body. The guerrilla is the military commander and the political theoretician all in one.

In Bolivia, Che said that he got very little help from the Communist Party there. The Communist Party wanted to be the mind, the Communist Party wanted to have full control of the guerrilla activity. But yet they weren't taking part in the practical work of the guerrillas. The guerrilla on the other hand is not only united within himself, but he also attempts to spread this to the people by educating the villagers, giving them political perspective, pointing out things, educating them politically, and arming the people. Therefore the guerrilla is giving the peasants and workers a mind. Because they've already got the body, you get a unity of the mind and the body. Black people here in America, who have long been the workers, have regained our minds and we now have a unity of mind and body.

MOVEMENT: Would you be willing to extend this formula in terms of white radicals; to say that one of their struggles today is to get back their bodies.

HUEY: Yes. I thought I made that clear. The white mother country radical by becoming an activist is attempting to regain his body. By being an activist and not the traditional theoretician who outlines the plan, as the Communist Party has been trying to do for ever so long, the white mother country radical is regaining his body. The resistance by white radicals in Berkeley during the past three nights is a good indication that the white radicals are on the way home. They have identified their enemies. The white radicals have integrated theory with practice. They realize the American system is the real enemy but in order to attack the American system they must attack the ordinary cop. In order to attack the educational system they must attack the ordinary teacher. Just as the Vietnamese people to attack the American system must attack the ordinary soldier. The white mother country radicals now are regaining their bodies and they're also recognizing that the black man has a mind and that he is a man.

MOVEMENT: Would you comment on how this psychological understanding aids in the revolutionary struggle?

HUEY: Until recently black people who haven't been enlightened have defined the white man by calling him "the Man." "The Man" is making this decision, "The Man" this and "The Man" that. The black woman found it difficult to respect the black man because he didn't even define himself as a man! Because he didn't have a mind, because the decision-maker was outside of himself. But the vanguard group, the Black Panther Party along with all revolutionary black groups have regained our mind and our manhood. Therefore we no longer define the omnipotent administrator as "the Man" . . . or the authority as "the Man." Matter of fact, the omnipotent administrator along with his security agents are less than a man because *we* define them as pigs! I think that this is a revolutionary thing in itself. That's political power. That's power itself. Matter of fact, what is power other than the ability to define a phenomenon and then make it act in a desired manner? When black people start defining things and making them act in a desired manner, then we call this Black Power!

MOVEMENT: Would you comment further on what you mean by Black Power?

HUEY: Black Power is really people's power. The Black Panther program, Panther Power as we call it, will implement this people's power. We have respect for all of humanity and we realize that the people should rule and determine their destiny. Wipe out the controller. To have Black Power doesn't humble or subjugate anyone to slavery or oppression. Black Power is giving power to people who have not had power to determine their destiny. We advocate and we aid any people who are struggling to determine their destiny. This is regardless of color. The Vietnamese say Vietnam should be able to determine its own destiny. Power of the Vietnamese people. We also chant power of the Vietnamese people. The Latins are talking about Latin America for the Latin Americans. Cuba *Si* and Yanqui *No.* It's not that they don't want the Yankees to have any power, they just don't want them to have power over them. They can have power over themselves. We in the black colony in America want to be able to have power over our destiny and that's Black Power.

MOVEMENT: A lot of white radicals are romantic about what Che said: "In a revolution one wins or dies . . ." For most of us it is really an abstract or theoretical question. It's a real question for you and we'd like you to rap about how you feel about it.

HUEY: Yes. The revolutionary sees no compromise. We will not compromise because the issue is so basic. If we compromise one iota we will be selling our freedom out. We will be selling the revolution out. And we refuse to remain slaves. As Eldridge says in *Soul On Ice,* "a slave who dies of natural causes will not balance two dead flies on the scales of eternity." As far as we're concerned we would rather be dead than to go on with the slavery that we're in. Once we compromise we will be compromising not only our freedom, but also our manhood. We realize that we're going up against a highly technical country, and we realize that they are not only paper tigers, as Mao says, but real tigers too because they have the ability to slaughter many people. But in the long run, they will prove themselves paper tigers because they're not in line with humanity; they are divorced from the people. We know that the enemy is very powerful and that our manhood is at stake, but we feel it necessary to be victorious in regaining ourselves, regaining our manhood. And this is the basic point. So either we will do this or we won't have any freedom. Either we will win or we will die trying to win.

MOOD OF BLACK PEOPLE

MOVEMENT: How would you characterize the mood of black people in America today? Are they disenchanted, wanting a larger slice of the pie, or alienated, not wanting to integrate into a burning house, not wanting to integrate into Babylon? What do you think it will take for them to become alienated and revolutionary?

HUEY: I was going to say disillusioned, but I don't think we were ever under the illusion that we had freedom in this country. This society is definitely a decadent one and we realize it. Black people are realizing it more and more. We cannot gain our freedom under the present system; the system that is carrying out its plans of institutionalized racism. Your question is what will have to be done to stimulate them to revolution. I think it's already being done. It's a matter of time now for us to educate them to a program and show them the way to liberation. The Black Panther Party is the beacon light to show black people the way to liberation.

You notice the insurrections that have been going on throughout the country, in Watts, in Newark, in Detroit. They were all responses of the people demanding that they have freedom to determine their destiny, rejecting exploitation. Now the Black Panther Party does not think that the traditional riots, or insurrections, that have taken place are the answer. It is true they have been against the Establishment, they have been against authority and oppression within their community, but they have been unorganized. However, black people learned from each of these insurrections.

They learned from Watts. I'm sure the people in Detroit were educated by what happened in Watts. Perhaps this was wrong education. It sort of missed the mark. It wasn't quite the correct activity, but the people were educated through the activity. The people of Detroit followed the example of the people in Watts, only they added a little scrutiny to it. The people in Detroit learned that the way to put a hurt on the administration is to make Molotov cocktails and to go into the street in mass numbers. So this was a matter of learning. The slogan went up; "Burn, baby, burn." People were educated through the activity and it spread throughout the country. The people were educated on how to resist, but perhaps incorrectly.

EDUCATE THROUGH ACTIVITY

What we have to do as a vanguard of the revolution is to correct this through activity. The large majority of black people are either illiterate or semiliterate. They don't read. They need activity to follow. This is true of any colonized people. The same thing happened in Cuba, where it was necessary for twelve men with a leadership of Che and Fidel to take to the hills and then attack the corrupt administration; to attack the army who were the protectors of the exploiters in Cuba. They could have leafleted the community and they could have written books, but the people would not respond. They had to act and the people could see and hear about it and therefore become educated on how to respond to oppression.

In this country black revolutionaries have to set an example. We can't do the same things that were done in Cuba because Cuba is Cuba and the United States is the United States. Cuba has many terrains to protect the guerrilla. This country is mainly urban. We have to work out new solutions to offset the power of the country's technology and communications: its ability to communicate very rapidly by telephone and teletype and so forth. We do have solutions to these problems and they will be put into effect. I wouldn't want to go into the ways and means of this, but we will educate through action. We have to engage in action to make the people want to read our literature. Because they are not attracted to all the writing in this country; there's too much writing. Many books make one weary.

THREAT FROM REFORMERS

MOVEMENT: Kennedy before his death, and to a lesser extent, Rockefeller and Lindsay and other Establishment liberals have been talking about making reforms to give black people a greater share in the pie and thus stop any developing revolutionary movement. Would you comment on this?

HUEY: I would say this: If a Kennedy or Lindsay or anyone

else can give decent housing to all of our people; if they can give full employment to our people with a high standard; if they can give full control to black people to determine the destiny of their community; if they can give fair trials in the court system by turning over the structure to the community; if they can end their exploitation of people throughout the world; if they can do all of these things they would have solved the problems. But I don't believe that under this present system, under capitalism, that they will be able to solve these problems.

PEOPLE MUST CONTROL

I don't think black people should be fooled by their come-ons because everyone who gets in office promises the same thing. They promise full employment and decent housing; the Great Society, the New Frontier. All of these names, but no real benefits. No effects are felt in the black community, and black people are tired of being deceived and duped. The people must have full control of the means of production. Small black businesses cannot compete with General Motors. That's just out of the question. General Motors robbed us and worked us for nothing for a couple hundred years and took our money and set up factories and became fat and rich and then talks about giving us some of the crumbs. We want full control. We're not interested in anyone promising that the private owners are going to all of a sudden become human beings and give these things to our community. It hasn't ever happened and, based on empirical evidence, we don't expect them to become Buddhists overnight.

MOVEMENT: We raised this question not because we feel that these reforms are possible, but rather to get your ideas on what effects such attempted reforms might have on the development of a revolutionary struggle.

HUEY: I think that reforms pose no real threat. The revolution has always been in the hands of the young. The young always inherit the revolution. The young population is growing at a very rapid rate and they are very displeased with the authorities. They want control. I doubt that under the present system any kind of program can be launched that will be able to buy off all these young people. They have not been able to do it with the poverty program, the Great Society, etc. This country has never been able to employ all of its people simply because it's too interested in private property and the profit motive. A bigger poverty program is just what it says it is, a program to keep people in poverty. So I don't think that there is any real threat from the reforms.

MOVEMENT: Would you like to say something about the Panthers' organizing especially in terms of the youth?

HUEY: The Panthers represent a cross section of the black community. We have older people as well as younger people. The younger people of course are the ones who are seen on the streets. They are the activists. They are the real vanguard of change because they haven't been indoctrinated and they haven't submitted. They haven't been beaten into line as some of the older people have. But many of the older people realize that we're waging a just fight against the oppressor. They are aiding us and they are taking a part in the program.

JAIL

MOVEMENT: Tell us something about your relations with the prisoners in the jail.

HUEY: The black prisoners as well as many of the white prisoners identify with the program of the Panthers. Of course, by the very nature of their being prisoners they can see the oppression and they've suffered at the hands of the Gestapo. They have reacted to it. The black prisoners have all joined the Panthers, about ninety-five per cent of them. Now the jail is all Panther and the police are very worried about this. The white prisoners can identify with us because they realize that they are not in control. They realize there's someone controlling them and the rest of the world with guns. They want some control over their lives also. The Panthers in jail have been educating them and so we are going along with the revolution inside of the jail.

MOVEMENT: What has been the effect of the demonstrations outside the jail calling for "Free Huey"?

HUEY: Very positive reactions. One demonstration, I don't remember which one, a couple of trustees, white trustees, held a cardboard sign out the laundry window reading "Free Huey." They say people saw it and responded to it. They were very enthusiastic about the demonstrators because they too suffer from being treated unfairly by the parole authorities and by the police here in the jail.

OPEN OR UNDERGROUND

MOVEMENT: The Panthers' organizing efforts have been very open up until this point. Would you like to comment about the question of an underground political organization versus an open organization at this point in the struggle?

HUEY: Yeah. Some of the black nationalist groups feel that they have to be underground because they'll be attacked. But we don't feel that you can romanticize being underground. They say we're romantic because we're trying to live revolutionary lives, and we are not taking precautions. But we say that the only way we would go underground is if we're driven underground. All real revolutionary movements are driven underground. Take the revolution in Cuba. The agitation that was going on while Fidel was in law school was very much aboveground. Even his existence in the hills was, so to speak, an above-the-ground affair because he was letting it be known who was doing the damage and why he was doing the damage. To catch him was a different story. The only way we can educate the people is by setting an example for them. We feel that this is very necessary.

This is a pre-revolutionary period and we feel it is very necessary to educate the people while we can. So we're very open about this education. We have been attacked and we will be attacked even more in the future but we're not going to go underground until we get ready to go underground because we have a mind of our own. We're not going to let anyone force us to do anything. We're going to go underground after we educate all of the black people and not before that time. Then it won't really be necessary for us to go underground because you can see black anywhere. We will just have the stuff to protect ourselves and the strategy to offset the great power that the strong-arm men of the Establishment have and are planning to use against us.

WHITE ORGANIZING

MOVEMENT: Your comments about the white prisoners seemed encouraging. Do you see the possibility of organizing a white Panther Party in opposition to the Establishment, possibly among poor and working whites?

HUEY: Well, as I put it before, Black Power is people's power and as far as organizing white people goes, we give white people the privilege of having a mind and we want them to get a body. They can organize themselves. We can tell them what they should do, what their responsibility is if they're going to claim to be white revolutionaries or white mother country radicals, and that is to arm themselves and support the colonies around the world in their just struggle against imperialism. But anything more than that they will have to do on their own.

PART THREE:

A New Revolution?

On Anti-authoritarianism

RUDI DUTSCHKE

The challenge to the established order of capitalist civilization originates at the moment in two markedly different sectors of the world population: the under class of the colonized peoples (including American blacks), and the middle-class youth of the mother countries. The former have scant need to theorize about their condition and needs; for them, the revolutionary imperative is all too clear. But the latter are not so sure of themselves. At least, very little in their world seems to go according to the classical Marxist program. Where one ought to find the locus of rebellion—the industrial working class—one finds instead (with some notable and much studied exceptions) either a virtual political silence or even an apparent reactionism. And on the other hand, where the assumptions of a strict materialism would predict indifference if not militant defense of the status quo, one finds widespread angst, *boredom, anger, rebellion. Why does this happen? What does it portend? Most important, what is the concrete basis of the curious alliance that seems to be materializing in today's world between the victims of neocolonial aggression and the aggressor's privileged children?*

Dutschke's essay by no means deals conclusively with such problems, and it leaves unopened the question of cross-class or student-worker politics within the world capitals. But his exploration of the concept of anti-authoritarian struggle, more Marcusean than Marxist in many of its features, is an important statement in the continuing debate about the role of the mother-country radical in a fight whose scope, as he says, is clearly global.

In 1968, inspired by the assassin of Martin Luther King, Jr., a young German rightwinger put several bullets in Dutschke's head and body. Dutschke survived. An incorrigible militant with a stereotypically German gift for theory, he has properly come to be seen as an embodiment of what is best in the Western-wide New Left movement.

USING ALL THE MEANS at its disposal, the existing System strives to prevent us from introducing those conditions in which men can live creative lives without war, hunger, and repressive work. Every radical opposition to this System must necessarily assume a global dimension today. In the current historical period, the globalization of the revolutionary forces is the most important task of those who are working for the emancipation of the human race.

The underprivileged in the whole world constitute the historical mass base of liberation movements. In them alone lies the subversive-explosive character of the international revolution.

The Third World, as the totality of peoples suffering under the terror of the world market system of the giant corporations, and whose development was prevented by imperialism, launched this struggle in the 1940's, completely under the influence of what Trotsky called the "betrayed" proletarian revolution in the Soviet Union. But it was marked by a crucial difference: the mass character and the permanence of the revolutionary process were already grasped in theory.

A new stage began in the 1960's with the revolutionary upheavals in Algeria and Cuba and the unbroken struggle of the South Vietnamese Liberation Front against the Diem dictatorship. Only the latter achieved world-historical significance for the worldwide opposition movement. The American aggression in Vietnam, too blatant and brutal to be overlooked, took place at a time when imperialism's various mechanisms for influence and control could no longer prevent the victory of the revolutionary liberation forces in South Vietnam. The historical bad luck of the American power elite—more exactly, of U.S. imperialism—consists precisely in the fact that it had to destroy its only "base of legitimacy," namely, the anticommunist ideology, in order to make the suppression of the social-revolutionary liberation movements at all possible under the banner of anticommunism. This apparent contradiction dissolves once we understand that imperialism had to recognize the ideology of coexistence, sponsored by the Soviet Union, in order to stabilize a calm zone of the System, at least in middle and western

Europe, and in order to "cover its rear" for the short-term and effective destruction of the revolutionary movements of the Third World. The historical guilt of the Soviet Union consists in its complete failure to grasp this strategy of imperialism in a deep and fundamental sense and to counter it in a subversive and revolutionary manner.

The aggression of U.S. imperialism in Vietnam, escalating from month to month, from year to year, materialized in the highly developed countries as the "abstract presence of the Third World in the metropolis" (O. Negt), as an intellectual productive force in the process of the development of an awareness of the antinomies of the present-day world.

When, in the middle 1960's, Vietnam became a living issue for us through lectures, discussions, films, and demonstrations, we revolutionary socialists were able historically to sublimate, so to speak, our guilt feelings over the existence of the Berlin Wall and of Stalinism in the German Democratic Republic by propagating the specific difference between seizing power through force, without, however, revolutionizing the masses and the collectivization of the idea of social liberation in the process of revolution, as in Vietnam. But in point of fact, Vietnam, *a priori,* presented more than just a means of compensation or a convenient rack on which to hang the activities of the leftist student groups. The world-historical significance of the struggle of the Vietnamese people, the exemplary significance of this conflict for subsequent struggles against imperialism, very soon became the focal point of the discussions of Vietnam. That this decisive aspect was able to penetrate into the students' consciousness so soon seems to have its material explanation in the students' specific relationship to the means of production. As students—although varying from faculty to faculty—we find ourselves in an intermediate position in the total social reproduction process. On the one hand, we are intellectually and educationally a privileged fraction of the people, but actually this privilege signifies nothing but frustration. Frustration because the student, especially the politically committed student, day after day experiences critically, and sometimes materially, the stupidity of the cliques of political hacks who do the bidding of the irrational authorities. Moreover, these anti-authoritarian students have not yet assumed any materially secure positions in society and are still relatively far from power interests and power positions. This temporary subversive position of the students by itself engenders a dialectical identity between the immediate and the historical interests of the producers. Hence, the vital needs and interests in regard to peace, justice, and emancipation can best materialize in these sociological positions. But students develop with real virulence only when they become politicized in the anti-authoritarian struggle against the bureaucracy within the milieu of their own university institution, when they more resolutely engage in the political struggle for their interests and needs. We must not forget the direct relationship of the student producer to his educational milieu. His learning situation in the university is determined by the dictatorship of examinations, rising in an inflationary way, and by the dictatorship of professordom. In turn, the professors are the servants of the State. The present-day nationalization of the whole society creates the basis for an understanding of the anti-state and anti-institution struggle of the radical extraparliamentary opposition.

Thereby Vietnam lost much of its apparent abstract character. The productive mediation between the direct and the historico-emancipationist interests of the anti-authoritarian students can only be effected in conflict, in the political struggle. The restrictive policy of the university bureaucracy, the brutal use of the West Berlin civil army in several demonstrations, our persistent efforts to illuminate our society's contradictions and actively and systematically to violate the groundrules of bourgeois society—all these created the anti-authoritarian position, an attitude which further drives the education and the self-education of the individual in the direction of the revolution. Thus it was the ruling clique itself which beat into us our anti-authoritarian attitude. Our opposition now is directed not against some small "mistakes" of the System. Rather, it is a total opposition, aimed at the whole way of life of the authoritarian state as it has existed up to now.

The anonymous terrorism of the state-societal machinery of force and violence is omnipresent in all institutions, but it possesses "no other power outside the government machine" (Marx). The *novum* of our situation lies only in the fact that we no longer accept this order as an incontestable and unchallenged necessity. Increasingly and ever more clearly, the State thus loses its apparent impartiality and exhibits itself as the "abominable machine of class rule" (Marx).

At the end of the so-called economic miracle, i.e., after the complete exhaustion of the available quantitative and qualitative manpower and occupational structure, the Federal Republic is characterized by its high unproductive state expenditures, subventions, etc., which during the period of prosperity could be handed out with relative ease by the state machine, in the process of establishing itself, to the representatives of the vested interests. At the end of the reconstruction period of West German capitalism, however, they suddenly appear as additional, mostly unproductive expenditures, as dead weight dangerous for the further development of the economy, as *faux frais* of capitalist production. The billions of "unprofitable investments" in the field of education (construction of new universities, schools, vocational schools, engineering schools, etc.) which might have been necessary for the creation of a quantitatively and qualitatively new vocational and educational structure in the present phase of West German capitalism are not available without sharpening inflation. In addition, there is the fact that the contradictory unity of the total apparatus of oligopolies, state-social bureaucracy, parties, lobby groups, etc., is not *really* guided by a "ruling will" affecting the totality of society.

The existence of stagnating production sectors incapable of accumulation (for instance, mining and agriculture, which go about "on crutches" and must be subsidized) and the underdeveloped status of the decisive bearers of the accumulation process in the 1970's (the historically new branches of industry such as electronics, space-research, aircraft construction, nuclear energy, etc.) hint at a long-term stagnation period of West German capitalism.

The evaluation of the social-economic situation of the Federal Republic and West Berlin is the precondition for a political-strategic discussion of the process of undermining and overthrowing the Federal Republic in the context of the international conflict between revolution and counterrevolution. It is increasingly clear that the "grand coalition," this last desperate attempt of the ruling oligarchies to "solve" the structural difficulties of the System, runs into objective barriers and is forced to protract the structural crisis by means of subsidies. It thereby lays the groundwork for ever-deepening contradictions in a long-term sense. We can view it as the new "party of order" whose direct business it is to keep the wage-dependent masses in a state of political immaturity and to shift the cost of the structural crisis onto them. In his remarkable historical essay, "The Civil War in France," Marx discusses the tasks of such a form of class-rule and states that its sole reason for being is the prevention of the "emancipation of the producing masses." For him, this form is "the most abominable of all political regimes." All fractions of the total apparatus—the former Fascists, certain sorts of resistance fighters, and the state-social bureaucracy—join forces in this coalition; the liberal bourgeoisie, the representatives of the monopolies, the betrayers of the workers from the labor unions, the Sickerts & Co., all embrace each other, and the centers of manipulation, the Augsteins and Springers, ensconce themselves within it. Together they form the "anonymous joint-stock company" to impose the usually subtle but, when necessary, the *manifest* terrorism of the class rule of late capitalism whose historical task is to transform the masses into a collective which reacts functionally in the interest of the rulers, to keep the masses utilizable and available at all times for military and civil purposes. But in the Federal Republic it is precisely this decisive task that late capitalism can fill to a lesser and lesser degree. The cultural revolutionary transition period which since June 2, 1967, at the latest, has mobilized decisive strata inside and outside the university has by no means come to an end; and it can be terminated only by the massive and brutal employment of all means of repression.

The ruling class has undergone a deep transformation. For a long time now it has no longer been identical with the nominal owners of the means of production. Marx had already seen the dawn of a new "class" of "industrial bureaucracy." This class cannot overcome the fundamental contradiction of bourgeois capitalist society. Rather, it brings it to a climax and ushers in its last phase, in which all capital functions have been socialized and delegated to certain groups and institutions. "The more a ruling class is able to absorb the most impotent men of the oppressed classes, the more solid and more dangerous is its rule" (Karl Marx, *Capital,* Vol. 3). The development has gone beyond this phase and has completed the repressive socialization of capital. Therein lies the strength and the weakness of the system of late capitalism. In fact, this development does not leave any groups outside the total context and tries to dominate all through "a system of concessions within the capitalistic framework" (Sering). This structural framework is guaranteed by the "dull compulsion of conditions," the internalized norms and ideas of bourgeois capitalistic society. But if a socially relevant fraction of the underprivileged outside the circle of vested interests, where the national product is distributed, bursts asunder this matter-of-course restriction of interests and needs to the ruling framework, the whole system is called in question. "Thus the breaching of false consciousness can provide the Archimedean point for a more comprehensive emancipation—on an infinitely small place to be sure, but the chance for a change depends upon the widening of such small places." (Herbert Marcuse, *Repressive Tolerance*).

We have begun with precisely this breaching of false consciousness. Through our political activity, our analysis, our provocations and mass actions, we structurally call in question the System's control and manipulation of individuals. This is why the "left-liberal critics" of the System, from the *Spiegel* to *Zeit,* are clearly beginning to turn against us politically. They understand the nascent danger for late capitalism, which will become a mortal danger once we are successful in arousing the spontaneity of the wage-dependent masses, destroyed by the parties, through an increasingly more effective dialectic of enlightenment and mass action. "That the workers maintain an attitude of neutrality towards the totalitarian order after the betrayal of their own bureaucracy since 1914, after the development of the parties into world-spanning apparatuses for the destruction of spontaneity, after the murder of revolutionaries, is no sign of stupidity." (Max Horkheimer: *Die Juden und Europa,* in *Zeitschrift fur Sozialforschung,* 1939.) The memory of the last fifty years of the German workers' movement can have an attraction only for the contemplative intellectual. For the masses it represents a chain of betrayal by leftist and rightist intellectuals, unbroken up to now.

Our historically correct limitation of our action to the university should not be made into a fetish. A revolutionary dialectic of the correct transitions must regard the "long march through the institutions" as a practical and critical action in all social spheres. It must set as its goal the subversive-critical deepening of the contradictions, a process which has been made possible in all institutions that participate in the organization of day-to-day life. There no longer exists a sphere in our society which would be exclusively privileged to express the interests of the whole movement in its cultural revolutionary phase.

The lukewarm opposition movement is dead, the spontaneous resistance—albeit it very often still in a completely unorganized form—has begun. Be it in Frankfurt or in Bremen, in Berlin or in Hamburg, the anti-authoritarian camp controls the links of the chain decisive for developing the political and social consciousness of people: the enlightenment rallies outside the universities, the plenary sessions of the students in the large universities, the meetings held by pupils in the secondary schools. The profusion of student newspapers is a mobilizing and educating force of the total movement. Everywhere "self-appointed vanguards" are being formed which have taken up the struggle against the manipulation and repression of man's creative capabilities, and they have not been organized by a central authority or otherwise manipulated. The strength of the anti-authoritarian movement lies precisely in the fact that the practical-critical activity of the anti-authoritarians is the real expression of their own needs and of the interests of individuals. The practical awareness of one's own needs in the making, of one's own interests and sufferings, prevents the monopolization of the historical interests of individuals in a membership party "representing" the masses. We already control the streets of the metropolises and easily find our way around in what Brecht called the "jungle of the cities." But the real collectivization of the idea of social-revolutionary liberation is still to come.

The first autonomous groups are being formed in the factories—loosely coordinated with the other groups according to the principle of mutual aid. This brings the anti-authoritarian methods picked up in the streets and during the study sessions into the centers of the production process for a direct fight against the authoritarian coerciveness of the factory structure.

The state-social bureaucracy is utterly helpless in all spheres. It sees the activities of ringleaders or a temporary conflict of generations in the socially mediated conflicts. It must personalize the problems because for it history exists only as the achievement of "great personalities," and for it the masses are only the "material" of the "elite."

Many leftists, on the other hand, often court the danger of absolutizing the "proletariat" or the "masses" in an almost metaphysical way. They do not grasp the concrete and difficult dialectic of developing the political and social consciousness of the masses and do not see the temporary separation between minor radical groups and the general masses. The other danger besetting us is that of intellectual arrogance, and in the last analysis, the fear of the creative capacity of the masses who have arrived at true consciousness. The practice of the historically correct activities lies between these two false alternatives.

The old concepts of socialism must be critically suspended, not destroyed and not preserved artificially. A new concept cannot yet be realized. It can be worked out and brought into being only in the practical struggle, in the constant mediation between reflection and action, practice and theory.

Today revolutionary science is possible only *within* the anti-authoritarian movement, as a productive force for the liberation of man from the uncomprehended and uncontrolled powers of society and nature.

Today we are not bound together by an abstract theory of history but by an existential disgust in the presence of a society which chatters about liberty and yet brutally oppresses the immediate interests and needs of individuals and peoples fighting for their social-economic emancipation.

This radical (because it affects the whole man) dialectic of the sentiment and the emotion (Marcuse), of which theory is the conscious expression, unites us more strongly than ever against the nationalized authoritarian society and makes possible a unity of radical action of the anti-authoritarians, and without a party program or a party's claim to monopoly of strategy and tactics.

Both the subtle and the brutal methods of social integration no longer work on us. In the struggle with the power structures of the System, with the state-local bureaucracy, with the police, with the law machinery, with the industrial bureaucracies, etc., the sentimental-emotional rejection becomes a practical-critical knowledge, a revolutionary will to destroy the autonomized productive forces, the inhuman machineries of war and of manipulation which, from day to day, spread death and fear in this world, from day to day can cause genocide on a worldwide scale. New radical needs develop during this struggle, as for instance the desire to liberate the totality of the forces of production from the fetters of capital and the bureaucracy, and which can free man from long working hours, manipulation, and misery, and to subject these forces of production, finally, to the conscious control of the producers.

But let us not succumb to any illusions. The worldwide net of organized repression, the continuity of power, will not be easily broken. The "new man of the twenty-first century" (Guevara, Fanon) who represents the preconditions of the "new society," will be the product of a long and painful struggle in which temporary upsurges will be followed by unavoidable "defeats." Viewed in terms of classical revolutionary theory, our cultural revolution is a transitional pre-revolutionary phase in which persons and groups still yield to various illusions, abstract ideas, and utopian projects. It is a phase in which the radical contradiction between revolution and counterrevolution, between the ruling class in its new form and the camp of the anti-authoritarian and underprivileged, has not yet matured in a concrete and immediate sense. What in America is already a clearly defined reality has a great significance for use, with some modifications. "This is no time for sober reflection but a time for adjuration. The *task of intellectuals* is identical with that of the organizer of the street, the conscientious objector, of the Diggers: *to talk with the people and not about the people.* The literature that leaves a mark is now the underground literature, the speeches of Malcolm X, the writings of Fanon, the songs of the Rolling Stones and of Aretha Franklin. All the rest sound like the Moynihan Report or a *Time* article which aims to explain everything, understand nothing, and change nobody." (A. Kopkind, *From Non-Violence to Guerrilla Warfare,* in *Voltaire-Flugschriften,* No. 14). We still do not have a broad, continuous underground literature, the dialogues of intellectuals with the people are still missing, that is to say, from the standpoint of the real, immediate, and historical interests of the people. There is the beginning of a desertion campaign in the American occupation army, but there is no organized desertion campaign in the *Bundeswehr.* We dare to attack American imperialism, but we do not yet have the will to smash our own power structure.

Comrades, anti-authoritarians, fellow human beings! There is not much time left. We, too, are being slain daily in Vietnam —and that is not an image, a phrase. If U.S. imperialism can convincingly prove in Vietnam that it is capable of destroying the revolutionary peoples' war, a long period of authoritarian world rule will start anew from Washington to Vladivostok. We stand before a historically open possibility. How this period of history will end depends primarily on our will. "If the Vietcong is not joined by an American, European, and Asiatic Cong, the Vietnam revolution will fail as others have before. A hierarchic state of functionaries will reap fruits it has not sown." (Partisan I, Vietnam, *The Third World and the Self-Deception of the Left,* Berlin, 1967). Frantz Fanon says for the Third World: "Come, then, comrades; it would be as well to decide at once to change our ways. We must shake off the heavy darkness in which we were plunged, and leave it behind. The new day which is already at hand must find us firm, prudent and resolute. (Frantz Fanon, *The Wretched of the Earth,* Grove Press, New York).

Let us, finally, accelerate our correct course. Vietnam is coming closer. In Greece the first units of the revolutionary liberation front are starting to fight. In Spain the conflict is coming to a head. After thirty years of Fascist dictatorship, a new revolutionary force exists among the workers and students organized in a united front.

The secondary school pupils in Bremen have shown how in the politicization of immediate demands of day-to-day life—

the fight against a fare hike—subversive explosive power can be developed.

Their solidarity with the wage-dependent masses and the correct handling of the contradictions and disputes with the authoritarian-militaristic police clearly show that great possibilities of struggle exist within the system of late capitalism. Such a confrontation in radical form is possible everywhere in the Federal Republic. It depends on our creative capability to deepen and politicize the apparent and immediate contradictions with courage and determination, to risk action, to unfold the initiative of the masses everywhere. True revolutionary solidarity with the Vietnam revolution consists in the actual weakening of the centers of imperialism and in their processual overthrow. The roots of our ineffectualness and resignation thus far lay in our theory.

The decisive precondition for the revolutionizing of the masses is the revolutionizing of revolutionaries.

(Translated by Salvator Attanasio)

The Battle of the Streets: "C'est Pour Toi Que Tu Fais La Révolution"

DANIEL AND GABRIEL COHN-BENDIT

Danny the Red, to whom the mass media's way of understanding history gave an international reputation, was of course no more the maker or the "leader" of the March–June 1968 French uprising than Mark Rudd was the leader of the Columbia University rebellion of the same period. But like Rudd he seems to have deeply embodied and projected the spirit of that important moment. Vigorous, happy, impertinent —even his breathlessness seems precisely right.

The two passages below both come from Obsolete Communism; The Left-Wing Alternative, *an analytic account of the March–June events co-authored by Daniel and his brother Gabriel Cohn-Bendit. The first comes early in the book; the last is the concluding chapter in its entirety.*

THE BATTLE OF THE STREETS

PARIS HAD KNOWN many recent demonstrations at the Place de la Bastille and Place de la République—some for higher wages, others against American aggression in North Vietnam. The authorities knew the strategy of the traditional Left and felt confident that, if they could deal with militant workers, they would have little trouble with a lot of "mere children."

The police were in full control of the streets, and the political battles were being safely fought in the ministries and in parliamentary committees. Hence it seemed a very simple matter to send the forces of law and order into the Sorbonne, occupy all the faculties, and arrest four hundred students. Emerging from their libraries, from their lectures, or simply strolling back to college along the Latin Quarter, students suddenly found themselves face to face with riot police (CRS) blocking the gates of the Sorbonne. Their reply was immediate, spontaneous, and quite unequivocal, and it was not even the students with the strongest political convictions who were the first to explode. Suddenly the walls were covered with such slogans as "Stop the repression," "CRS = SS," while the ranks of demonstrators swelled to unprecedented proportions. All hell broke loose when the first police vans left the Sorbonne filled with students being taken off for questioning.

"In the Latin Quarter at about 6:00 P.M., violent incidents occurred as students joined battle with police contingents." (*Le Monde*, May 5–6, 1968).

All night, special police squads poured into the district, every civilian was stopped, and anyone who even vaguely resembled a student was clubbed down mercilessly. More than one passerby who had nothing whatever to do with the demonstration spent an uncomfortable night in the police cells.

Hence the "riotous scenes" everyone talked about that night. What was so remarkable about the events of May 3 was the spontaneity of the resistance—a clear sign that our movement does not need leaders to direct it; that it can perfectly well express itself without the help of a "vanguard." It was this day that really mobilized student opinion; the first great ripple of a swelling tide. And not unexpectedly, the Communist students, bound to their party like Oedipus to his fate, did their utmost to stem that tide:

"Irresponsible leftists use the pretext of government inefficiency and student unrest in order to subvert the work of the faculties and to impede the mass of students from sitting for their examinations. These false revolutionaries behave, objectively, as allies of the Gaullist authorities and represent a policy that is objectionable to the majority of students, above all, to the sons and daughters of the working class." Clearly the Communists would do anything rather than try and understand the real issues.

I have said that the events of the day brought about an awakening of political awareness in many students. Take this eye-witness account published in the June issue of *L'Evènement:*

> "Are you a member of the March 22 Movement?" they asked me.
>
> I was still a little embarrassed, the speakers had talked of Marx and someone called Marcuse, of whom I had never even heard. The first time they mentioned that name I

> asked them to spell it for me. I looked him up in Larousse, but I could not find him there.
>
> I was told: "The Movement has proved its strength by boycotting the examinations." But to boycott partial exam-tions is something anyone can do—you can always sit them again. And in my case, I was quite happy to give mine a miss for personal reasons. And then one day, quite suddenly, I felt like jumping on to the platform and shouting: "I have been an imbecile, I always thought that personal revolt was the only way of telling the authorities to go and jump in the lake. But you have shown me that we can all stick together in Nanterre, that we need no longer be alone, and that no one has to wield the big stick to make us act in unison."
>
> There were no membership cards, no followers, and no leaders. From then on everything went like greased lightning. Meetings, leaflets, and then we went out among the workers in Nanterre . . .

The unwelcome presence of the police on the campus gained the students the support of the University Teachers' Association (SNESUP), and also of four professors in Nanterre: Messrs. Lèfevre, Michaud, Touraine, and Ricoeur, who declared themselves willing to undertake the defense of those students who had been summoned to appear before the Disciplinary Committee in the Sorbonne on the following Monday. Their moral support took the press completely by surprise and did much to gain the students fresh sympathizers.

On Saturday, May 4, the police swooped again, and on Sunday, May 5, an emergency court sent six student demonstrators to jail. Proclamations in the press and over the radio then made it known that the demonstrations in support of the condemned students which had been called for Monday at nine o'clock were officially banned.

"On Monday, Paris saw its most impressive and threatening demonstration for many years. Even during the Algerian war there has never been a movement of such breadth and above all of such staying power." (*Le Monde,* May 8, 1968).

"We cannot allow those who are openly opposed to the university to seize that institution. We cannot tolerate violence in the streets, for violence is no way of starting any kind of dialogue." (Charles de Gaulle, May 7, 1968).

Many people have asked themselves how it was possible that so vast a movement should have erupted from what was apparently so unimportant an event as the closure of a university and the intervention of the police in student affairs. It is therefore important to explain how a relatively small number of students succeeded in broadening the struggle against police repression to such an extent that it culminated in the occupation of the universities and the total rejection of their function in capitalist society. Learning through action plays a basic part in the genesis and growth of all revolutionary movements. From analyzing what is closest at hand, we can come to understand society at large.

The complexity of modern life and the frustration it brings in its wake are such that we are forced most of the time to submerge our deepest aspirations. Students, who have to swallow humiliation every day, are particularly subject to these frustrations, and so react all the more violently once they are aroused. Lull them with sweet promises about the future and they may be prepared to put up with petty restrictions, false values, hypocritical doctrines, and the lot, but bring out the police against them and you will find that you have stirred up a hornet's nest. The students started demonstrating at 9:00 A.M. and by the time they dispersed fourteen hours later, a mere trickle had swelled into a torrent, and "barricades" had sprung up in the streets. The students' determination, and above all their willingness to take on the police, was truly astonishing. They asserted their right to enter their own university, and to run it themselves for the benefit of all. The almost continuous confrontation with the police merely hardened their determination not to go back on their first claims: the release of all the imprisoned demonstrators, withdrawal of the police, and reopening of the faculties. I must add in parentheses that during the "Long March" of May 7, and during the demonstrations at the university annex at the Halle aux Vins, the various factions of the Left tried desperately to insinuate their own marshals in the vain hope of taking control. There were some 35,000 demonstrators present in the Champs Elysées alone and—*mirabile dictu*—they managed without any leaders at all. Unfortunately, the bureaucratic officials of UNEF, that moribund Student Union, who had been frustrated in their earlier attempts to take over the Movement, now called in the help of the trade-union bureaucrats who, at the Halle aux Vins and in the demonstrations that followed, were able to divert the Movement away from its original aim: the recapture of the Sorbonne. I do not want to pass an opinion on the strategic and tactical possibilities of capturing the Sorbonne at this point, but merely to show that all hierarchical and bureaucratic organizations must necessarily pervert all activities in which they participate to their own ends. Thus Alain Geismar explained to the General Assembly of the March 22 Movement on May 8, how trade-union officials had used every trick in the book to force the student movement to opt for a program that would divert the struggle into purely reformist channels. In this they were greatly helped by Communist students and lecturers, who played a particularly treacherous part on May 8 at the Place du Luxembourg, when they called upon the students to disperse. This might well have spelled the end of the Movement, long before it had a chance to express its real demands: the overthrow of repressive society. Luckily the revolutionary students were not taken in; they realized that they themselves had the power to beat repression, even in the face of Communist Party and other bureaucratic obstruction. Indeed, UNEF, by launching appeals to "reason" and issuing communiqués through the press, merely mobilized an ever larger number of demonstrators. And so when Roche announced he would reopen the Sorbonne under police protection, the students replied with an improvised "teach-out," assembled in their thousands, and completely stopped the traffic in the Boulevard St. Michel. This teach-out was the first attempt to turn the Latin Quarter into a "public forum." Those responsible for the dispersal of the students in the Place du Luxembourg during the previous night were severely taken to task and asked to explain their actions. Direct democracy was being put into effect—under the very noses of the police. All the political and strategic problems of the past few days were brought up for discussion and thrashed out, not least among them the role of the university of the future. As the students stood talking they were joined by scores of passers-by, among them Louis Aragon, that venerable bard and prophet of the Communist Party, the man who had sung paeans of praise to OGPU and Stalinism, and who had come to take his place among those who "remind me so movingly of my own youth." A group of students recognized him and greeted him with cries of "Long live OGPU! Long live Stalin, the father of all the people!"

The Aragon episode, in itself banal and without political importance, nevertheless shows how politically aware the young demonstrators had become. They would have no truck with members of a party whose official organ, *L'Humanité,* had launched what could only be called a smear campaign against French youth. The revolutionary movement did not deny the importance, and even the necessity, of a dialogue with the rank and file of the Communist Party, but it did try to unmask the opportunist strategy and counterrevolutionary attitude of its leaders, including Louis Aragon, the poet laureate of the personality cult. He could not make himself heard simply because those participating in the "teach-out" knew that he had nothing in common with them. His bold assertion that he was in the Party "precisely because he was on the side of youth" merely turned him into a laughing stock. By refusing to act honestly for once in his life, and to denounce the machinations of his Party, he threw away his chance to join the student movement, and incidentally saved his leaders a great deal of embarrassment.

Luckily the dialectic of events did not have to wait on an Aragon: we knew that the issue would be decided by the demonstrations called for next day and not by some Party demagogue or other. The people were clearly sympathetic, the National Assembly was divided, and we saw our chance to prove that the power of General de Gaulle would collapse like a house of cards if we went about it the right way. And here the police force itself came to our aid: by barring the route we had planned to take, they forced us into the Latin Quarter. Once there, we were determined not to disperse until all our demands had been met. And so we found ourselves drawn up in front of the CRS, facing their clubs—30,000 of us standing united and ready for action, but with no definite plan. No one seriously envisaged attacking the Sorbonne, no one wanted a massacre. All we knew was that we had to defend ourselves where we stood; we split up into small groups, so that the police services were unable to launch a single, directed attack. Every barricade became a center of action and of discussion, every group of demonstrators a squad acting on its own initiative. Barricades sprang up everywhere; no one felt the lack of a general in charge of over-all strategy; messengers kept everyone informed of what was happening on the other barricades and passed on collective decisions for discussion. In our new-found solidarity our spirits began to soar. For the first time in living memory, young workers, young students, apprentices, and high-school pupils were acting in unison. We could not guess what turn the events were going to take, but that did not bother us—all that mattered was that, at long last, we were all united in action. The Gaullist regime proved completely helpless in the face of this youthful demonstration of strength, and this was only a beginning! None of the lies that have been told since, nor yet the final sell-out by the CGT, can detract from this achievement. In a society which seeks to crush the individual, forcing him to swallow the same lies, a deep feeling of collective strength had surged up and people refused to be browbeaten. We were no longer thousands of little atoms squashed together but a solid mass of determined individuals. We who had known the nagging ache of frustration were not afraid of physical hurt. This "rashness of youth" did not spring from despair, the cynicism of impotence, but, on the contrary, from the discovery of our collective strength. It was this feeling of strength and unity which reigned on the barricades. In such moments of collective enthusiasm, when everything seems possible, nothing could be more natural and simple than a warm relationship between all demonstrators and quite particularly between the boys and the girls. Everything was easy and uncomplicated. The barricades were no longer simply a means of self-defense, they became a symbol of individual liberty. This is why the night of May 10 can never be forgotten by those who were there. For bourgeois historians, the barricades will doubtless become symbols of senseless violence, but for the students themselves they represented a turning-point that should have its place among the great moments of history. The memory of the raids, the gas grenades, the wounds, and the injuries will surely remain, but we will also remember that night for the exemplary bravery of the "*communards*" or "*sans culottes*" of the rue Gay-Lussac, of young men and women who opened a new and cleaner page in the history of France.

C'EST POUR TOI QUE TU FAIS LA RÉVOLUTION

There is no such thing as an isolated revolutionary act. Acts that tend to transform society take place in association with others, and form part of a general movement that follows its own laws of growth. All revolutionary activity is collective, and hence involves a degree of organization. What we challenge is not the need for this but the need for a revolutionary leadership, the need for a party.

Central to my thesis is an analysis of the bureaucratic phenomenon, which I have examined from various viewpoints. For example, I have looked at the French workers' unions and parties and shown that what is wrong with them is not so much their rigidity and treachery as the fact that they have become integrated into the over-all bureaucratic system of the capitalist state.

The emergence of bureaucratic tendencies on a world scale, the continuous concentration of capital, and the increasing intervention of the State in economic and social matters, have produced a new managerial class whose fate is no longer bound up with that of the private ownership of the means of production.

It is in the light of this bureaucratization that the Bolshevik Party has been studied. Although its bureaucratic nature is not, of course, its only characteristic, it is true to say that Communists, and also Trotskyists, Maoists, and the rest, no less than the capitalist state, all look upon the proletariat as a mass that needs to be directed from above. As a result, democracy degenerates into the ratification at the bottom of decisions taken at the top, and the class struggle is forgotten while the leaders jockey for power within the political hierarchy.

The objections to Bolshevism are not so much moral as sociological; what we attack is not the evil conduct of some of its leaders but an organizational set-up that has become its own and only justification.

The most forceful champion of a revolutionary party was Lenin, who, in his *What Is To Be Done?*, argued that the proletariat is unable by itself to reach a "scientific" understanding of society, that it tends to adopt the prevailing, i.e., the bourgeois, ideology.

Hence it was the essential task of the party to rid the workers of this ideology by a process of political education which could only come to them *from without.* Moreover, Lenin tried to show that the party can only overcome the class enemy by turning itself into a professional revolutionary body in which everyone is allocated a fixed task. Certain of its infallibility, a party appoints itself the natural spokesman and sole defender of the interests of the working class, and as such wields power on their behalf—i.e., acts as a bureaucracy.

We take quite a different view: far from having to teach the masses, the revolutionary's job is to try to understand and express their common aspirations; far from being Lenin's "tribune of the people who uses every manifestation of tyranny and oppression . . . to explain his Socialist convictions and his Social Democratic demands," the real militant must encourage the workers to struggle on their own behalf, and show how their every struggle can be used to drive a wedge into capitalist society. If he does so, the militant acts as an agent of the people and no longer as their leader.

The setting up of a party inevitably reduces freedom of the people to freedom to agree with the party.

In other words, democracy is not suborned by bad leadership

but by the very existence of leadership. Democracy cannot even exist within the party, because the party itself is not a democratic organization, i.e., it is based upon authority and not on representation. Lenin realized full well that the party is an artificial creation, that it was imposed upon the working class "from without." Moral scruples have been swept aside: the party is "right" if it can impose its views upon the masses and wrong if it fails to do so. For Lenin, the whole matter ends there. In his *State and Revolution,* Lenin did not even raise the problem of the relationship between the people and the party. Revolutionary power was a matter of fact, based upon people who are prepared to fight for it; the paradox is that the party's program, endorsed by these people, was precisely: All power to the soviets! But whatever its program, in retrospect we can see that the party, because of its basic conception, is bound to bring in privilege and bureaucracy, and we must wash our hands of all organizations of this sort. To try and pretend that the Bolshevik Party is truly democratic is to deceive oneself, and this, at least, is an error that Lenin himself never committed.

What then is our conception of the role of the revolutionary? To begin with, we are convinced that the revolutionary cannot and must not be a leader. Revolutionaries are a militant minority drawn from various social strata, people who band together because they share an ideology, and who pledge themselves to struggle against oppression, to dispel the mystification of the ruling classes and the bureaucrats, to proclaim that the workers can only defend themselves and build a socialist society by taking their fate into their own hands, that political maturity comes only from revolutionary struggle and direct action.

By their action, militant minorities can do no more than support, encourage, and clarify the struggle. They must always guard against any tendency to become a pressure group outside the revolutionary movement of the masses. When they act, it must always be with the masses, and not as a faction.

For some time, the March 22 Movement was remarkable only for its radical political line, for its methods of attack—often spontaneous—and for its nonbureaucratic structure. Its objectives and the role it could play became clear only during the events of May and June, when it attracted the support of the working class. These militant students whose dynamic theories emerged from their practice, were imitated by others, who developed new forms of action appropriate to their own situation. The result was a mass movement unencumbered by the usual chains of command. By challenging the repressive nature of their own institution—the university—the revolutionary students forced the State to show its hand, and the brutality with which it did so caused a general revulsion and led to the occupation of the factories and the general strike. The mass intervention of the working class was the greatest achievement of our struggle; it was the first step on the path to a better society, a path that, alas, was not followed to the end. The militant minorities failed to get the masses to follow their example: to take collective charge of the running of society. We do not believe for a single moment that the workers are incapable of taking the next logical step beyond occupying the factories—which is to run them on their own. We are sure that they can do what we ourselves have done in the universities. The militant minorities must continue to wage their revolutionary struggle, to show the workers what their trade unions try to make them forget: their own gigantic strength. The distribution of petrol by the workers in the refineries and the local strike committees shows clearly what the working class is capable of doing once it puts its mind to it.

During the recent struggle, many student militants became hero-worshippers of the working class, forgetting that every group has its own part to play in defending its own interests, and that, during a period of total confrontation, these interests converge.

The student movement must follow its own road—only thus can it contribute to the growth of militant minorities in the factories and workshops. We do not pretend that we can be leaders in the struggle, but it is a fact that small revolutionary groups can, at the right time and place, rupture the system decisively and irreversibly.

During May and June, 1968, the emergence of a vast chain of workers' committees and subcommittees by-passed the calcified structure of the trade unions, and tried to call together all workers in a struggle that was their own and not that of the various trade-union bureaucracies. It was because of this that the struggle was carried to a higher stage. It is absurd and romantic to speak of revolution with a capital *R* and to think of it as resulting from a single, decisive action. The revolutionary process grows and is strengthened daily not only in revolt against the boredom of a system that prevents people from seeing the "beach under the paving stones" but also in our determination to make the beach open to all.

If a revolutionary movement is to succeed, no form of organization whatever must be allowed to dam its spontaneous flow. It must evolve its own forms and structures.

In May and June, many groups with these ideas came into being; here is a pamphlet put out by the ICO, not as a platform or program for action, but as a basis for discussion by the workers:

> The aim of this group is to unite those workers who have lost confidence in the traditional labor organizations—parties and trade unions.
>
> Our own experiences have shown us that modern trade unions contribute towards stabilizing and preserving the exploitative system.
>
> They serve as regulators of the labor market, they use the workers' struggle for political ends, they are the handmaidens of the ruling class in the modern state.
>
> It is up to the workers to defend their own interests and to struggle for their own emancipation.
>
> Workers, we must try to understand what is being done to us all, and denounce the trade unions with their spurious claims that they alone can help us to help ourselves.
>
> In the class struggle we intervene as workers together, and not on the basis of our job, which can only split our ranks. We are in favor of setting up committees in which the greatest number of workers can play an active part. We defend every nonsectarian and nonsectional claim of the working class, every claim that is in the declared interest of all. We support everything that widens the struggle and we oppose everything that tends to weaken it. We are in favor of international contacts, so that we may also get in touch with workers in other parts of the world and discuss our common problems with them.
>
> We have been led to question all exploitative societies, all organizations, and such general problems as state capitalism, bureaucratic management, the abolition of the state, and of wage-slavery, war, racism, socialism, etc. Each of us is entitled to present his own point of view and remains entirely free to act in whatever way he thinks best in his own factory. We believe in spontaneous resistance to all forms of domination, not in representation through the trade unions and political parties.
>
> The workers' movement forms a part of the class struggle because it promotes practical confrontations between workers and exploiters. It is for the workers alone to say how, why, and where we are all to struggle. We cannot in any way fight for them; they alone can do the job. All we can do is give them information, and learn from them in return. We can contribute to discussions, so as to clarify our common experience, and we can also help to make their problems and struggle known to others.

> We believe that our struggles are milestones on the road to a society that will be run by the workers themselves. (*Information et Correspondance Ouvrières*).

From the views expressed by this and other groups, we can get some idea of the form that the Movement of the future must take. Every small action committee, no less than every mass movement which seeks to improve the lives of all men, must resolve:

(1) to respect and guarantee the plurality and diversity of political currents within the revolutionary mainstream. It must accordingly grant minority groups the right of independent action—only if the plurality of ideas is allowed *to express itself in social practice* does this idea have any real meaning;

(2) to ensure that all delegates are accountable to, and subject to immediate recall by, those who have elected them, and to oppose the introduction of specialists and specialization at every step by widening the skill and knowledge of all;

(3) to ensure a continuous exchange of ideas, and to oppose any control of information and knowledge;

(4) to struggle against the formation of any kind of hierarchy;

(5) to abolish all artificial distinctions within labor, in particular between manual and intellectual work, and discrimination on grounds of sex;

(6) to ensure that all factories and businesses are run by those who work in them;

(7) to rid ourselves, in practice, of the Judeo-Christian ethic, with its call for renunciation and sacrifice. There is only one reason for being a revolutionary—because it is the best way to live.

Reaction, which is bound to become more and more violent as the revolutionary movement increases its impact on society, forces us to look to our defenses. But our main task is to keep on challenging the traditional bureaucratic structures both in the government and also in the working-class movements.

How can anyone represent anyone else? All we can do is to involve them. We can try and get a few movements going, inject politics into all the structures of society, into the Youth Clubs, Youth Hostels, the YMCA, and the Saturday night dance, get out on to the streets, out on to all the streets of all the towns. To bring real politics into everyday life is to get rid of the politicians. We must pass from a critique of the university to the anti-university, open to all. Our challenge of the collective control of knowledge by the bourgeoisie must be radical and intransigent.

The multiplication of nuclei of confrontation decentralizes political life and neutralizes the repressive influence of the radio, television, and party politics. Every time we beat back intimidation on the spot, we are striking a blow for freedom. To break out from isolation, we must carry the struggle to every market place and not create Messianic organizations to do the job for us. We reject the policy committee and the editorial board.

In the vent, the students were defeated in their own struggle. The weakness of our movement is shown by the fact that we were unable to hold on to a single faculty—the recapture of the factories by the CRS (with the help of the CGT) might well have been halted by the working class, had there been a determined defense of a single "red base." But this is mere speculation. What is certain is that the Movement must look carefully at its actions in May and June and draw the correct lessons for the future. The type of organization we must build can neither be a vanguard nor a rearguard, but must be right in the thick of the fight. What we need is not organization with a capital O, but a host of insurrectional cells, be they ideological groups, study groups—we can even use street gangs.

Effective revolutionary action does not spring from "individual" or "external" needs—it can only occur when the two coincide so that the distinction itself breaks down. Every group must find its own form, take its own action, and speak its own language. When all have learned to express themselves, in harmony with the rest, we shall have a free society.

Reader, you have come to the end of this book, a book that wants to say only one thing: between us we can change this rotten society. Now, put on your coat and make for the nearest cinema. Look at their deadly love-making on the screen. Isn't it better in real life? Make up your mind to learn to love. Then, during the interval, when the first adverts come on, pick up your tomatoes, or if you prefer, your eggs, and chuck them. Then get out into the street, and peel off all the latest government proclamations until underneath you discover the message of the days of May and June.

Stay awhile in the street. Look at the passers-by and say to yourself: the last word has not yet been said. Then act. Act with others, not for them. Make the revolution here and now. It is your own.

The Appeal from the Sorbonne

THE OPEN ASSEMBLY OF JUNE 13–14, 1968

The Appeal is not really marred by the few flagrant inconsistencies that appear in it (e.g., Thesis 10 holds that the revolution "will not be made." Thesis 11, equally self-assured, holds that "we must make the revolution." Radicals have faltered before in that space between fate and will). In its abrupt formulations, it evokes the gathering mood of combative anticipation and at the same time draws up a nearly definitive agenda for the forthcoming trial of Western identity; for it is clear that a form of civilization is henceforth in suspense about its survival and its right to survive, and that its survival somehow depends upon its ability to do away with itself.

THESIS 1

THERE ARE NO student problems. The "student" is a limited notion. We are privileged persons because we alone have the time, the material, and physical chance to understand our state and the state of our society. Let us abolish this privilege and act so that everyone may become privileged.

Students, we must not let ourselves be taken in again.

Students, we must be conscious of what we all did in confusion and haste in the streets.

Students, we must be clear and not accept being bought back, assimilated, or understood in our small problems as privileged persons.

Student, we are adults, we are workers, we are the responsible. Let us take the time to understand what we want and to show it clearly.

THESIS 2

Let us not cut ourselves off from the professors and other classes of society. Let us not isolate ourselves as a class of students with its problems of economic and social integration. *We are workers like the others.* We are an investment capital for the society. We must be paid and viewed as every other worker with a social function. Let us not be treated as parasites. Let us refuse to be mama's boys, that is, to be economically dependent.

THESIS 3

We reject the consumer society, but we are partly wrong. We do wish to consume—but to consume only what we have decided to produce.

THESIS 4

Let us not yield to "workerism." The working class as a whole has not sold out as some are trying to sell us out now. They have not been given the means of choosing, that is, the education necessary for industry.

THESIS 5

Let us refuse to compromise with the union leaders. They have also let themselves be seduced and have thus betrayed the workers by making blind consumers of them. No one has made them grasp the importance of this banality. The worker consumes only what he produces. The forty-hour work week has been voluntarily refused by the working class because consumption has been presented to it as an ultimate goal, an end in itself.

THESIS 6

The embourgeoisment of the working class has been an enterprise of modern capitalism around the world. It has made its own privileges seem accessible to all, thus initiating the infernal cycle of needs and "pseudo-needs." It has thus been able to divide the world in two: the secure, and all those who might be made secure, against the "provisionally excluded" of this world, the so-called "underdeveloped nations." Thus, the solidarity of the bourgeoisie and the proletariat is set against the lumpen proletariat of the Third World.

THESIS 7

We are the lumpen proletariat of the consumer society. Let us accept our historic function. Let us do away with ourselves and with all the lumpen proletariats.

THESIS 8

Let us not give in to the blackmail of being apolitical. Our struggle has always been political and can only be that. Let us refuse the palliatives of understanding, of paternalism—the "reasonableness" which is demanded of us.

THESIS 9

We must continue the struggle for a radical change of society.

THESIS 10

Let us refuse "revolutionism." It is not a question of making a revolution—because it will not be made. *Revolution is not a luxury nor even an art—it is a historical necessity when all other means are impossible.*

The revolution is the continuation of a dialogue when that is no longer possible.

THESIS 11

We must make the revolution. It will be long and hard. We must not allow ourselves to be duped. Revolution is not several more lecture halls and professors. We can change nothing about our situation in society because our social condition is only the product of the state of society in its entirety.

THESIS 12

If our situation leads us to violence, that is because the entire society is violent towards us, because the foundation of society is violence.

THESIS 13

We should refuse the violence of "happy times"—this scandalous "happy times" of supplementary hours of trading, of the work force, and of the life force exchanged for some toys and TV's in black and white and in color which serve only to deprive us of our humanity.

THESIS 14

We alone can refuse because we are privileged in not yet being fully integrated into this infernal cycle of consumption. No one will help us because no one can. Before, we were only a small minority of privileged agents, necessarily and easily cooptable. We are now too big a minority. Such is the contradiction in which we are placed. Such is our revolutionary force.

THESIS 15

Let us count only on our youth, our "immaturity," our lack of responsibility to win everyone over to a clear view so that everyone can truly become adult, mature, responsible.

THESIS 16

Let us not let ourselves be fooled by those who would do our thinking for us. We must think for ourselves because we alone have the means to do it. We alone have the possibility to say no. The other responsible workers—political, syndical, governmental—have already said yes in accepting totally their respective roles. They quarrel among themselves only to make themselves feel more unified, only in order not to question the rules of the jockeying for position in which they exhaust themselves.

THESIS 17

It is necessary that everyone have rights, not "roles." Let us be other than characters in a tragi-comedy which is no longer even comical.

THESIS 18

Let us accept the means to our ends. If we want a radical change, we will not obtain it by a dialogue; that has not existed for a long time. If we wish simply an arrangement of our privileged future as part of the ruling class, let us continue our apprenticeship and let us not give the illusion of "revolution."

THESIS 19

We must liberate our comrades and resume our "professional activities." That is our first goal in the order of priorities, but it is neither the only one nor the most important.

THESIS 20

We must refuse the unheard dialogue of words, but we must also refuse the dialogue of brutal and conventional force! To go to the butcher is to begin a dialogue in which we start out as losers.

THESIS 21

Take on our responsibilities to ourselves and to others. Categorically, let us refuse the ideology of efficiency, of progress, and of pseudo-forces of the same name! Progress will be what we want it to be. Let us refuse the integration of "luxury" and "necessity," stereotypically imposed upon all those who consume and produce at the same time that consumers and producers are divided arbitrarily.

THESIS 22

Let us close up all these divisions, perpetrated either consciously or unconsciously, of proletarian and bourgeois, of intellectual, laborer, and manual laborer. If the intellectual laborer is not simply a laborer, that is only because it was once necessary that work be dehumanized through the concentration of the means of production and technical progress. It was therefore necessary to glamorize the only remaining thing: the brute work, the force, the violence.

THESIS 23

Refuse also the division of science and ideology, the most precious of all since we foster it ourselves. We hide it from ourselves. This division claims to be scientific to the extent to which science is the dominant ideology and the guarantee of all the abuses and setbacks of the scientific ideology.

THESIS 24

Refuse also the glibness of rhetoric, the revolutionary verbiage which is only an instrument of assimilation and a refusal to deal with the problems. Let us ask what revolution is.

THESIS 25

Refuse to answer when they ask us to say where we are going. We are not in power. We do not have to be positive to justify our excesses. If we refuse to answer, that means also and above all that we chose the means of our ends, that is, the power from which every form of violence and repression can be excluded as the foundation of its existence and the means of its survival.

THESIS 26

Let us not allow our goals to be assimilated as those of the proletariat have been. We do not wish to control only the means of production, but also those of consumption; to have a real, not a theoretical, choice.

THESIS 27

The proletariat, like the bourgeoisie in its time, has been revolutionary in knowing that it could have a dialogue only by radically transforming the society. The proletariat has lost this power everywhere in the world. A new ruling class has been born, a synthesis, in fact, of the proletariat and the bourgeoisie. This "association of interests" seeks to conserve the ideology of the last century in its entirety as a guarantee of its new privileges.

THESIS 28

If we are treated as privileged persons, it is to attempt to integrate us into this industrial bureaucracy—the technocracy of the foundations, of progress through the "economic-scientific" imperatives. The ambiguity of this privilege then appears in all its nakedness. For the proletariat, we can only be *petits bourgeois*. For the ruling class, ingrates. The points of departure differ; the reasoning is the same.

THESIS 29

The bourgeois revolution was judicial; the proletarian revolution was economic. Ours will be social and cultural so that man can become himself.

THESIS 30

Refuse the ideologies and utopias of total man which propose a goal, a stopping point, and which propose this in the name of progress only in order to refuse all the better our forward motion.

Students, we are the revolutionary class, the carriers of the dominant ideology, because our goal is to do away with ourselves insofar as we are a class. *We do not wish merely to be young workers.* This is a position which we can propose to the thousands of young workers, intellectual or manual, so that they can be like us and we like them.

Once again, it is necessary for us to abolish all privileges, all hidden barriers, and to struggle with all our forces and by all our means toward that victory which can be final only temporarily.

Three Student Risings

TOM FAWTHROP, TOM NAIRN, AND
DAVID TRIESMAN

The July–August 1968 issue of New Left Review, *the best radical journal being published in English, opens with a lengthy, brilliant survey of England's national culture by editor Perry Anderson. Its opening words: "A coherent and militant student movement has not yet emerged in England. But it may now be only a matter of time before it does. Britain is the last major industrialized country which has not produced one." It is from the same issue of* NLR *that the following student reports are reprinted.*

HULL

Tom Fawthrop

ON SATURDAY, JUNE 8, after a ten-day campaign unique in the history of the University of Hull, the overwhelming majority of students voted at a union general meeting to occupy the administration buildings. For once, union policy was promptly implemented; by Saturday night the power-center of the university had been taken over; a sign on the entrance, "Under New Management," announced this new fact of life.

Yet only a few weeks before the event, few students at Hull would have imagined student power being demonstrated in Humberside. At that time Hull students seemed to reflect the passive and inert nature of most other students in the country, and the actions of Paris seemed far away.

But suddenly that scene changed dramatically, and more than a thousand students were involved during the campaign. This, of course, was profoundly disturbing for the bureaucrats on all sides, i.e., university administrators and the students' union. Naturally, bureaucrats fear nothing more than spontaneity—people acting for themselves.

The initial sit-in (May 30) only lasted a few hours, and

after a tactical withdrawal the next stage of the campaign began by setting up commissions responsible *to general meetings of the union.* These commissions, in effect, posed an alternative model of organization to the traditional students' union bureaucracy (of council and executive). During the next ten days "the campus" at Hull became the center of continuous debate, discussion, and argument—the political character of the student body had been transformed. What was once a corpse, was now a vigorous body. In spite of exams, numbers at general meetings of the union exceeded eight hundred and they continually reiterated their support for the eight demands. But although the demands were reformist in many respects, they soon came to assume some "revolutionary" implications. The demand for representation became the demand for equal representation—and this in turn became our central demand, and remains union policy even after the sit-in. The main governing board of Hull University is the senate (composed of forty-seven members of the academic hierarchy); so we decided to elect forty-seven student senators who would take their place on senate within one week (after May 31—General Meeting of Union)—or else we would take direct action.

After ten days of procrastination by the senate, and compromise by the students, we finally reoccupied the administration center on Saturday, June 8. The sit-in lasted five and a half days.

The Eight Student Demands

1. Basic reform of the examination system now, in consultation with students and members of staff in accordance with union policy.
2. The immediate formulation of staff-student committees on a departmental basis to consider questions of syllabus, assessment, and the possibilities of extending teaching techniques.
3. No increase in residence fees, meal, or buttery prices except by prior agreement.
4. Stop *in loco parentis,* in line with the Latey Report, i.e., treat students as adults.
5. Democratic student control of the Lawns Centre Block—no removal of cooking facilities from the Lawn Halls.
6. Direct student representation on council, senate, and all administrative bodies of the university. The students to have equal executive power.
7. End secret diplomacy throughout the whole system and open all accounts and minutes of the university.
8. That the Vice-Chancellor and all members of staff should

in no circumstances, other than academic, inform or instruct LEA's to withhold student grants, so that there can be no penalization of the individual demonstrating political views.

Clearways Campaign Step by Step

Thursday, May 30th. The Socialist Society expresses solidarity with the French students. Hull students also air grievances and dissatisfaction with this university. A march to administration block and subsequent sit-in takes place, students holding open discussion with the Vice-Chancellor. A first outline of the eight points to be delivered to senate is drawn up. The name May 30th Committee is given to this movement of Hull students for spontaneous and independent organization. In the evening commissions are proposed to clarify the situation and to make information available to students throughout the university.

Friday, May 31st. An unofficial meeting of over seven hundred students discusses the eight points outlined the previous day and subjects them to formal ratification at the next union meeting. Commissions are set up to investigate and report on the various demands. The meeting demands that senate meet by the following Wednesday to discuss seating our union senators at a further meeting on Friday, and sixty union senators are elected.

The Long Weekend. The commissions meet and discuss practical purposes. The Departmental Commission suggests "immediate formulation of staff-student committees with executive power on a departmental basis, working through student meetings, departmental committees, and more personal contact with tutors and supervisors." The Exam Commission suggests various alternatives to the present examination system including over-all assessment, verbal exams, and dissertations. The Lawns Commission outlines several long-term proposals including reformation of the Lawns Management Committee to include more student representatives. The Coordinating Commissions visit halls of residence to explain events and to dispel certain rumors such as "violence and damage to property."

Tuesday, June 4th. A general meeting of the union decides to postpone any militant action until Friday's union meeting as senate is unable to meet before Thursday afternoon. Thirteen of the union senators withdraw since at the present time there are only forty-seven members of the university senate. A Press Commission is set up to avoid misuse of information and misquoting. The "Clearway" sign is adopted, implying the slogan: "No stopping until equal representation!"

Thursday, June 6th. The senate meets and discusses our eight points and the possibility of seating our representatives at its next meeting. In the evening union senators discuss senate's proposals as soon as they are made known.
Friday, June 7th. An open staff-student meeting in the university lecture theater is initiated by sympathetic staff to discuss the student case. So far twenty-three staff sponsors from ten departments have lent their support to this meeting.
2:15. A general union meeting is held to discuss the statement from the Vice-Chancellor on behalf of senate and to consider any further action. Friday's vote goes against a sit-in.
Saturday, June 8th. The proposals of the members of senate are rejected. The sit-in recommences. The real occupation of the administration building takes place.
Thursday, June 13th. Sit-in ends after narrow defeat in union meeting.

Lessons of Our Struggle

Strategy. Other student confrontations (e.g., LSE, Essex), have largely been based on a defensive strategy arising from the victimization of particular students. At Hull the issues were taken to the authorities rather than the other way round, and Clearways Campaign has been based throughout on an *offensive* strategy. This has important implications for developments elsewhere: students do not have to wait for the authorities to provoke the student body.
Politics of the Campaign. Although the Socialist Society played some part in initiating the campaign, after the first day every effort was made to enlist the support of all students within a truly broad-based movement. A clear choice confronted us at Hull: either an ineffective campaign by a minority, or an effective campaign by a majority. The militants opted for the latter, and revolutionary socialists fell in behind the banner of democracy. We chose the real politics of revolutionary democracy as opposed to the sham politics of revolutionary semantics. Every real struggle, every engagement with the power structure is worth a hundred revolutionary slogans.
Role of the Student Union Bureaucracy. In a student union the president is generally the most influential figure—certainly at Hull his role was important (cf. the role of the president at Leicester). Whilst supporting all the eight demands and accepting the *de facto* control of union by Clearways Campaign (union facilities, duplicating material, etc.), the president played an ambiguous role during the actual course of the cam-

paign for a sit-in, by long and private conversations with the Vice-Chancellor (contrary to the spirit of the Movement—"end secret diplomacy"). In some sense the Movement up to the main sit-in succeeded in "capturing the bureaucracy" by rendering it relatively impotent. However, once the general meeting of the union knew that senate had not met our demands, and the call to implement our promise of direct action was made, the old union structure reasserted itself by attempting to divide the Movement. The very clear lesson is that the mass of students should always be wary of this elite, who will nearly always in the end compromise with the university oligarchy,[1] rather than back up union policy with student power.

But the impact of the sit-in would probably have been much less if the union bureaucracy had not been carried that vital distance to the edge of their own personal abyss, i.e., the demise of their own bureaucratic status and their absorption into the common ranks of all those actually sitting-in. *The issue of secret diplomacy between the students and the university should be viewed as the crucial factor in any similar confrontation.*

The Demands. The two vital aspects of our demands were:

1. The synthesis which related all the demands together under the banner of a "Democratic University,"
2. The fact that each individual demand was felt as a very real grievance by large numbers of students.

The first factor is, of course, the essential basis for an offensive strategy, if the student body is to hold the initiative. In this way, the Hull campaign was never a single-issue campaign, and the demand for student power (equal executive representation on all decision-making bodies) was always related to the other seven demands. In practice this meant that student power was not reduced to an abstract slogan, but became the description of a concrete program for the democratization of the university. It should also be stressed that the democratic university meant to Hull students not just democracy for the students, but for the lecturing staff as well. Indeed, why have professorships at all? The staff hierarchy is nothing less than a structure of academic status and snobbery.

One of the explicit demands concerned the wages of porters in the union, but we affirmed support for representation of maintenance staff, catering staff, cleaners, and all other work-

[1]Several members of the union executive supported the sit-in; every movement should encourage and cater for defections from the Establishment.

ers at the university on those committees that affected their working conditions.

These demands were treated as necessary reforms by the majority of students, although the number of students whose perspective encompassed a thorough-going transformation of our institutions, fluctuated considerably during the course of grand debates between five hundred to a thousand.[2]

Role of the Lecturing Staff. The number of lecturers that signed our sit-in visitors book totaled forty-nine.[3] Most of these could be described as sympathizers, with about a dozen providing active support. This group of solid supporters suffered incredible abuse at staff meetings, and were generally referred to as the "traitors," supporting "the other side." Their support proved invaluable, and our experience suggests that the ultimate success of such campaigns may often be assisted by splits and divisions among the staff, as the latter are confronted with the contradiction between the real aims of teaching and education, and their complicity in the prostitution of learning for the purpose of perpetuating the academic hierarchy, and the goals of a technological capitalist society.

The Performance of the Vice-Chancellor. The way in which the mass of students views the Principal or Vice-Chancellor is of great importance. Certain students will often tend to regard him in terms of a "father-figure," a person there to help, explain, and advise. This paternalistic role was played with great dexterity by Brynmor Jones at Hull, and it was largely his intervention during the final meeting that succeeded in swaying the students against the sit-in.[4]

When it came to the "crunch" rather more students blindly trusted the V.C. and had faith in his assurances than the rest—and next day the sit-in came to an end.

Containment of Student Unrest. The main tactic adopted by the authorities throughout was that of procrastination. This is their trump card. They are unable to grasp the nature of a mass movement, and expect and wait for the enthusiasm to fade, and the spontaneity to be suffocated by their own machinery of negotiations.

This is a very real danger only if the mass of students becomes showered with technicalities, and the Movement loses

[2] Total number of students is 3,550.

[3] Total number of staff 450.

[4] Wednesday, June 12 (fourth day of the sit-in), General Meeting of Union took place with 1,600 students present. By a majority of about 180 votes, the amendment to continue the sit-in was lost.

touch with its original ends. Certainly at Hull, the senate has made an ingenious attempt to do just this—to sidetrack us from our original intent. Instead of meeting our demands, they have come out with proposals for parallel structures throughout the university, on which students would have equal representation. However, these would only be "dummy committees," from which a certain number of students would be allowed to sit on the real committees, for the duration of the minutes of the parallel committee (this proposal applies to all levels—departmental, faculty, and senate).

This proposal may well be regarded as a prototype for the containment of student unrest. It is ingenious in that it presents the illusion of power, without giving away any of its reality.

The proposals are nothing but a sophisticated exercise in the practice of deceit. They represent a systematic attempt to undermine the movement for real power, to emasculate our demands, and to isolate the militants from the mass of students. Our task is to communicate that beneath the complexities of these apparently generous proposals, lies a cynical fraud. Our opponents are too clever to say no to our demands. They offer neither rejection nor acceptance but instead offer to discuss alternative proposals—and to discuss at length. The pedagogic gerontocracy is adept at playing for time—students must be aware of this.

We Are Impertinent. This became our slogan for challenging authority. In spite of all the sell-outs, the compromises, the betrayals, and the Vice-Chancellor, "at the end of the day" (the fourth day of the sit-in) 635 students still voted to continue the sit-in. It was not enough to win the motion, but it was enough to produce a distinctly uncomfortable feeling deep down inside those irresponsible individuals who form together in the university an *unrepresentative minority* called senate (government not by election but by appointment).

In this sense the sit-in can be regarded as a triumph, in that the university will never be the same again. Our commissions continue to operate, and departmental activity is springing up everywhere. The concept of the "Free University" has been born in Hull, and five hundred people who participated in the sit-in have been through a fantastic experience that we will never forget, and that senate will never understand—the experience of spontaneous activity, impromptu speeches, and living in close cooperation with nearly four hundred other people at one time. For the first time we sensed that we belonged to a real community—and our triumph was to succeed in creating it.[5] Now the campaign continues in the same spirit, as this time we work toward creating not just a partial community, but a total free university as the intellectual bridgehead to a different type of society.

HORNSEY

Tom Nairn

Hornsey Art College in North London has been the scene of the most successful student-power movement yet in Britain. The terms of this success are well known, thanks to the great publicity the takeover attracted. At the time of the writing, the students had occupied the college for six weeks—and the occupation was both complete (i.e., involved every aspect of the institution, not only the teaching areas) and continuous (i.e., twenty-four hours a day, with a permanently open canteen and a considerable number of students sleeping-in). The Movement is running an important exhibition-*cum*-teach-in at the gallery of the Institute of Contemporary Arts, and has called a National Conference of Art Colleges to extend the revolution and change the whole system of art education from below.

Potentialities of Student Power

The achievements of the Hornsey *coup* are remarkable, by any standards. Seen from inside, the changes brought about—in people and attitudes, rather than simply in administration—were astonishing. It is only yesterday that art students were paragons of self-satisfied apathy, further removed (even) than most other British students from any sort of political consciousness.

Yet, the Hornsey movement has been very widely criticized, within the student political Left. Militants have tended to dismiss it as "unpolitical," or "corporative," concerned only with the problems of art education and indifferent to wider issues. The Hornsey students confined themselves to stirring up other art colleges, and trying to establish a permanent control of power inside their own institution, instead of provoking a general crisis of British capitalism (or, at least, of the British Higher Education system). Why such narrow-mindedness?

[5] The Hull struggle has not gone unnoticed in other parts of the globe—on Wednesday, June 12, we received some flattering comments on Peking Radio.

Does this not show indeed (in the words of R. Kuper)[1] how ". . . Student struggles *more than* any other form of struggle are less able to bring meaningful advances, unless we really believe in the nonsensical view of islands of libertarian communities in a sea of corporate organizations."

There is a very important point at issue here, which is bound to affect one's view of the correct strategy for student revolutionary movements in Britain. Hornsey is indeed an archetype of "corporate" development, in this sense. Again and again, the students there showed themselves hostile to "politicization," in the terms offered by the existing left-wing groups. They consciously tried to confine the revolution to their own sector, to win significant and permanent victories within it rather than orient the Movement toward the formation of a general revolutionary situation. But just how much importance do such limited movements have? How much weight will student power have politically, if it sticks to apparently "trade union" forms like this?

In confronting this problem of revolutionary strategy, the first important point to note is the precise significance of a "corporate" consciousness among students in Britain. It is rather absurd to dismiss a "mere trade-unionist" awareness, when the overwhelming majority of students don't possess even this, and are still in a completely fragmented "proletarian" condition whose only relief is the rag-day or the union hop. Traditional student "union" activity of course did nothing to change this condition, it was a part of it. In Britain, a student takeover represents a very radical break with the past—however "limited" it is. Therefore, a revolutionary strategy must wholeheartedly encourage such movements—in the same way as in the nineteenth century it was necessary to back trade unions—as a basis for future developments.

But—pursuing the analogy with the trade unions—it may be objected that the same thing could happen here. Could not student-power movements be isolated, in the same corporative way, as harmless "islands" inside capitalist society—all the more easily, because of the middle-class background of most students?

The second point which ought to determine real revolutionary strategy is, surely, the recognition of the extreme unlikelihood of this happening, even in Britain. True, such a hope clearly

[1] "Crisis in Higher Education: the Roots of Revolt," in *Teach Yourself Student Power,* ed. D. Adelstein (RSA Publications, 1958).

animates the attitude of Authority toward the Hornsey revolt—because it has occurred among art students, seen as a marginal sector of Higher Education touched by bohemianism and so unlikely to contaminate those philistine bastions of intellect, the universities. But the point is, that in the long run—whatever happens at Hornsey—such hope is illusory. There is no real possibility of a successful student corporativism becoming isolated, or a conservative barrier to further development.

There are two reasons for this. All movements of this type, however "limited," are movements toward *power*, toward control of the process of mental production in which students are involved. This is just where the analogy with the unions—valid up to a point—disappears. Secondly, the process itself is a vital one for the entire functioning of society. As David Adelstein points out: "The prime function of higher education used to be the recruiting and cultural buttressing of the social elite. Nowadays it has an added dimension—the fundamental role it plays in the economy. For skilled manpower is the scarcest resource of industrial society. It is in this fact that collective student action gains its significance."[2] To this, one should add that in "industrial society" the intellectuals produced by higher education also have an increasingly important general *social* role as creators of the consensus required by the machinery of repression. This is outside the "economy," traditionally conceived—though it can also be seen as meaning that today's "economy" is universal, and coextensive with "society."

Capitalist society could foster forms of corporative existence in the instrumental class which it created to work its apparatus of material production; autonomy within its "brain" is another matter altogether. Traditionally, exploitation in the sphere of material production was maintained (especially under conditions like those in Britain) by a parallel machinery of mental production (ideology, etc.). Under the circumstances of late capitalism—as the events of May showed—a crisis in the latter sphere can be literally catastrophic. The British ruling class, confident in its successful past strategy of containment, naturally does not realize the dimensions of the new threat. Here, as in so many other respects, it is living out past routines.

But it is wrong for would-be revolutionaries to do the same. Student-power movements are potentially revolutionary in character—whether they have yet acquired a full consciousness of this fact and its implications, or not. It is obvious that, in

[2]*Ibid.*

British conditions, they are likely to evolve such a consciousness fairly slowly. How could it be otherwise? One college—or even a fairly widespread sectoral movement, as this has become—cannot overcome the entrenched defects of an entire political culture. To criticize students for such a "failure" is a serious tactical blunder, whose effect (as at Hornsey) is simply to delay the awakening of the awareness in question.

An increasingly explosive situation is developing in the advanced capitalist countries today. The fact is, however, that the "revolutionaries" available to exploit this situation are—barring nobody—all products of the stagnant, nonrevolutionary situation of many decades past. During this long ice-age, inevitably, revolutionaries were forced to identify the revolution with *themselves*. In other words, "sectarianism" was a necessary, defensive reflex protecting the spirit of revolution throughout this era. But in the thaw, this reflex is becoming truly disastrous. The problem has become, urgently, that of educating the educators—and no movement which fails to recognize the problem will have any grip whatever upon coming events. Except, naturally, the negative, obstructive one which was fortunately fairly slight at Hornsey (and this was an important constituent in the Movement's success).

Still deeply convinced that they were the revolution, some outside speakers went to Hornsey to guide the Movement into their orbit with the appropriate slogans and abstract ideas. They did not take the trouble to inquire into the actual conditions of what was happening, the existing state of mind of the majority, the real possibilities offered by the situation as it was (which are always "limited"!). It did not occur to them that their job, as revolutionaries, was to be educated by what was happening—by the revolution before their eyes—as well as to educate. Is it surprising that they encountered a hostile reaction? Having no living sense of relationship to what was happening—without which it is not possible to *be* a revolutionary, in such a situation—they were incapable of elaborating any tactic of generosity that could at once encourage the Movement and push it just the distance further that was possible, then and there, toward an ultimate political consciousness.

There will be more Hornseys, under British conditions. It is clear that, under these conditions, the correct strategy for revolutionaries is to encourage the student-power trend to the utmost, however "corporative" it may be, and to participate in it wholeheartedly with the aim of ensuring that its revolutionary potential is realized and that reformist pitfalls are avoided. For the time will come, if revolutionary students play the role that they can and should, when such movements develop a more adequate awareness of their meaning, in a wider revolutionary situation. Student power will transcend itself, as an idea and as a fact. It can't be *made* to do so immediately, by the brandishing of ice-age adages. To amend a well-known adage from before the ice-age: the emancipation of the students must be the work of the students themselves.

Context and Lessons of the Hornsey Occupation

Britain has no CRS, and her policemen go unarmed. Authority has worked traditionally through the consent of its victims, in other words. Getting their minds early on, it rarely needs to cudgel their skulls later. The slave who believes in gentlemanly fair-play is the safest bet of all: he will always feel that revolt is not quite the decent thing to do. And anyway, if the mystification breaks down at any point, the cudgel is always there.

The Hornsey occupation has demonstrated certain aspects of this British situation in rich comic relief. Probably as student revolt grows the cudgel will come to be used more, and more rapidly. But for the present, the Hornsey experience is full of valuable lessons for sitters-in.

It began as rebellion against the educational Authority in the college. The May 28th teach-in made itself permanent, and became a kind of living illustration of Marshall McLuhan's theses on modern education:

> We now experience simultaneously the drop-out and the teach-in. The two forms are correlative. They belong together. The teach-in represents an attempt to shift education from instruction to discovery, away from brain-washing instructors. It is a big, dramatic reversal . . . The teach-in represents a creative effort, switching the educational process from package to discovery . . .

The majority of the teaching staff reacted well to the reversal. They enjoy the creative effort and atmosphere, once they get used to it. But the higher echelons—from Heads of Departments upward via the Vice-Principal and Principal to the Board of Governors—are a different story.

Of course, their immediate and lasting reflex is simple: to stop it. But the whole point about the British situation is that one can't stop it *at any cost.* To use too much force too crudely, or too publicly, disqualifies the normal mechanisms of servility. It permanently damages the mystification. If they had rushed the fuzz up Crouch End Hill instantly to battle in front of the TV cameras and pressmen, nobody would ever have "consented" to anything again, in that sense. As for the watching world . . . how soon would LSE have struck in sympathy, how many other art colleges would have been affected?

Here is the first lesson: if the revolt is big enough, and has good public relations, it can make Authority retreat, and wait. Obviously this is easier in London, closer to the centers of the media. Further away, or where a smaller percentage of student opinion is mobilized—as at Guildford Art College—it may crack down at once.

However, crossing this first threshold of violence is a deceptive victory. At Hornsey, Authority did not retreat so much as vanish away into thin air. The Principal at the time of writing had not been seen for three weeks. Governors, and representatives of the Haringey Borough Council (directly responsible for the college) occasionally appear with fixed, slightly uneasy smiles, and say it is all very interesting. The deposed court (known simply as "Versailles") meets now and then at a safe distance from the revolution, to launch measures of harassment, all ridiculous. They distributed the classical McCarthyite loyalty oath among the staff, only to withdraw it under a hail of abuse. They sent the health inspectors to get the heart of the revolt, the student-run canteen, closed down. It turned out to be more hygienic than before. But all this farce must not be allowed to lull one into complacency: behind it, there is the real, waiting strategy of power.

This is the second lesson: Authority may retreat, but it assumes that it can afford to, because time is on its side. And so it is. Sooner or later, a vacation will come along; the impetus of the revolution will slacken, people will become tired, and have the feeling of getting nowhere; then "the Rule of Law will be restored," quietly and easily, in the words of Alderman Cathles, Chairman of Haringey's Education Committee. A reliable observer states that the smile with which Cathles uttered these words hasn't left his face once in the last fifteen years. Then, the troublemakers can be dealt with, the agitators will have their contracts ended, or their grants stopped . . . the children will have had their fun, and things will go back to "normal." In Britain, Authority may agree to lose a battle now and then; precisely because it is so profoundly sure of winning the war.

This is the situation which must determine a revolutionary strategy. Revolutions usually develop in constant combat with their enemy: they sustain their drive and define their aims in the heat of tooth-and-claw battle. Where power feels smug enough to retreat, the revolt is thrown much more on to its own resources. Somehow, it has to feed off itself, maintain its subjective tension, its cohesion, its aims, through its self-activity. In many ways, this is the severest test.

The trouble is, the resources aren't enough. How could they be? Revolutions make new men, but not from one day to the next. It takes a long time. Inevitably, the culture one is thrown back upon—even at eighteen—is basically that of the old regime. The enemy is within.

Third lesson: recognize the enemy within, and concentrate on him when Authority outside plays the waiting game. British revolutions are serious, orderly, moral affairs, admirable in their fairness and tenacity. What they tend to lack is a similar confidence in *imagination*. Big ideas remain unreal: Jerusalem can't be built yet, because we haven't worked out the drainage system. Shall we appoint a committee to work out some practical, concrete proposals about it? British practice-fetish, British distrust of the philosophical idea and the moving vision—scourges of every left-wing group we have—don't just evaporate in a revolutionary situation. They have to be fought, with a program of intensive cultural activity. Even in an art college, the typically British revolutionary problem isn't restraining the mad intellectuals: it consists in finding them, and encouraging them to speak up. How can one defeat a Haringey Borough Council (or a House of Commons), if one carries it around inside oneself? And what would be the point?

Postscript

Early in the morning of July 4 Haringey Borough Council sent security police with guard dogs to surround and close the art college. At the time only two dozen students were in the building. After reoccupying his office the Principal offered a string of "concessions" to the students, including a commission on the future of the college. A meeting of the students eventually accepted this situation, with the more militant among them going to join the occupation of Guildford Art College.

ESSEX

David Triesman

On May 7, two hundred students and staff demonstrated against a talk to be given by Dr. Inch of Porton Down, the government germ-warfare establishment on Salisbury Plain. On the 10th, despite the fact that the demonstration was eventless, the Vice-Chancellor suspended three of us. A mass meeting convened within minutes of the suspension and, aside from a break for the weekend, carried on continuously until the 20th. On Friday the 17th, students jubilantly acclaimed a victory because, by a technical device, Pete Archard, Rafi Halberstadt, and I were reinstated. But what in fact had we won, and what had we lost?

A number of conflicts were highlighted by these expulsions. First, there was a conflict which greets every demonstration here. We are on a remote campus near a remote town in which political activity is nonexistent. Not, lamentably, having created political situations in town, we have engaged in demonstrations against particular political objectives on campus. The result is that we are always acting within the bounds of control of the university. Secondly, there is a critical difference between the cultural attitudes of the senate members and ourselves. They are from a generation which is paranoid about both communism and fascism on the grounds that they inhibit "free speech"—a mystified absolute. We are a post-CND generation taught our final lessons in Grosvenor Square. Against Inch we knew the value of demonstrations, and would repeat the demonstration tomorrow.

The issue around which the mass meetings coalesced was the fact that three people were victimized without even being told what they were supposed to have done. Essentially this is a liberal issue if it is not seen that the university is engaged in manufacturing degrees, and the investors in the factory will not tolerate dissent. (Here they won't even tolerate a company union.) In an effort to keep the entire body of students and staff together in a group for the whole week, the Left allowed themselves to be conned into a game of consensus politics. The cost is plain enough. When the issue died and senate waved exams at us, the students went back to the library without maintaining their challenge to senate, which they had literally robbed of any legitimacy by Thursday, the 16th. They had had the senate reduced to incompetent incoherence, but they let the chance to take over the university slip away. Although there were some gains—more politicized cadres, more radicals with less respect for authority within the institution—there was a defeat, and the fault lies with the Left. We must take the blame and learn the lessons.

The lessons are these. We must not be afraid of polarization. If there is a moderately large minority committed to action, as there was, they must begin as soon as is possible to hold sanc tions over the university. We had a chance to do this on Monday, the 13th, taking part of the building and confiscating the property of the administration, but we mistimed the attempt. Secondly, the staff must not be encouraged to come in too soon. They cannot help being a moderating influence since they can scarcely incite us to seize the university. What we should do, if the situation were to arise again, would be to behave as provocatively as necessary and to effectively sanction the university to the extent that they *need* to use force, probably the police. Complete occupation of offices rather than corridors will achieve this. It is at this stage that the administrations commit their ultimate folly, and it is at this stage that the staff and less political students will feel encouraged to enter a situation already politically structured.

The crucial point is this. Universities are linked to a set of productivity norms which, in order to be met, need a system as authoritarian as any other factory. Expose that, by linking it with outside repressive forces, police, demands for action from the University Grants Committee and so on, and the first cracks will appear in the façade. When the outside insists on coming inside, we will know two things. One, we will lose; but the loss of "socialism on one campus" is inevitable and should stimulate support in all the others during the really hard struggle. Two, we will have won, because we will force the Administrations to openly show their relation to the capitalist machine, and the institutions' implicit aim of producing a new generation of managers to rule the working class. Maybe, at that point, the students who will go from a position of militancy into the outside world—who will be expected to fit in, to teach children to leave school at sixteen to work the rest of their lives on a shop floor, to socially engineer the decaying capitalist structure to keep the whole nauseating apparatus from collapsing—will ask exactly what the point of their education was, and what use it could be toward making a socialist society. And maybe the workers will begin to ask why they are bearing the brunt of the cost to finance the production of their future governors.

Columbia: Notes on the Spring Rebellion

MARK RUDD

Liberal critics of the student movement claim to identify a cynical opportunism in the fact that student disruptions, aiming at racists and militarists, strike most painfully at the presumptively innocent campus itself. Their suggestion is that the militants should learn to distinguish better between their targets and their sanctuary.

The stereotype of ivory-tower detachment was nowhere better promoted than at ivy-league Columbia University. Nowhere was it more conspicuously empty a myth. The Columbia strike of spring 1968 achieved what then was the most concrete unification yet of the antiracism and antiwar fights, and this happened, quite simply, because of the extent to which Columbia, as an institution, was complicit in both crimes. There is nowhere in New York a slumlord more voracious and cold than Columbia. For generations, its bureaucracy has driven the black people of Harlem into tighter, fiercer, and more expensive ghettoization. And Columbia's ties with the Institute for Defense Analyses (since broken) typified the mode and manner of American scholardom's general servitude to the priorities of the warfare state. Institutional innocence was loudly claimed. Complicity was too deep to miss. The bitterness of the struggle which erupted there was in part a measure of this hypocrisy of the clerks.

Rudd's role in the strike began properly when he and a few other militants walked out of an SDS meeting which had voted all but solidly against militant support of the black students who had taken Hamilton Hall. The issues which were joined in that vote, that walkout, and the subsequent liberation and defense of other buildings are developed with exceptional authority in the following essay, written almost a year after the events unfolded.

REVOLUTION IS THE BEST EDUCATION FOR HONORABLE MEN
—CHE GUEVARA

BEFORE AND DURING the Columbia rebellion, the SDS chapter faced situations very similar to those encountered by other chapters around the country. Questions of militancy *vs.* isolating yourself from the base, questions of relating to a black students' movement, questions of student power *vs.* a radical position on the university, questions of how to work as a radical within mass political situations, all came to the forefront in our experience at Columbia. They also became the key questions at places like Brooklyn College, Kent State in Ohio, San Francisco State, Brandeis, and literally hundreds of other campuses where the Movement is at various stages of building itself. Had we had the collective experience of Movement organizers who had gone through similar situations before us, we would have made far fewer errors than we did; this article is being written with the belief that our experiences can be absorbed and used, and, what is most important, the Movement can go on to higher levels, evading old mistakes in order to commit the mistakes of the future. Thus far very little has been written about Columbia for *organizers;* in fact, very few of the questions posed above have ever been answered in print. This is a long overdue attempt to do just that.

This article cannot be considered a complete review of what happened at Columbia. It was originally meant as a reply to certain points, especially on "radical student power" and the "failure of mass politics" in Eric Mann's article which appeared in the fall edition of *Our Generation* and was reprinted in the November *Movement*. Eric's article can be read for its in other respects outstanding description of the rebellion after the April 30 bust and of its nationwide significance in answering the McCarthy threat.

BASE-BUILDING AND MILITANCY

New Left Notes this fall reported a split which had occurred in the Ann Arbor, Michigan, chapter of SDS, between advocates of a liberal-radical position on student power and "base-building" (called "The Radical Caucus"), and advocates of struggle and aggressive action in exposing the imperialist and racist university and building a radical movement ("The Jesse James

Gang"). Little known to activists around the country was the fact that a roughly parallel split in the Columbia chapter in March had prepared the way for the militant and aggressive stance of SDS which led to the blow-up of April 23. For years SDS nationwide has been plagued by the "base-building *vs.* militant action" debate—it took the revolution in the chapter at Columbia and the subsequent mass student rebellion to show the essential unity of the two lines, and the phoniness of the debate. (Recently, Progressive Labor Party has pushed this stupid debate to discredit the "right-wing, anarchist, Debrayist, mindless activists" it sees everywhere. The only result of this, based especially on the experience of Columbia, should be to discredit non-struggle PL as the real right wing.)

From April, 1967, to March, 1968, the SDS chapter had been led by a group of people who tended to stress "organizing" and "base-building" above action and "confrontation." Though possessing a "Marxist" analysis, they believed that the way support is gained is by going out to people and talking to them about this analysis. Various pieties about the necessity to build the base before you take action and the dangers of isolating yourself from the base were incessantly pronounced in the name of the "Marxist analysis." The word "politics" was used as a bludgeon with which to beat unruly upstarts into place and to maintain control over the chapter. One example will illustrate this point.

In early March, at a meeting of the SDS Draft Committee (which had been doing something called "political draft counselling"—a total dud as far as building a radical movement goes), the question came up of what to do when the head of the Selective Service System for New York City came to speak at Columbia. Someone suggested that SDS greet the Colonel by attacking him physically—which would clearly define the fact that we consider him to be an enemy. The idea was defeated by a vote of thirty-to-one after the old leadership of the chapter argued that an attack on the Colonel would be "terrorist, apolitical, and silly," and especially would not communicate anything to anyone (since the action had "no political content"). It was decided that the Draft Committee would be present at the speech to "ask probing questions."

Several SDS members and nonmembers then organized clandestinely the attack on the Colonel. In the middle of his speech a mini-demonstration appeared in the back of the room with a fife and drum, flags, machine guns, and noisemakers. As attention went to the back, a person in the front row stood up and placed a lemon-meringue pie in the Colonel's face. Everyone split.

Only two groups on campus did not dig what became known as "the pie incident." First, there was the administration of Columbia University, which disapproved for obvious reasons. Second, there was the old leadership of Columbia SDS, which disapproved because the action was terroristic and apolitical and would jeopardize our base on campus. Meanwhile, almost everyone on campus thought that this was the best thing SDS had ever done (though we disavowed any part in it and said it was the New York Knickerbockers who had done the job). People understood the symbolism in the attack and identified with it because of their own desires, often latent, to strike back at the draft and the government. This was, in symbolic miniature form, the same dynamic of exemplary action by a small number and then mass identification which worked so well during the rebellion one month later.

In a criticism session held after the pie incident, members of the chapter began to learn the difference between the verbal "base-building," non-struggle approach of the old leadership (now called the "Praxis Axis" after the supplement to *New Left Notes* edited by Bob Gottlieb and Dave Gilbert, of whom many of the old leadership were self-styled followers) and the aggressive approach of those who saw the primacy of developing a movement based on struggle. This latter group, centered around myself and John Jacobs as well as others in and out of SDS, came to be known as "the Action Faction" due to the never-ending search for symmetry.

Subsequent to the ascendancy of the ideas of the Action Faction, the chapter began engaging in more and more militant confrontations—an illegal demonstration on March 27 against IDA (Institute for Defense Analyses), in which we chased two vice-presidents around the campus, the disruption of a memorial service for Martin Luther King in order to expose the fact that while Kirk and Truman were eulogizing King, their university was completely racist toward the community and toward its employees. The open letter I wrote to Grayson Kirk, printed in the chapter newspaper *Up Against the Wall* on April 19 (and later reprinted in the *Guardian*), was an attempt to express to the entire campus the spirit of militancy and struggle guiding our chapter.

This prominence of militancy and the aggressive approach should not be interpreted as a victory for the action side of the action *vs.* base-building dichotomy. In fact, action and education (verbal and otherwise) are completely united, two aspects of the same thing (call it "base-building," "organizing," "building the movement," whatever you like). A leaflet or dorm-canvassing is no less radical activity than seizing a building—in fact, both are necessary. At Columbia, we had a four-year history of agitation and education involving forms of activity from seminars and open forums on IDA to militant confrontations over NROTC (Naval Reserve Officers Training Corps) and military recruiting. All went into developing the mass consciousness that was responsible for the Columbia rebellion. The point I wish to emphasize, however, is that we had to develop the willingness to take action, minority action, before the tremendous potential of the "base" could be released. In addition, the vanguard action also acted as education for many people not yet convinced. The radical analysis never got such a hearing, and a sympathetic one, as during the rebellion.

There are no sure ways to know when the base is ready to move. Many militant actions which expose the participants will result only in an educational point entering the consciousness of the people, without developing mass support. An example of this is the sit-in against the CIA which took place at Columbia in February, 1967, involving only eighteen people (led by the Progressive Labor Party, before it had turned right). This seemingly isolated action (even the SDS chapter did not participate) helped ready people for the direct action to come one year later by making a first penetration into students' minds that direct action is both possible and desirable. (For a fuller discussion on the complex and significant history of the Movement at Columbia, see *Columbia Liberated.*)

We had no way of knowing whether the base was ready at Columbia: in fact, neither SDS nor the masses of students actually were ready; we were spurred on by a tremendous push from history, embodied in the militant black students at Columbia.

THE ROLE OF THE BLACKS

Before April 23, the Students' Afro-American Society and Columbia SDS had never joined together in a joint action or even had much cross-group communication. SAS had been mostly a cultural or social organization, in part reflecting the class background of its members (SDS's position on campus likewise reflected its members' middle-class background—the tendency toward over-verbalization instead of action, the reliance on militant, pure, revolutionary rhetoric instead of linking up with the people). It was only with the death of Martin Luther King that SAS began to make political demands—though still mostly about the situation of black students at Columbia. Another important factor in the growing militancy of SAS was the struggle of the Harlem community against Columbia's gym in the form of demonstrations, rallies, and a statement by H. Rap Brown that the gym should be burnt down if it somehow was built.

The push to the whites and Columbia SDS I spoke of came in its first form from the assassination of Martin Luther King, Jr., which spurred SDS on to greater militancy. Second, and more immediate, was the speech at the sundial at noon, April 23, by Cicero Wilson, the chairman of SAS, at which we were honky-baited, but also at which people developed the anger and the will to engage in direct action—i.e., tearing down the fence at the gym site. This one symbolic act opened the floodgate of anger and strength and resolve against the racism and prowar policies of the university, and set the stage for the occupation of Hamilton Hall which followed.

The pivotal event of the strike, however, was the black students' decision to barricade Hamilton the night after the joint occupation began. In this decision, the blacks defined themselves politically as members of the Harlem community and the black nation who would fight Columbia's racism to the end. It was also this action that gave the whites a model for militancy and, on a broader scale, forced the whites to wake up to the real world outside themselves (i.e., become radicals).

At the time that the black students in Hamilton Hall announced they were going to barricade the building, SDS' goal was the same as it has always been—to radicalize and politicize the mass of white students at Columbia and to create a radical political force of students. This self-definition, however, led to the conclusion that we did not want to risk alienating the mass of other white students by confronting them, say, from behind a barricade. Part of our decision not to barricade must also be seen as a remnant of the earlier timid and nonstruggle attitudes so common in the chapter.

The blacks, for their part, had decided that they would make a stand alone, as a self-conscious black group. This decision was also prompted undoubtedly by the lack of militancy on the part of the whites in Hamilton and especially our lack of discipline and organization.

After leaving Hamilton, a change came over the mass of

white students, in and out of SDS. People stayed in Low Library "because we can't abandon the blacks." Not only did people see the model for militancy in the black occupation of Hamilton, but they also began to perceive reality—a world outside themselves—and the necessity to fight, to struggle for liberation, because of the situation in that world.

The essence of liberalism is individualism and subjectivity—"if I'm unhappy, it's my own fault; if I can get ahead in the world, everyone can make it," etc., etc. At the point that people begin to perceive that the real world transcends the individual, that people are affected as classes, and that they can join together to fight back as classes, then the first barrier toward radicalization is broken. It was the action of the black students at Columbia—a group outside the individual fragmented "middle-class" students at Columbia—that woke these students up to the fact that there is a world of suffering, brutalized, exploited people, and that these people are a force willing to fight for freedom. Especially important to this realization was the power of Harlem, both manifest and dormant. Now the liberal universe—the isolated self—was shattered, and the mass occupation started by a handful of whites, the twenty-three who stayed in Low, grew to be the natural response of well over a thousand people who wanted to fight back against the oppression of blacks, Vietnamese, and themselves.

From another point of view, the militancy of the SDS whites forced others to reconsider their position and eventually to join the occupation. But the SDS occupation itself hinged on that of the blacks, and the overwhelming presence of the black students and Harlem itself in proximity forced us to keep the image of the real world—away from which middle-class white students can so easily slip—clear and bright in our minds. Because of the blacks, we recognized the immediacy and necessity of the struggle: Vietnam is far away, unfortunately, for most people, and our own pain has become diffuse and dull.

In addition to the vanguard position of blacks toward whites, the example and vanguard role of whites vis-à-vis other whites must also be stressed. When neutral or liberal or even right-wing students see other students, very much like themselves, risking careers, imprisonment, and physical safety, they begin to question the political reasons for which the vanguard is acting, and, concomitantly, their own position. Here, education and propaganda are essential to acquaint people with the issues, and are also the rationale for action. At no time is "organizing" or "talk" more important than before, during, and after militant action.

One of the reasons why people joined *en masse* was the fact that white students, with the same malaise, alienation, unhappiness about this society and their lack of options in it, and the same hatred for the war and racism, saw a way to strike back at the enemy in the actions begun by a few. This was the same enemy, the ruling class and their representatives, the Board of Trustees of Columbia, that had been oppressing blacks and Vietnamese. So, with a little class analysis, articulated by SDS, hundreds of whites saw how they had to move, for their own liberation as well as that of others.

This is not to deny the importance of black militancy, but only to emphasize the complex and dialectical relationships existing between blacks, white militants, and "the base." In struggle after struggle on campuses and in shops, the blacks have been taking the initial and even vanguard role. San Francisco State, where the direction and militancy of the struggle has been given by the Black Students' Union and the Third World Liberation Front, is the best example of the most oppressed taking the vanguard. Kent State in Ohio, Brandeis, the high-school students' strike in New York City, and numerous other cases, similarly show the importance of black vanguards. This is not an empirical fact peculiar only to schools, but in shops and in the army, too, blacks have been taking the lead and whites following—e.g., the Dodge Revolutionary Union Movement, which gave rise to a white insurgent caucus in the United Auto Workers, and the Fort Hood 43.

The implication of the primacy of the black movement is not that whites should sit back and wait for blacks to make the revolution. It is, rather, that we should study and understand the roots, necessity of, and strategy of the Black Liberation Movement in order to understand how our movement should go. At Columbia, our understanding of the dynamics at work was at best intuitive: we knew that whites and blacks had to organize their own (Stokely had said so) but we didn't know how this worked in practice—separate tactics, separate organization. At some schools, such as Kent and San Francisco State, the white militants did as well or better than we to the extent that they were conscious of their own role in relation to black militants.

This question "in relation to" has at least two clearly differentiable pitfalls. First, because of the intensive and all-pervading racism in the United States, white radicals are sometimes unwilling to follow black leadership. This was the situation during the recent United Federation of Teachers' boycott of the New York City schools over the issue of community control. Both the Progressive Labor Party and their arch-enemy, The Labor Committee, manifested their racism by refusing to support community control on the grounds that it was a cooptative plan designed by the ruling class to split the working class (both racist teachers and black parents are "workers" primarily, according to PL). Neither grouplet saw the class nature of a united black community fighting for better schools against the racist ruling-class school board and racist teachers union. The implication of this blind spot on the part of PL is that blacks are too stupid to figure out when community control turns into cooptation, and therefore, they should follow the dogmatic and unreal line of PL: black parents and white teachers unite to fight for better education (a position which ignores both the racism of many white teachers and the fact that blacks already are fighting for better schools). SDS, because of its internal factional warfare, lost numerous opportunities to support the black struggle and also to begin educating the white community about its own racism, both of which are absolutely necessary.

The second pitfall "in relation to" the black movement is a passivity based on the opposite side of the traditional white leadership syndrome. Blacks are often unwilling to take the leadership or vanguard position in a struggle, having had white leadership thrust on them for so long, or else feeling isolated (as they, in fact, are at many white schools), or else having assimilated traditional middle-class values of success (this latter point is both the most common and the most complex. For a fuller discussion of this phenomenon, see James Forman's new book, *Sammy Younge, Jr.*[1]). White radicals at many places feel that blacks must initiate antiracism struggles, and that they will follow in support. The origin of this feeling is both the desire to see blacks taking leadership positions, a good thing, and also the attitude that racism is a "black problem" and cannot be raised legitimately by whites as a "white issue."

But any anticapitalist or "revolutionary" program must fight in the interests of the most oppressed—the blacks and the Vietnamese—as well as in the interests of the working class in

[1] New York: Grove Press, 1969.

general. Thus our movement must be consciously antiracist if it is ever to advance beyond short-term self-interest or economism or reformism or any of the myriad other liberal errors. Racism must become a conscious "white problem," and must be fought at every point. This was our belief at Columbia, when Columbia SDS took independent action against the administration of Columbia for its racism by disrupting the Martin Luther King memorial service. The black students did not take part in this disruption, but the disruption did help shock SAS into action, along with other factors, especially the demonstrations of the Harlem community against Columbia. Similarly, at Kent State in Ohio, the demonstrations against the Oakland Pig Department recruiters, as antiracist demonstrations, were initiated by the white SDS chapter and picked up by the black students. At both Kent and Columbia, the black students then went on to take dominant and even decisive roles.

At school after school, white radicals are waiting for black students to take the lead. Since racism must be combatted, they are in error in not taking the initiative, giving both black students and the mass of whites the impetus to carry the struggle forward. They must also, however, know when to follow the lead of blacks, and when to work parallel. At Columbia, inadvertently sometimes, we did all three: initiating, following, and paralleling.

STUDENT POWER OR HOW TO LIVE DOWN AN OLD SLOGAN

One of the things we learned at Columbia is the old SDS dictum, "People have to be organized around the issues that affect their lives," is really true. Not in the way it has always been meant, i.e., student-interest-type demands like dorm rules, bookstores, decisions over tenure, etc., but in the broadest, most political sense. That is to say, that racism and imperialism really are issues that affect people's lives. And it was these things that people moved on, not dorm rules, or democratizing university governance or any of that bullshit.

The general public, and the Movement in more subtle ways, has been subjected to a barrage of propaganda trying to show conclusively that the rebellion at Columbia (as well as other rebellions) was due to campus unrest over archaic administrative procedures, lack of democracy in decision-making, and, above all, an immense failure of communication among students, faculty, and administration. It is unnecessary to document this beyond referring the reader to any article about Columbia in *Time Magazine* or *The New York Times.*

This student powerization of the Columbia rebellion and the New Left in general is an attempt on the part of the ruling class to de-fuse the social and political content of our Movement —rip its guts out, tear off its balls, and substitute some sort of faggoty, wimpy, tepid, "we-love-your-system-but-it-needs-reform," McCarthyite gook in its place. In general, the Left itself has understood the primacy of revolutionary anti-imperialist politics present in the core of the rebellion, but few have had access to our arguments concerning student power and "restructuring" of the university, and thus many have believed either: 1) we admitted the necessity for reform and at least partially worked toward it, or, 2) the supposed failure of the Movement in the fall was due to the failure of Columbia SDS to respond to the mass movement for restructure and reform; in other words, we were coopted by the new liberal administration and Students for a Restructured University. Neither is the case.

Every militant in the buildings knew that he was there because of his opposition to racism and imperialism and the capitalist system that needs to exploit and oppress human beings from Vietnam to Harlem to Columbia. It was no accident that we hung up pictures of Karl Marx and Malcolm X and Che Guevara and flew red flags from the tops of two buildings. But there was some confusion over our position toward the university itself. We were engaged in a struggle that had implications far beyond the boundaries of the campus on Morningside Heights—and, in fact, our interest was there, outside the university. We did want to stop the university's exploitative racist and pro-imperialist policies, but what more? This unsureness over program toward the university reflected a political confusion that only became solved as the radicals discussed more among themselves and were faced with a greater number of self-appointed liberal reformers who wanted to "save the university."

Two days after the liberation of the buildings began, I was asked, in the middle of a crowded faculty meeting, the following crucial question by Professor Alan Silver, a good liberal who always considered himself a radical: "Mr. Rudd, is there nothing in the university worth saving?" Had I been as sure then as I was several weeks later, after much study, experience, and discussion, the answer *No* would have come readily. As it was, neither I nor any of the six or so SDS people present had any answer. We had to decide what is the value of a capitalist university, what is its function in society, and what are the contradictions which can possibly make it useful to a revolutionary movement?

Given that the capitalist university serves the function of production of technology, ideology, and personnel for business, government, and military (we had hit at these functions in our exposure of IDA and expansion), the question of "saving" the university implies capitulation to the liberal mythology about free and open inquiry at a university and its value-neutrality. Whatever "good" function the university serves is what the radical students can cull from its bones—especially the creation and expansion of a revolutionary movement. The university should be used as a place from which to launch radical struggles—anything less now constitutes a passive capitulation to social-democracy and reformism, whatever the intention of the radicals involved.

This position on the university leads to a clear position on "restructuring": *it is irrelevant.* Tremendous pressure on the coalition strike committee was brought by liberals who proclaimed the creation of a "new, just, democratic Columbia University" as their goal. Professing revolution as another one of their goals, they saw reform of the University as one of the many "steps" toward revolution. Behind this conception, of course, was the traditional liberal view of reform of institutions, one by one, which would through evolution lead to enough reform, somehow called revolution. Also present was a healthy fear of both the personal and social effects of struggle.

The radical answer to the liberal onslaught is somewhat as follows. Demands about democratizing the university are *procedural*—forms which of necessity will be empty and easily coopted by an extraordinarily powerful ruling class and its representatives, the Board of Trustees and Administration. What we are after is *substantive* change—such as, for example, embodied in the six demands and especially the demands on IDA and the gym. This is where our fight for power is located. How can any reforms in procedures ever mean power to change the university's exploitative function if we can't even win our direct demands on that function now? For radicals who were somewhat confused, we added, one of our main goals is the building of a radical movement that can engage in fights, that can struggle against capitalism and expose it and its institutions to more and more people and also gain support. Will our fighting over some petty little tri- or bipartite committees do this? Or will we just be coopted into some silly little liberal game, deflecting the focus of our movement, and depoliticizing it?

Eric Mann, in his *Our Generation/Movement* article, criticizes the strike position on student power by saying, "leaving the issue of student power to the liberals is a bad mistake." According to Eric, there is a "radical position on student power," though it never gets explained beyond some vague phrasing of "structural changes within the context of the (radical) critique (of the university)." What are these radical structural demands? What will they accomplish?

Leaving aside the first question, one possibility for the goal of "radical student power" demands is to co-opt liberals to the Left, instead of to the Right. At this stage of history, however, people can only be coopted to the Right, since consciousness is necessary for revolutionary politics. This position can be described as "opportunism."

The other possibility for the "why" of radical student power is closer to the one Eric puts forward. According to Eric, there are *two valid categories* of issues: 1) off-campus-type issues, such as embodied in the IDA and gym demands, 2) on-campus reform issues, which Columbia SDS left to the liberals. "Building alliances with off-campus groups is an important task for the radical student movement," but this second type is also important. Much work was done by ad-hoc liberal-radical groups on departmental reform, but ultimately, the political content of this work was null in terms of building a revolutionary movement.

The validity of campus reform issues implies an understanding of the tasks of a student movement which is different from ours at Columbia and also that of the most advanced elements of nationwide SDS. We see the goal of the student movement not as the creation of an eventual power base, involving all students around all their concerns, radical and otherwise, which is a very old conception of what we're up to, but rather, building a radical force which raises issues for other constituencies—young people, workers, others—which will eventually be picked up on to create a broader, solider revolutionary movement. Since the working class will be the agency of change, it is these people who must be addressed by any action initiated by students. This is very different from "creating alliances." It means the entire content of our Movement must be radical—i.e., anti-imperialist, anticapitalist—not concerned with the parochial, privileged needs of students. This use of the student movement as a critical force is exactly what began to happen at Columbia; no power base was carved out; rather, good, solid, radical issues were raised for the community, the city, and, in fact, the entire nation. To the extent that our issues lacked a focus and a target other than students, they were not consciously "revolutionary." This criticism should be discussed more.

The reason we went so far with "restructuring" demands —we added the demand for participation in restructuring to our six demands (after the Trustees had already called for a student committee on restructuring, I might point out)—was both because of a certain amount of confusion along the lines of Eric's thinking described above, and because we misread the extent of the liberal base on campus for "student power," very much as Eric Mann does in his article. Self-proclaimed liberal "leaders" kept coming to the strike committee saying that their constituencies wanted restructuring and the strike committee was going to lose their support if their demand wasn't supported. Throughout the summer we considered the arch-liberal Students for a Restructured University to be the main competition to the radical movement on campus. But we were totally mistaken.

After people have been exposed even peripherally to a movement that fights for meaningful goals—an end to racism, an end to exploitation, the creation of a better world—how can they go back to their old liberal ideas about reform of institutions? We had underestimated the relevance of the radical movement at Columbia, and how deeply it undercut all the liberal sops. This fall, the fifteen student, faculty, administration, and trustee committees on restructuring held hearings on plans to reform Columbia. Out of a university of 17,000, 40 people showed up. Columbia College, the undergraduate liberal arts division, held elections for candidates to various restructuring committees. Out of a student body of 2,600, only 240 voted. Don't blame the turnout on apathy—15 per cent of the College was busted in the demonstrations last spring. The answer is clear—"restructuring" is not only irrelevant to radicals, it's irrelevant to everyone.

The liberals who set up SRU were supported with $50,000 from Ford and other foundations as well as with publicity from *The New York Times*. Yet the people who founded SRU were both incapable of organizing masses—at Columbia, at least, only radicals can do that—and incapable of projecting interest in their reformist crusades. One of the reasons was that their crusade was prompted not out of any material interest in the university with which others could identify (does anyone identify with the university?), but rather out of ego-interest. These were the liberal ego-freaks, the student-council opportunist types that abound on every middle-class campus, and take on the self-appointed title, "Student Leader." On every campus in the country, these people can be found both in and out of SDS, usually pursuing the most reformist politics so as to gain the most personal fame and power. Sometimes these people attack SDS, very often they are found licking our asses. It is also these people whom you find pushing "student power"—look at the national leadership of the National Student Association—so they can wear three-piece suits, striped ties, have sherry with the Deans, and be the future administrators and CIA agents of America. SDS must by-pass the freaks-on-the-make and reach out to other students and working people with politics that, indeed, are relevant. This was done at Columbia, until the time when we began to worry more about the student-power freaks than about the people.

Analysts of the New Left, both in and out of the Movement, are fond of saying that Columbia SDS failed to revive the strike because of Administration co-optation. Randy Furst, in a celebrated mis-article in the *Guardian* wrote, "Strike fizzles as liberals take over." James P. O'Brien, writing an all-inclusive history of the New Left, makes this authoritative remark, "The SDS chapter has been baffled by a liberal new president (Cordier) and by a proliferation of student proposals for structural changes in the university that have little relevance to the questions (still raised by SDS) of the university's relationship to society." And Eric Mann, in his article, warns of the SRU/liberal/cooptation threat. Don't our comrades realize that this position that our movement was coopted is exactly the left-liberal position of *The New York Times* in what it hopes is the obituary for the New Left? It is a liberal position which denies the integrity of our original struggle, saying that the radicals who were interested in real issues were only a tiny minority in the strike, and the other thousands were just protesting the lack of communication and democracy in a great but archaically administered university. Of all possible reasons for the failure of the strike to revive, this one of liberal cooptation is the least important. In fact, Cordier is a fat, imperialistic joke (once when he appeared at an outdoor meeting on campus to "meet the people," the people kept yelling, "Speak to the issues," to which he replied, "Yes, there are many issues, and there seems to be more of them every day"). I've already cited some data on the extent of interest in restructuring. Of course there are many reasons why the Movement waned this fall, an analysis of which should be done separately when enough people have discussed the subject. Included in this discussion should be the effects of the baseless Liberation School, the repression playing on fear of further arrest and being thrown out of school, the escalation in rhetoric by SDS, the rise of an elite leadership in SDS, the insane sectarian faction fighting forced on the chapter by first the Labor Committee sectarians and then by Progressive Labor Party members who moved into Columbia (there was one member over the summer). Most of all, the failure of many students to see where the whole Movement is going, how a revolution will be made, and what are the life-alternatives for people within the Movement are questions which the Movement itself is only now in the process of answering.

FAILURE OF "MASS POLITICS"

After the police bust which cleared over a thousand people from five buildings, the rebellion faced a critical turning-point. The mass of students, faculty, community people, and others spontaneously demanded a strike against classes, shutting down the university. But the political basis for this strike—its demands, tactics, and organization—was still unclear. Radicals wanted the strike to maintain the original six demands, as a means of keeping the political focus on racism and imperialism, while liberals pushed for as broad a strike as possible—"You've got a good thing here, don't blow it, everyone's with you, but don't force your politics onto people" was a typical liberal remark.

The real danger, despite the chorus of liberal warnings, was in watering down the politics and the tactics of the strike. This the radical strike committee knew (this was the same strike committee that had been established during the liberation of the buildings, with two representatives from each building), and yet the result of the expansion of the strike committee, even with the politics of the six demands, was the eventual weakening and loss of mass base which occurred in the weeks after the bust.

In brief, the story of the expansion of the strike committee is as follows. The original committee called for a mass meeting for Wednesday night, the day following the bust. This meeting was attended by over 1,300 people, all vigorously anti-administration, and most of whom were ready to follow radical leadership. At that meeting, the strike committee proposed a two-part resolution:

> 1) Expand the strike committee to include representatives of any new constituency groups to form on the basis of one representative to seventy members. Groups could join if they supported the original six demands.
> 2) Restart the university under our own auspices by running liberated courses, and eventually establishing a provisional administration.

Debate centered around the question of requirements for joining the strike committee: the radicals thought they were absolutely necessary in order to maintain some political coherence, while the liberals, centered around the graduate-faculties student council grouping, wanted, as usual, the broadest base possible, and no requirements. A full description of the political and psychological vicissitudes of this meeting is given by Eric Mann in his article, but in brief, through a misunderstanding, I capitulated the strike committee position to the liberal one, establishing an apolitical strike committee. This error in itself did not have to be fatal; nor was it, since the radicals did go out and organize like hell the next day, both in the constituent groups which were being formed and in the new strike committee itself. The new committee passed almost unanimously the six demands, plus a seventh demand on being able to participate in restructuring, so it looked to us (the radicals) that we had "reinjected" politics back into the committee. One good aspect of the error, which should not be underestimated, was that the liberals were prevented from organizing themselves into an opposition for two whole weeks. They had had plans to walk out of the original meeting described above and form a rump strike committee, but those plans were blocked by my "co-optation."

The failure to deepen and expand the radical base which had formed during the occupation of the buildings, however, lay at the root of our problems. Instead of maintaining the communes as the bodies with effective power, they became only the left wing which sent delegates to a coalition strike committee organized much like a student council. Not only political sharpness, but also the militancy which defined our strike by struggle was lost.

The people in the buildings had fought. Many were new to the radical movement, many were just learning—this was a time of openness, of new experiences and life-situations. If ever the phrase "practice outran theory" was true, this was such a time. People seizing buildings, yelling "Up Against the Wall, Motherfucker," fighting cops, committing their lives and careers to a movement for liberation—this was all new and unexplained in political terms. During the liberation of the buildings, too, the frantic pace had kept discussion on too much of a tactical level (Should we barricade? Should we negotiate with the cops?), often focused away from the broader questions that would tell people why, where this is all going, how it fits into a broader, worldwide struggle. After the bust, there was more time, yet two important factors relating to the formation of the coalition strike committee intervened: 1) The communes were kept together, but their function became more and more a combination veterans' organization and discussion group rather than power source. In the buildings the knowledge that political decisions had to be made, and that no one else would do it, held the discussions together. Now, through a system of representative democracy, and also the sharing of power with liberal groups, people in communes, feeling powerless, said, "So what?" The communes should have been given effective power. 2) The radical leadership was kept occupied in the nightly torture sessions called "Strike Coordinating Committee Meetings." Here we had to constantly fight the ego-freaks and others among the liberals to whip them back into line around such basic issues as amnesty and restructuring, which had been fought hundreds of times before. This was totally wasted time since the strike committee, instead of being a source of strength for the strike, was really the weakest element. Vis-à-vis the needs of the radical constituency, the strike committee kept the leadership tied up instead of free to talk with and "organize" the real base, working with the people, the real power.

This denial of power to the militants and reliance on the coalition strike committee resulted in the lack of militancy which sealed the fate of the strike and kept it from becoming a struggle as intense and sustained as that of San Francisco State. At the time classes resumed, approximately one week after the bust, the strike, still with the base of hundreds of militants who had been in the buildings, was faced with the question of whether to block access to classes. The strike coordinating committee passed a resolution calling for nonobstructive picketing for Monday. An assembly of "communards" met and concurred with this position, primarily because none of the strike "leaders" spoke for obstruction and militant confrontation. The thinking of the group centered around the desire to involve more and more "liberals" in our strike, and also the necessity to maintain the coalition strike committee as a front for legitimacy's sake. Only intuitively did we realize that the front was sapping our Movement of its energy and momentum for struggle: the morning the picketing began, picket captains gave two sets of orders—private, to certain groups of militants calling for experiments in obstruction, and the other open and official calling for nonobstruction. The "experiments," in fact, went quite well and resulted in a further confrontation with the Administration, which threatened an injunction. At no point, however, was the pressure kept up, since there was no unified support for the small groups that obstructed.

That night, in the strike coordinating committee, the liberals, most of whom had not been out on the picket lines, were up in arms, threatening to appoint cops to make sure the lines remained nonviolent. Here again, in the interests of unity, the radicals made the fatal concession and backed down. There were many of our number who saw the mistake, but their counsel to "escalate at all points," certainly the wisest strategy in a struggle where radical politics has the upper hand and the initiative, went ignored.

How does a mass radical movement involve greater and greater numbers in decision-making? How does it maintain its radical politics when faced with demands for coalition? These problems are still unanswered, though the experiences of Columbia and San Francisco State do help provide some ideas.

SIGNIFICANCE OF THE COLUMBIA UPRISING

In these notes I've tended to emphasize the errors we made in order to communicate some of the lessons learned during what was for all of us the most intense political experience of our lives.

The failure to establish mass, militant, long-term radical politics has at least in part been answered by the experiences of San Francisco State and other schools. Martin Nicolaus, writing in *The Movement* has also pointed out that the Third World/Liberation Front/Black Student Union movement at San Francisco State has purposely allowed no leader/symbol/star figures to emerge through the mass media. Both politically and personally this has been a bad error in the Columbia struggle, though it has had some advantages.

The confusion over the radical position on the university, and the function of a student movement in building a revolutionary movement, has begun to be cleared up by the Revolutionary Youth Movement proposal passed by the Ann Arbor–Winter NC. The ideas in this resolution have not been completely clarified in SDS, but the departure from both student-movement-in-itself and also worker-student alliance politics is clear to most. This proposal is, in a sense, the ideological successor to Columbia.

The victories of the Columbia struggle, however, were great. It was the most sustained and most intense radical campus struggle up to that time, around the clearest politics.

At a time when the radical movement was the most disheartened and disspirited due to the grins of McCarthy, the Columbia rebellion broke through the gloom as an example of the power a radical movement could attain. It is no coincidence that the McCarthy movement at Columbia, starting off with over six hundred members the first day, has never been able to revive after the rebellion of the spring. Liberal politics were exposed as just so much shallow verbiage and wasted effort when compared to the power of a mass radical movement, around significant issues such as racism and imperialism. The radical "base," for the first time ever at one campus, attained a number in the thousands.

Nationwide, Columbia and Chicago provided the models for militancy and energy which attracted masses of students after the total failure of conventional politics this summer and fall. The content of that politics, too, the compromises and reformism of McCarthyism, were juxtaposed to the thoroughgoing analysis of the Left on imperialism, racism, poverty, the class nature of the society. This all was highlighted by Columbia.

At Columbia, our two principal demands, the ending of construction of the gym in Morningside Park, and the formal severing of ties with the Institute for Defense Analyses, were, in fact, met. This laid the basis for broadening the demands this fall to ending all defense and government research, and stopping all university expansion into the community.

Perhaps the most important result of the rebellion, in terms of long-term strategy for the Movement, was the creation of new alliances with student, nonstudent, community, and working-class groups throughout the city. A chapter that had been mostly inward-looking and campus-oriented suddenly opened up and began to realize the tremendous importance of the various types of hook-ups—support, tactical alliance, coalition

—which would broaden the radical movement beyond its white, "middle-class," student base.

First of all was the tactical alliance with the black students in Hamilton Hall, sometimes close, sometimes more distant, but always working parallel toward the same goal. This was described at the beginning of this article, but it is worthwhile reiterating the tremendous importance of the experience as a model for the different types of relationships possible with militant black students.

Backing up the black students as a source of power, and to some extent behind the whites as well, was the Harlem community, sometimes mobilized, sometimes lying in wait. This force proved not only the greatest single deterrent to a police bust, but also provided *all* demonstrating students with support in the form of mass rallies and demonstrations, manpower, money, food donations, and morale boosting. Black high-school students sparked the militants in Fayerweather Hall, then returned to their own schools and within two weeks had created the most militant high-school antiracist strikes New York City has seen in recent times. A strike committee member spoke at a rally at Seventh Avenue and 125th Street in Central Harlem, the first white person to do so within anyone's memory. Since the rebellion, the relationship between New York SDS and the New York Black Panther Party has grown increasingly closer.

As a result of the liberation of the buildings, anti-Columbia organizing activity in the mostly white Morningside Heights neighborhood revived to an all-time high. The Community Action Committee, organized completely by community residents, provided support to the students in the form of demonstrations and even a rent-strike of tenants in Columbia's tenements. On May 14, the CAC liberated an apartment in a tenement on 114th Street in an effort to dramatize the decimation of the community by Columbia's racist expansion policies. The CAC led numerous actions over the summer, all working closely with students at the Liberation School. The work of the CAC was not all a bed of roses: problems developed over the fact that the organizers were mostly middle-class young people who were estranged from both white working-class residents who were threatened and the middle-class residents whose buildings were not in jeopardy.

As a direct result of the strike, cafeteria workers, mostly Spanish-speaking, ended their thirty-year battle with Columbia, one of the most repressive employers in the city, with the formation of a local of Local 1199 of the Drug and Hospital

Workers' Union, one of the few antiwar unions in New York City. Student organizers, all SDS members, or student "Marxist-Humanists," did most of the work for Local 1199, and red-baiting by the bosses was effectively turned against Columbia since the workers knew the students would be on their side if the Union was denied.

More general off-campus results of the uprising, though important, are hard to estimate. Despite the distortions of the press, many people began to see that students are willing to fight militantly for good goals—ending racism, ending the war. Though no mass or general strike erupted in the nation around our demands, we feel the Columbia rebellion helped break down the antagonism of working people toward students fighting only for their own privilege (at least where the truth got through).

Internal changes in the chapter took the form of the wealth of experience absorbed by hundreds of individuals. It is almost a truism at this point to cite the incredible changes in consciousness that took place through the action ("Revolution is the best education for honorable men"—Che). The rebellion trained new leaders, some of whom have left Columbia to provide other local movements with leadership. From my travels around the country, I've seen that the level of political discussion at Columbia is as high or higher than anywhere else in the country, including the radical "center" in the Bay Area. The number of militants active in the chapter is much greater than last year, and, in addition, a chapter member with many years' experience recently commented that the entire undergraduate school and most of the graduate students look to SDS for political leadership, and, most important, see SDS as acting in their interest. This is perhaps the only campus in the country where the SDS chapter can call the whole school its "base."

Our strength was greatest at the time of our greatest militancy. It was also the time that we resolved to fight—to disregard all the liberal Cassandras warning us of the horrors of the police bust and the right-wing reaction. In a sense it was a time when we overcame our own middle-class timidity and fear of violence. We, of course, were following the lead of the blacks, but we were also forging new paths where elite white students had never been before. At that time nothing could defeat us, not the police, not the jocks, not the liberal faculty, so treacherous and yet so impotent, only our own (we found out later) weakness and bad political judgment. The liberal world was paralyzed; radicals had a vision of what victory seems like.

Of course we made mistakes, dozens of them. At the lowest points, feeling that the Movement itself had erred in irreconcilable ways (such as leaving Hamilton Hall, which we at that time did not understand as inevitable and even a source of strength), we found the strength to go on in the knowledge that somehow, history was carrying us forward. Also important was the observation that after making forty-three mistakes, forty-four wouldn't make any difference, so we threw ourselves into the next crisis.

Above all, we learned almost accidentally the great truth stated by Chairman Mao Tse-tung, "Dare to struggle, dare to win."